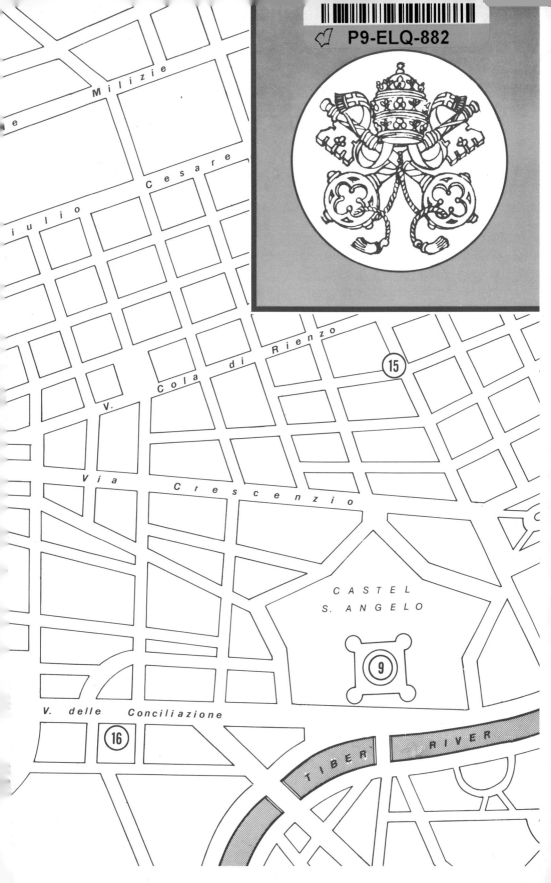

P9-ELQ-882

Milizie

Cesare

iulio

e

V. Cola di Rienzo

Via Crescenzio

15

CASTEL
S. ANGELO

9

V. delle Conciliazione

16

TIBER RIVER

The Making of the Popes 1978

Andrew M. Greeley

The Making of the Popes 1978
The Politics of Intrigue in the Vatican

Andrews and McMeel, Inc.
A Universal Press Syndicate Company
Kansas City

First printing April 1979
Second printing June 1979

Library of Congress Cataloging in Publication Data

Greeley, Andrew M   1928-
   The making of the Popes 1978.

   1. John Paul I, Pope, 1912-1978.   2.   John Paul II,
Pope, 1920-   3. Popes--Election.   I.   Title.
BX1378.4.G73   262'.136   79-14714
ISBN: 0-8362-3100-7

For All Those Who Helped
—Especially "Deep Purple"

Acknowledgments

I am grateful first of all to all my Roman sources, for whom I shall show my gratitude by preserving their anonymity.

In addition, I am grateful to the following for their assistance at various stages of the project:

At Universal Press Syndicate: James F. Andrews, Conger Beasley, Jr., Thomas Drape, Betty Fitzpatrick, Donna Martin, Alan McDermott, John P. McMeel, Rowena Nichols, and Lee Salem.

In Rome: Dominic Mariani, Edward Grace, Judith Fisher, Grace Ann Barry, Alain Woodrow.

At the National Opinion Research Center: Christian Jacobsen, James Coleman, Kenneth Prewitt, Virginia Reich, Julie Antelman, Toshi Takahashi, Mary Okazaki, Irene Edwards, Christopher Lonn, Jane Martin, Kenneth East, Mary Kotecki, and—especially for establishing my total dispensability—my student, colleague, and now boss, William McCready.

From the Press: Lillian Block of Religious News Service and George Cornell of AP for making post release material available to me, Jordan Bonfante of *Time*, James Hoge and Roy Larsen of the *Chicago Sun Times*, Chris Wallace of NBC News, Dan Herr of the Thomas More Association, Desmond O'Grady, Sheila and Kevin Starr of the *San Francisco Examiner*, and Peter Nichols of the *Times* of London.

For Roman Hospitality: Il signor Cardinale and L'ancien évêque du Manchester.

For sharing the heavy burden of sorrow at the time of Gianpaolo's death—my traveling companions Jack and Sue Saletta and Andy and Mary Burd, all of whom go back a long time.

None of the above is going to be allowed the slightest credit for the good things that might be said about the book, so they should be dispensed from all censures, literary or canonical.

Contents

The Making of the Popes 1978

Cast of Characters

Alfrink, Bernard–born 1900, retired archbishop of Utrecht; former head of the Dutch church; one of the leading figures of the Second Vatican Council; scripture scholar with a publication list of more than seventy articles; he guided the Dutch skillfully through troubled times despite harassment from the Roman Curia. He retired in 1976 as archbishop of Utrecht and was replaced by Cardinal Johannes Willebrands.

Arns, Paulo Evaristo–born 1921, archbishop of São Paulo in Brazil; a Franciscan priest; theologian, of German ethnic ancestry; one of the moderate progressive leaders in the Latin American church; admired for his pastoral zeal and his social concern and personal holiness.

Baggio, Sebastiano–born 1913, prefect of the Congregation for Bishops; Vatican diplomat with wide experience in the Americas; as apostolic delegate to Canada, he appointed progressive bishops, mostly for pragmatic reasons, a policy he has continued as head of the Congregation for Bishops. Widely traveled and sophisticated, Baggio would be thought moderate or even liberal in the terms of the Roman Curia. He was instrumental in the campaign to replace Cardinal Cody in Chicago.

Benelli, Giovanni–born 1921, archbishop of Florence, former undersecretary of state to Paul VI; Vatican diplomat; one-time secretary to Paul VI when the latter was himself undersecretary of state; diplomatic service in Dublin, Paris, Rio de Janeiro, and Madrid; tough-minded, energetic, hard-driving pragmatist, whose principal task was to force the Curia to do what Paul VI wanted it to do.

Bernardin, Joseph–born 1928, archbishop of Cincinnati; former general secretary and president of the National Conference of Catholic Bishops; twice elected to the Permanent Council of the Synod of Bishops.

Bertoli, Paolo–born 1908, papal diplomat, served in Turkey, Colombia, Lebanon, and France (where he clashed with Benelli, who was a member of his staff). Resigned in protest as prefect for the Congregation for the Causes of Saints. Moderate curialist, committed to the Second Vatican Council.

Casaroli, Agostino–born 1914, secretary of the Council for the Public Affairs of the Church in the Secretariat of State. Casaroli has been called the Vatican Kissinger because of his responsibility for its "foreign policy"; he is the one who has presided over Ostpolitik, the Vatican's attempt to reach accommodations with the socialist regimes in Eastern Europe.

Colombo, Giovanni–born 1902, archbishop of Milan, where he had served in 1960 as an auxiliary bishop to Cardinal Giovanni Battista Montini (Paul VI). Seminary teacher and rector for much of his life, he maintained greater openness to the foreign bishops at the Second Vatican Council than did many other Italian bishops.

Confalonieri, Carlo–born 1893, the oldest member of the College of Cardinals and, hence, its dean; formerly prefect for the Congregation for Bishops. One of the least reactionary of the curialists in his day, he could not vote at the conclaves because he was over the eighty-year age limit. Nevertheless, he exercised influence because of his seniority and position.

Cordeiro, Joseph–born 1918, archbishop of Karachi in Pakistan, a small Catholic diocese in a country of several million people; the most influential and outspoken of the Asian cardinals.

Enrique y Tarancón, Vicente–born 1907, archbishop of Madrid; the most important leader in the Spanish church; had an influential and important role in the Second Vatican Council and decisive impact on the liberalization of the Spanish church.

Felici, Pericle–born 1911, prefect of the Supreme Tribunal of the Apostolic Signatura (papal appellate court); quintessential curialist. Felici writes poems, takes his own pictures, develops his own photographs, and delights in his video tape recorder; secretary of the Second Vatican Council, he consistently tried to manipulate the council to favor the curial party. After the council he was head of the commission responsible for revising the code of canon law; worked tirelessly to neutralize the most powerful effects of the council through the new code of canon law.

Hoeffner, Joseph–born 1906, archbishop of Cologne, a sociologist of a sort and a conservative, if not reactionary, influence inside the German church; implacable enemy of Swiss theologian Hans Küng; the sort of man who sends agents to listen to lectures by visiting authors from other countries.

Hume, George Basil–born 1923, archbishop of Westminster; Benedictine abbot and ecumenist who was appointed to England's largest Catholic diocese in his early fifties; scholarly, personable, charming, the darling of the English and French press corps at the conclaves.

Jadot, Jean–born 1909, apostolic delegate to the United States; Belgian missionary and chaplain, he entered the diplomatic service through an unconventional route and was apostolic delegate to Southeast

2

Asia and then in West Africa; sent to the United States in 1972 when Paul VI became alarmed at the deteriorating condition of the American church. An unorthodox diplomat who speaks little Italian and is distinctly uninterested in a Roman position, Jadot has revolutionized the American church by the "pastoral" appointments made during his term and has earned the lasting enmity of the old guard in American Catholicism (most notably Cardinals John Krol and John Cody). It was said of him by one of his staff that "that man has learned more about the American church in six months than his predecessors did in all their years here."

Jubany Arnau, Narciso–born 1913, archbishop of Barcelona; another one of the liberal Spanish churchmen who emerged during the 1950s and 1960s; close ally of Enrique y Tarancón and an important figure in the transition of the Spanish church.

Koenig, Franz–born 1905, archbishop of Vienna; one of the giants of the Second Vatican Council and longtime progressive leader among Western European bishops, he is in a most strategic position in Vienna and influential in Eastern Europe. In addition, he is president of the Secretariat for Non-Believers in the Curia; his academic field is the history of religions.

Lorscheider, Aloisio–born 1924, archbishop of Fortaleza; a Franciscan with German ethnic background, Lorscheider is one of the giants of the contemporary church despite poor health; most influential of the Latin American cardinals, tireless worker, and member of the Council of the Synod of Bishops (to which he was elected in 1977 on the first ballot, as was America's Joseph Bernardin).

Marty, François–born 1904, archbishop of Paris, leader of the French cardinals and one of the more influential of the modern European liberals.

Oddi, Silvio–born 1910, one of the "Piacenza mafia" (two other curial cardinals, Opilio Rossi and Antonio Samore are also from Piacenza); papal diplomat; he ended his career as apostolic nuncio to Belgium and was rewarded with a red hat even though Paul VI did not like him and refused to give him any top level responsibility; one of the more influential of the curial reactionaries.

Palazzini, Pietro–born 1912, moral theologian and canon lawyer; the principal representative in the College of Cardinals of the Spanish quasi-secret religious order of Opus Dei; as secretary to the Congregation for the Clergy, he was a constant embarrassment to his superior, Cardinal John Wright; solid member of the curial conservative block; strongly disliked by many non-curial cardinals, who felt that he typified all that was wrong with the Curia.

Pappalardo, Salvatore–born 1918, archbishop of Palermo; papal diplomat, sometime nuncio in Indonesia; professor and then president of the Pontifical Ecclesiastical Academy, where papal diplomats are trained; performed brilliantly in difficult tasks as archbishop in Palermo; noted as an intellectual and liberal despite his curial background.

Pellegrino, Michele–born 1903, retired archbishop of Turin, so progressive and so sympathetic to the cause of the poor and the worker that he had been called "red archbishop" of Turin; deeply admired for his courage, his charm, and his personal sanctity; specialist in the study of St. Augustine; leader of the strong, if often silenced, liberal element in the Italian clergy and hierarchy.

Pignedoli, Sergio–born 1910, president of the Secretariat for Non-Christians; sometime chaplain in the Italian navy; papal nuncio to Bolivia and Venezuela; auxiliary to Archbishop Giovanni Montini (later Paul VI) in Milan; apostolic delegate to Canada; most widely traveled and most progressive of the curial cardinals and hence cordially disliked by most other curial cardinals.

Pironio, Eduardo–born 1920 in Argentina of Italian parents; called to Rome to be head of the Congregation for Religious and Secular Institutes from his diocese of Mar del Plata in Argentina, where he was on the death list of right-wing terrorists; one of the most influential of the progressive Latin American bishops.

Poletti, Ugo–born 1914, cardinal vicar of Rome, the pope's administrator for the city of Rome; from the city of Novara in southern Italy. Poletti has been forced in Rome to steer a narrow path between his own open and progressive orientations and the watchful hostility of the Roman Curia. A seminary teacher and parish pastor, he would like many of the other Italian residential bishops to be much more liberal and open-minded than his Italian colleagues in the Curia.

Ratzinger, Joseph–born 1927, one of the most influential of the younger theologians at the Second Vatican Council; later broke with many of the other conciliar theologians and took a much more conservative stand, allegedly because of his shock at the student unrest in German universities in the late 1960s. He became a staunch theological defender of Paul VI and was rewarded in 1977 by being made archbishop of Munich and a cardinal five days later. Scholarly, retiring, at times even suspicious, he has not been popular with the priests of Munich but has a powerful influence with the German hierarchy. There is strong antipathy between him and many of the more progressive German theologians.

Cast of Characters

Siri, Giuseppe–born 1906, archbishop of Genoa; an archbishop for thirty-two years and a cardinal for twenty-five, Siri was the leader of the conservative forces at the Second Vatican Council and, despite his relative youthfulness at the time, a principal candidate against Montini in the 1963 conclave; he has been the unquestioned leader of those conservative forces in the Italian church which resisted the council and harassed Paul VI's attempts to modernize the church.

Suenens, Leo Josef–born 1904, archbishop of Mechelen-Brussels; theology professor and vice-rector at the Catholic University of Louvain; he was on the Gestapo's death list at the end of the Second World War. He served as one of the "moderators" of the Second Vatican Council and was, according to many, the most influential of all the council fathers, in particular influencing the content of the council's famous *Constitution on the Church in the Modern World*. He was one of the Great Electors for Montini in the 1963 conclave and was rumored as the prime candidate for secretary of state at that time. He was ostracized in Rome for mild suggestions about developing coresponsibility between bishops and pope in governing the church on the grounds that he had dared to be critical of Paul VI. Nonetheless, he has maintained wide influence through his travels, his personal charm, and, in recent years, his influential role in the charismatic movement.

Ursi, Corrado–born 1908, archbishop of Naples; seminary rector and parish priest, Ursi is an enthusiastic Italian and residential bishop who has had extraordinary influence on the difficult diocese of Naples. He is a progressive by Italian standards.

Vagnozzi, Egidio–born 1906, president of the Prefecture of Economic Affairs of the Holy See; former apostolic delegate to the United States; influential curial reactionary whom many think responsible for a lot of the troubles in contemporary American Catholicism. In the years immediately after the Second Vatican Council he was principally responsible for the appointment of American archbishops and bishops who were considered to be "safe," a tactic by which the American church was punished for the surprisingly progressive stands its leaders took at the Second Vatican Council.

Villot, Jean–born 1905, secretary of state; a mild-mannered and influential progressive during the Second Vatican Council, Villot was called to Rome from Lyons in France as prefect of the Congregation for the Clergy; and then was promoted to secretary of state when Paul VI was intimidated by Siri and other Italian conservatives from appointing Suenens. It was to be Villot's job to reshape the Curia so that it would be

5

an effective tool for Paul VI's plans. However, he lacked the vigor and the willpower necessary for such a monumental task and was for many years a mere figurehead while the real power was exercised by his undersecretary, Giovanni Benelli—a relationship which Villot did not particularly enjoy.

Willebrands, Johannes–born 1909, archbishop of Utrecht, president of the Secretariat for Christian Unity; one of the early Dutch ecumenists during the Second World War. In 1960 he was appointed by Pope John XXIII as the secretary of the new Secretariat for Christian Unity, where, under the leadership of Cardinal Augustin Bea, Willebrands helped to organize and formalize the Catholic ecumenical movement. Widely admired and respected, Willebrands commutes between Utrecht and Rome and is one of the unquestioned leaders of the Western European church.

Wyszynski, Stefan–born 1901, archbishop of Gniezno and Warsaw; primate of Poland for thirty years, Wyszynski—who fought the Nazis during the Second World War—has fought the Communists ever since that war; a stern, rigid, authoritarian man, he also has great personal courage and indomitable willpower. The Stalinist regime kept him in prison for years and did not permit him to go to Rome to receive the red hat when he was made cardinal. Released by the revolution that accompanied the Poznan riots in 1956, he has slowly but surely won ever greater freedom for the church in Poland but has resisted change in the Polish church, partly in the name of unity against the party, but also because of his own profoundly conservative orientation. He is one of the three remaining cardinals who participated in the election of Pope John XXIII. He was a strong supporter of Cardinal Roncalli in that conclave, appearing next to him on the balcony when John XXIII gave his first blessing. (The other two cardinals who participated in the conclave that elected John XXIII are Siri of Genoa and Paul Léger of Montreal.)

Overture

It was the year of the three popes, a year of shattering changes in the papacy. The cardinals assembled in August, took a big gamble, and won, more spectacularly perhaps than they had expected. Then death wiped out the September smile and the cardinals came back and took an even bigger gamble. At the present moment, they seem to have won that one too.

Cardinals are not usually high-stake gamblers.

The sluggish and weary church of Paul VI's declining years was swept through two dramatic revolutions in three months, spinning a few dazzling somersaults in the process. It now stands hesitant and uncertain—not quite sure what comes next. As Karol Wojtyla (John Paul II) ruefully commented in one of his early talks, not even he knows of what sort his papacy will be. Presently, those who have watched the poetry-writing, folk-singing, mountain-climbing bear of a man who is the new pope are predicting that the surprises have only begun.

The Catholic church has not produced all that many surprises in the last decade and a half, much less poetry-writing, guitar-playing Polish surprises.

This is the story of the three months of the three popes: August, September, and October, 1978. It is also the story of how one maverick—but in good standing—American priest, who is also a sociologist and a journalist, tried to understand the political process of church government and elections. Rereading my notes from the years of research before August, 1978, I can trace the pattern of events which produced the dramatic moments of late summer and early autumn 1978. In retrospect the hints were all there. As George Orwell would have said, all Vaticanologists are wrong (save the National Opinion Research Center's IBM 370/165 computer), but they are wrong in different ways.

The threads of the story were lying around Rome for several years, often in tangled knots. An example: papal campaigning, everyone said, required travel, meeting people, shaking hands. The principal Italian candidates were visibly engaged in such activities. Other men were traveling and being seen often for reasons which had nothing to do with a desire to be pope (and neither of the John Pauls thought of himself as papabile or even wanted the job when it was thrust upon him). For this election, unlike others, it was possible to be a candidate and engage in candidatelike behavior without realizing that one was in fact doing the things a papabile ought to be doing. Only in retrospect would the threads straighten out. A future pope had to travel, even if, as in the case of Albino Luciani (John Paul I), the trips outside of Europe were not numerous. The unknowns who were elected were not all that unknown . . . save in Rome.

Let it be clear, then, that I am not going to hide the mistakes I made in trying to put together this story. The bad predictions are going to appear alongside the good ones. Since I am accepting blame for the mistakes, you'd better believe I'm going to take as much credit as I can for the successes—and I'll accept apologies from all the journalists, especially Italian and English, who laughed at the "hopeful holy man who smiles" job description in August.

I gave this summary as part of a social science "job description" to a couple of hundred reporters in the press conference in the Columbus Hotel on a hot Sunday morning the day after Pope Paul's funeral. The Committee for the Responsible Election of the Pope had sponsored the job description and organized the press conference. My attempt to approach the papacy from a sociological analysis of the "public image" of the pope in a world of mass communications was dismissed by most of the reporters (especially the Italians and the English) as American public relations "puffery." In retrospect, I should be so lucky as to have all my social science hypotheses so spectacularly validated—and so soon as the "Smiling Pope."

The purpose of the story, though, is not to set up a ledger sheet of successes and failures in predictions. It is rather an essay in understanding, an attempt to grapple with go-for-broke cardinals, a Pinocchio-quoting pope, self-destructive curialists, and then a Polish pope who writes learned philosophical articles and canoes down turbulent rivers.

So my story will be an attempt to explain surprises, a fascinating if ultimately frustrating enterprise. But the surprises are fun; and one tries to explain them if only to enjoy them all the more.

It will be evident that I don't like the way the Catholic church has been run—great comedy but poor church. However, my criticism is not that of a detached outsider but of a passionately committed insider. The bride is not without spot till the bridegroom comes, says the Scripture, speaking of the church. But that doesn't mean we complacently accept the blemishes. Composed of humans, the church will have human faults, but those who love it are committed to reducing the faults, not covering them over with a protective secrecy whose dishonesty comes close to being blasphemous. We wash our dirty linen in public because that is the only way to get it clean.

It is just as well that I could not interview all the cardinals. It is part of the conspiracy of dishonesty and secrecy that surrounds papal elections and papal government that cardinals are not supposed to tell the truth. There are exceptions, thank God. I learned about what happened from "sources" whose lives and careers would be destroyed if their names were revealed (I thought of calling one source "Deep Purple"). So much for an institution whose Founder talked about working in the open and speaking on the housetops. The reader will have to accept that my sources are well informed, and that I quote them accurately. I have so obscured their identity, however, that it would be pointless for anyone to try to break through the disguises. In using material from confidential sources which was critical of the various actors in the conclave drama, I followed the *Washington Post*-Woodward-Bernstein rule of not including allegations which could not be confirmed by two independent sources. In addition, in several cases I asked some of those in a position to know about such allegations to read them in manuscript form to correct any inaccuracies which might have crept in. I omitted one particularly juicy raw dossier which was given to me by a major Vatican agency on an Italian cardinal, even though I was able to obtain partial confirmation, because I was not satisfied with the precision of the documentation.

This is the true story, as best I can tell it, of the year of the three popes. I tell it in the conviction that, as Pius XI said, "The Catholic Church has nothing to fear from the truth."

Sitting on a beach in the summer of 1975, lamenting the high water level of Lake Michigan and other cosmic evils, it occurred to me that Theodore White was doubtless gearing up to write his book on **The Making of the President** *during 1976.*

Too bad, some spirit whispered into my ear, that we don't

have parallel material on **The Making of the Pope.** *From the title came the idea and from the idea in about fifteen minutes a phone call to the publisher, Jim Andrews.*

He suggested that the first step in preparation would have to be a trip to Rome to brush up on the Vatican's inner workings, set up sources, and find out what people there were saying about the issues and the candidates in the next conclave. I agreed.

In the autumn of 1975, regretting the impulse of the phone call, I left our research shop (at the National Opinion Research Center) in the wise and able hands of Bill McCready and, with my cassette recorder in a flight bag, embarked for Leonardo da Vinci airport at Fiumicino. [1]

Researching a papal election is a tricky business—especially since no one knows when the election will be held. Many times I envied Teddy White for his easier access to candidates and influential figures in studying American presidential elections. My activities were about one-third social science, one-third journalism, and one-third espionage. At times when I saw Pope Paul in Rome it seemed a ghoulish project. I traveled around the United States interviewing American bishops, made a baker's-dozen trips back and forth to Rome and to various European countries—like France, Germany, Austria, England, Belgium, the Netherlands, and Ireland (where there was lots of interesting information to be consumed—along with other materials)—talked with cardinals, archbishops, bishops, monsignors, abbots, priests, laity, apostates, pagans, Jews, Protestants, and full professors. Because of the papal deaths and conclaves during the summer and fall of 1978, I spent four months on jet lag and tried in despair to peddle the project back to the publisher. I probed the inner resources of the Vatican with "sources" who were willing to trust their careers to my hands, partly because they were so disgusted at what they saw happening to the church. In the meantime, my colleagues and I at NORC continued our national sample survey research on American Catholicism, providing statistical data to back up the field work I was doing between jet flights. I kept a diary of events dictated into various kinds of tape recorders (which got blessedly smaller with each passing year), a diary which ran over a thousand pages of transcription. I dictated enough memos and reports and collected enough clippings and research reports to fill several packing boxes. I tested hypotheses and theoretical perspectives with professional colleagues in both journalism and sociology and badgered several staff seminars at NORC with ideas. James S. Coleman and I even tried to build a mathematical model of the conclave, an exercise which turned out to be uncanny in its accuracy—despite my slowness in believing its success.

Throughout the project I had access to the full journalistic resources of Universal Press Syndicate. During the two conclaves I led a UPS task force and wrote daily dispatches for over one hundred daily newspapers throughout the world.

It was exhausting, discouraging, demoralizing work, and I'm glad it's over. It was also exciting, fascinating, and enormous fun, and I'm sorry it's over. I hope Jan Pawel has a long and successful administration so that we won't have another conclave for a long time.

But I'll miss Rome . . .

Prologue

Scene I

It was not merely social science curiosity nor journalistic diligence that motivated me to begin studying the "Making of the Pope"—any more I daresay than it was merely curiosity and diligence that moved Theodore White to begin his Making of the President series. White tells us in his In Search of History that he passionately cared about the outcome of the events he was studying . . . sometimes to his own undoing. We hardly needed his memoirs, however, to know that he was personally involved in the election campaigns he reported. His concern leaps out of the pages.

So, too, I was profoundly concerned about the church and worried about the implications of the erosion of papal credibility after 1968. John XXIII and the Second Vatican Council had occurred in my young years as a priest. My eyes were opened in those days to the possibilities of a dramatic revival of the Catholic heritage of the sort which had occurred only a few times before in history. At the same time the American Catholic church was moving through an exciting era as it shifted from the church of the despised immigrant working class to the church of the upper-middle-class suburban professional class. In my first parish assignment in the Beverly Hills district of Chicago—a magic neighborhood to begin with—I was swept up by the heady euphoria of the changes from slum to suburb and from Counter-reformation to Ecumenical Age. I was deeply influenced by the liturgical and social action innovations permitted in the Archdiocese of Chicago by Cardinals Samuel Stritch and Albert Meyer. The latter sent me to graduate school at the University of Chicago in 1960 just at the time that Pope John was convening the council and John Kennedy was running for president. Prospects for the church to which I had committed my life looked bright and challenging.

Then it all fell apart. The hopes of the council era were spectacularly shattered as the council fathers went home and the Curia set about the task of reestablishing its control of the church. Disillusioned priests and nuns resigned by the thousands. Mediocrities replaced the great leaders of the council years as heads of the major archdioceses in the United States.

Pope Paul, from whom so much had been expected, seemed

somehow incapable of responding to the euphoric enthusiasm of the Catholic clergy and people. He seemed determined to reassure us that things were not moving too fast when, in fact, most of us thought they were not moving fast enough.

Then, as enthusiasm declined, and frustration increased, there came on a summer day in 1968 the long-expected birth control encyclical. Like many other American Catholics I could not believe either the conclusion or the arbitrary sweeping away with a wave of the papal hand the reasons which the pope's own commission had advanced for a change in position. I told friends at Grand Beach that people would not accept the encyclical and that it would be a disaster for the church.

How many of them would not accept it and how great a disaster it would be, however, came as a shock six years later when my colleagues at the National Opinion Research Center, William McCready and Kathleen McCourt, and I did a "before and after" study of the Vatican Council's impact on Catholic schools. We had anticipated that it was the council which had led to the decline in church practice that everyone was observing. There seemed to be little doubt in the conventional Catholic wisdom—both liberal and conservative—that the council produced the crisis American Catholicism was suffering; the only difference was over whether it was the council itself or the slow pace of its implementation.

But our research demonstrated that the council had been a huge success and that the decline in church practice could be accounted for almost entirely by reactions to the birth control encyclical. The American hierarchy pooh-poohed our research and so did many of the Catholic Wise Persons who referred vaguely to long-run "secularization trends." But no one found anything wrong with our mathematical models; and one archbishop who had repeated the party line in public told me privately, "You're right, of course; I can't sleep often at night because of what that goddam encyclical did in my diocese."

So by the summer of 1975, with twenty-one years in the priesthood, I was still an intensely committed Catholic and an irrevocably committed priest—but also a frustrated and disillusioned one. The church was in the process of muffing a golden opportunity. Given its present structure any change to make it more effective—a better witness to the Gospel it is supposed to preach—would still have to come from the top down. There had been a failure of nerve at the top during the years of Paul VI. Those years were coming to an end. The next papal election would be of enormous importance. I didn't figure I could influence the outcome; but I thought I could at least watch the drama up close. I did not anticipate, thank heaven, that for a few terrifying October days, the issue would seem to become, not the continued reform of the church, but the sheer survival of the Vatican Council as its enemies mounted one final desperate and brilliant attack against it.

Unlike a lot of other clergy-scholars of my generation I still cared about the papacy. As a sociologist I saw it as the most important religious leadership position in the world; the years of John XXIII had given a hint of what the pope could do if he understand its world-impact potential. I also believed in the importance of leadership in any human institution; I had seen what happened to my own diocese when the religious leader lost credibility among his clergy and people. I was watching the same thing happen in the whole church. Perhaps we'd had too much emphasis on the pope, as a number of my European colleagues argued; perhaps another unsuccessful pontificate would be a good thing because it would complete the elimination of the "cult of personality" from the pope's office. But I doubted it. The issue in my mind was (and is) not whether we need a pope in Christendom but what kind we need (if we didn't have an office like that of pope, we would have to invent it); the question is not whether we can dispense with papal leadership but what style of leadership would be most effective given the circumstances of our time.

On the first of October, 1975, six weeks before my first scouting expedition to Rome, Pope Paul VI issued the apostolic constitution "On Electing a Supreme Pontiff." It was a great disappointment to those who had expected a modernization of the process and a broadening of the participants beyond the membership of the College of Cardinals. While cardinals over eighty years of age were excluded (much to their chagrin), there were no other changes in the composition of the electorate. Apparently, Cardinal Giuseppe Siri, who always had the evil eye on Paul VI, had raged—while the proposed reforms were in the early stages—that they would destroy the "ancient traditions of the church," an argument which, as Siri and others well knew, would get to Paul. The result was a rigid and legalistic document, in which the requirements of secrecy (an ancient tradition dating to 1903 and designed to keep the Austrian emperor Franz Josef I from affecting the outcome of the conclave) were made tighter than they had ever been before.

This despite the fact that there isn't an Austrian emperor anymore.

ROME

Saturday, November 15, 1975

Rome—The night of November 15. I am in a state of incoherence. The damn Germans, for all their efficiency, are unable to keep their airfields from getting fogged in. So after a very pleasant flight across the Atlantic, a good night's sleep on the plane (all my new schemes for coping with jet lag were operational), I found myself at nine o'clock in the morning, not at Frankfurt but in Cologne. They thereupon put me on a bus and dragged me across the German countryside for three hours, and then made me sit in the airport in the fog for three more, and I got into Rome late tonight, thoroughly bedraggled and confused.

The Hotel Michelangelo, where I put up, is in the shadow of St. Peter's. (Incidentally, the cab driver who drove me in referred to the Vatican as a *grande bordèllo*.) The Michelangelo is nice, as hotels go . . . no, it's not "nice," it's primitive.

Anyhow, I had supper with Father Carter. A fascinating man—a scholar, deeply pious, a shrewd politician, very witty and urbane; a graduate of Oxford, with a velvet accent that brushed melodiously against my ears; a most remarkable looking man as well—tall, stately, with an aquiline nose and finely chiseled features, and a pair of slender, aristocratic hands that punctuated every third or fourth sentence with finger flicks as deft as a rapier thrust.

We went to a little Italian restaurant around the corner here where I began to fight my certainly losing battle against pasta.

During the dinner, Father Carter said that it would be a mistake to think there is any significantly organized conspiracy in the Vatican at this point. Most things happen erratically, unpredictably, spontaneously. There is no "mafia," no power elite, nothing like the Cook County Democratic Committee or Richard J. Daley. Clout in the Vatican is neither concentrated, institutionalized, nor well organized. For example, Ugo Poletti, the cardinal vicar of Rome, denounces Communism, pleading with the Italians not to vote Communist in the election. At the same time, Agostino Casaroli, the Vatican Kissinger,[1] is up in East Berlin dealing with the Communists. This is not Machiavellian; it is rather the result of a lack of any systematic organization and policy. The Curia is so crazily decentralized that the right and left hands operate unaware that coordination is required.[2] The young people in Rome, Father Carter says, scoff at this inconsistency on Communism, but it doesn't bother the Vatican at all; they don't even feel that it is inconsistent.

(Incidentally, the public opinion polls suggest that a lot of the Communist gains of the last election were a protest vote, and that when it comes to a parliamentary election, the Communists will not do all that much better than they did the last time, despite many liberal journalists who report on Italy for the United States.)

Also, there is a rumor about that the pope sent a memo to Archbishop Benelli, his chief of staff, that nineteen new cardinals will be made some time in the next couple of weeks. They will be such that the next papal election will be tipped in a conservative direction. This memo is apparently in the hands of some of the enemies of the pope, and is burning a hole in their pockets. Whether it will be leaked to the press or not remains to be seen. The Vatican is very conscious now of leaks. Everything leaks; it's as bad as the White House under Nixon. The new rules which came out several weeks ago on the election of the pope (leaked to the Italian press the day beforehand) have all kinds of precautions against bugging the papal conclave. Pope Paul is unaware of the technology of bugging. All you have to do is get one cardinal to come in there with a little microphone clipped to his cardinalatial robes with someone outside picking up the signals, and there's no way to debug the place.

There is, says Carter, campaigning going on for the papacy, but it is all very subtle. If you think you might like to be pope, you make sure you do a lot of traveling so that the other cardinals get to know you or at least are able to link a name with a face. If you are serious about such ambitions, you also are very careful about what you say and what you don't say. Cardinals Franz Koenig and Sebastiano Baggio, for example, both recently praised the Opus Dei, a right-wing quasi-secret secular institute founded in Spain which has enormous underground power in the church. (It was Opus Dei–affiliated laymen who were the technical experts in Spain during the last days of the Franco regime. I've had some personal experiences with them in the United States and find them dishonest and untrustworthy.) However, the best way to run for pope is not to say very much at all, but to limit yourself to pious generalities and platitudes as you make your appointed rounds— one strategy with a precise parallel in American presidential campaigns.

There is also negative campaigning, which is far more important, says Carter. It consists of eliminating other candidates, usually by innuendo, rumor, and character assassination. "Poor Cardinal so-and-so, he is such a great man, he works so hard, he has done marvelous work in his diocese, he is so enlightened, so open-minded, so pious. Too bad that the mental strain in that position has been so great. Oh yes, didn't you know he had to spend a week in a Swiss clinic last year recuperating. . . ."

Father Carter says that those who want an Italian pope don't so much push people as attack other people. They destroyed Cardinal Leo Josef Suenens of Belgium by saying he does peculiar things and the pope no longer approves of him. They are now working on Archbishop Jean Jadot (the progressive Belgian who has been apostolic delegate to the United States since the early 1970s and has been responsible for the appointment of many open-minded and pastoral bishops), who a lot of people think would make a good papal secretary of state. They are pointing to Jadot's statements on the acceptability of "altar girls" in liturgical functions as indications that he is frivolous and dangerous. It's an endless campaign of backbiting and tearing down, which is both aimed at Pope Paul (so that the people who are supposed to be papabili lose favor in his eyes) and also aimed at others (so that they will think the papabile has already lost favor).

The powerful people on the curial side are people like Cardinals Pericle Felici and Egidio Vagnozzi, who formerly was the apostolic delegate to the United States. Vagnozzi has nothing to do in Rome (his position in the finance office is a figurehead-one requiring little work); he has no important jobs, and all of his time, according to Father Carter, is aimed at furthering his plans for the next papal election. Vagnozzi doesn't seriously think he is going to be the pope, but he has a scheme in mind as to who ought to be pope: somebody who is Italian, somebody who will slow down the pace of change, somebody who will work not so much for the repealing of the work of the Second Vatican Council as for deadening the effects of it. Vagnozzi, Felici, and some of the other Italian curialists think the Vatican Council was a mammoth mistake. They think so in principle (they do have some convictions on the matter) and also because the Council is a threat to their own power. They want a pope who is Italian, who has come up through the diplomatic service.

Of the people who are candidates for the papacy, it is said that Sebastiano Baggio is the current favorite of Paul VI. He is Italian, a former member of the diplomatic corps, a kindly, friendly, sophisticated man of the world (according to Carter, he hasn't read a book in years—his talks are embarrassing); he could be depended upon to keep the church open enough to be presentable—but not changing very much. Certainly, he would not repeal the birth control encyclical, *Humanae Vitae*; certainly, he would not give any notable power to the Synod of Bishops.

Somewhat to the left of him is Cardinal Sergio Pignedoli, who is also said to be one of the pope's choices. Pignedoli would not be acceptable to the curialists like Vagnozzi and Felici, but they might settle for him because he is a diplomat and an Italian. What they live in mortal terror of is either a non-Italian or one who didn't come up through the same career ranks they did and who might destroy the whole world as they know it.

Very high on Father Carter's list of possible compromise candidates are Ugo Poletti, the cardinal vicar of Rome, and Eduardo Pironio, an Argentinian, born of Italian parents, who is supposed to take over the Congregation for Religious and Secular Institutes in December. The pope told him to show up by December 8, which leads everybody to think that the new consistory for creating the rumored new set of nineteen cardinals will be shortly thereafter. If made a cardinal, Pironio would be an outside candidate whom the more moderate and progressive forces in the College of Cardinals would favor. On the other hand, Karol Wojtyla, from Cracow, could be an outside candidate with whom the curialists could live. Carter thinks Wojtyla is a fine man, having met him in Cracow recently. The Curia folks, he said, would be in for a real surprise if they bring him into town. Father Carter also thinks what might happen as the conclave opens is that someone like Cardinal Leo Suenens would rise up and say, "Before we begin the selection of the pope, should we not consider retirement? Should we not consider limiting the term or office? Should we not consider whether the pope as bishop of Rome really need be an Italian?" Apparently, there are even a fair number of Roman cardinals who think these issues ought to be settled at the beginning.

The Third World cardinals will not be much of a threat, particularly the Latin Americans. The Asians and the Africans might make a little more trouble. The Italians are reasonably well organized (though, as I said before, nothing here is all that well organized), whereas the non-Italians (and they outnumber the Italians three-to-one) have no leader or organization. Vagnozzi, for example, could be counted on to have a major influence on the American cardinals, since they are all his creatures. Carter thinks there is something badly flawed about Paul VI; intellectually he stands for progress and change, but when it comes to administrative decisions, he is very timid and most likely to be strongly influenced by the last person he has talked to, which is surely the sign of a weak administrator.

An interesting story concerns Archbishop Annibale Bugnini, who was instrumental in such liturgical reforms as the translation of the mass into English and the drastic changes in the mass ceremonials. He was sacked and is living in Rome with no appointment at all. The curialists, particularly Felici, set out to get him because of the liturgical reforms of the council. Paul VI defended him for a while, but finally Bugnini fell as a victim to the character assassination that goes on in the Curia, and Paul withdrew his support.

Character assassination seems to be the standard technique by which the Curia destroys those whose power it fears or those whom it sees as enemies. Again, it's very much a small town—the village approach to politics—and not very Christian. Paul VI himself (when he was Archbishop Montini) was repeatedly the victim of such attacks. That's why Pius XII sent him up to Milan without making him a cardinal. Granted that the Curia is not the well-organized monster it is thought be be, and granted also its confusion and chaos, it still doesn't sound like a very pleasant group of people.

I asked Father Carter whether in the midst of all its machinations and conspiracies there was anybody in the Curia who had an idea of how bad things were in the church—in other parts of the world. He replied no, he didn't think so. Some men like Cardinal Benelli, who sent Jadot to the United States, might detect some of the problems; most do not. In a tour of the United States in 1970, Benelli was reportedly shocked by the low morale of the American clergy and the rapid deterioration of lay acceptance of church teaching. It is alleged that he felt the apostolic delegates in Washington for the past few decades had not been reporting accurately the conditions of the American church and had been making inept episcopal appointments. He therefore persuaded the pope that a man with an entirely different approach was needed, and Jadot, a Belgian priest who had not been trained in the regular diplomatic pattern but had served as a missionary and an army chaplain and then as papal representative in Southeast Asia and in Africa, was sent to Washington.

I told Carter that Bishop Ernie Primeau[3] had sent me tickets for the canonization tomorrow; there are all kinds of canonizations as part of the tourist spectacle for the Holy Year (held every twenty-five years). In fact, one of the alleged reasons for Cardinal Bertoli's resignation from the Congregation for the Causes of Saints is that he was being forced to push through the canonizations too fast. Forced by Benelli, of course. (Primeau, by the way, sent me two tickets. He must think I am traveling with a wife or a mistress. I'm not.) Carter said that the canonization is worth seeing if only for the ending—when Pope Paul is helped (his arthritis is so bad he can't walk by himself) around the altar and stands by himself facing the crowd out in the Piazza San Pietro, the crowd goes wild; for a brief few moments, he is not a man torn by ambivalences and harassed by an unsympathetic and immobile bureaucracy, but the religious leader of the world. That, said Carter, is the papacy at its best.

Sunday, November 16

The pope seemed a weary old man at the mass today, led around by the various bustling little monsignors. I settled in at the edge of the benches in the piazza so that I could sneak away early (looking very important as one must always do when leaving church before mass is over) without having to climb over too many of the Holy Year's pilgrims who crowded the piazza. They seemed as bored as I was by the long ceremony. I felt like telling the restless Austrians near me that canonizations were a lot longer in the old days. I believe in saints all right, I've even met a few, but I don't believe in making them this way.

But I stayed to the end anyhow and there was a surge of applause for the pope as he came around the altar to wave a feeble greeting to the people. For a moment he was the religious leader of humankind, the incarnation of the Catholic tradition, a symbol of the commitment of the congregation. He was caught in the wild enthusiasm of their response, smiled wanly, seemed to hesitate as though he wanted to say something, and then tottered off in the keeping of the little monsignors.

As much an enigma as he was twelve years ago, Paul VI is a bundle of contradictions. Even those who like him seem to feel obliged to defend him even before the criticism begins; and those who tend to dislike him are not merely honoring ecclesiastical protocol when they begin with praise for his accomplishments. I am convinced that he has repeatedly missed wonderful opportunities. Yet he stopped the Curia from undoing the work of the council and, however grudgingly and incompletely, has institutionalized its reforms so that they are probably irrevocable.

His problems are not merely problems of style. The birth control decision was a substantive one both in its content and in the view of the papacy which produced it. Yet even in this most fateful act, the personality, the style, the wrenching anguish of Paul VI seem to have been behind the decision. He began by looking for a way out of a bind, then when he was given a brilliantly reasoned way out was prevented from taking it by his strangely anguished conscience. Indeed it often seems that he is only confident that a decision is the correct one when it adds to his already overwhelming personal anguish.

In recent years he has tried bravely to smile because men like Benelli and Macchi, his secretary, have told him he ought to smile; and the smile is that of a man who is doing it because he ought to do it; not fake, surely, but somehow unpersuasive. You know that though he is trying to look happy he is actually suffering intensely; and that the suffering is made worse by the need to pretend that he is not.

Whence the anguish and the need to impose it on others? The papacy is a tough job, but his predecessor seemed to enjoy it. His

24

dismissal to Milan by Pius XII is alleged to have been a trauma from which he never completely recovered, but why should it have been that kind of blow? He knew the risks, and Milan is not after all the end of the earth. Whatever the cause, the torn, suffering soul of Paul VI is a classical tragic flaw. He is a man of intelligence, conviction, experience, courage, and, I am told, intense personal charm in a face-to-face relationship. He should have been a great pope. Yet he turns ordinary people off and has missed the possibilities of the age because of a personal torment which seems to be almost a self-fulfilling prophecy.

Walking back to the hotel after the ceremony was over I wondered if the obsessive-compulsive rules he laid down a few weeks ago for the election of his successor—as clear a manifestation of his anguished torment as one could imagine, with all its oaths and rules and regulations and penalties—may impose his style on us for the rest of the century.

Sunday afternoon

Around two o'clock, a large black Mercedes with Vatican license plates swept up to the hotel. The chauffeur stepped out and bowed as he held the door open for me. I was whisked a short distance to the Vatican, through a number of courtyards and arches, a quick turn through the Vatican gardens and then to another courtyard. The chauffeur stepped out, opened the door again, and bowed as I dashed through the rain to the door which led up a flight of very old stairs to the office of my good friend, Father Adolpho.

The Vatican hasn't changed much since the last time I was here. There are pilgrims wandering around, old nuns, old priests, dessicated-looking Vatican bureaucrats, young Swiss Guardsmen in their splendid uniforms, carefully clipped green grass, the Vatican railway station, in which a train has not stopped for thirty-five years, I'm sure. The huge dome of St. Peter's floats over it all.

Father Adolpho, whom I've known for many years, always reminds me of a Spanish nobleman out of a movie by Luis Buñuel. Tall, with very erect posture despite his advanced middle age, he greets me with a fervent handshake and an ironic twinkle in his eyes. His white shock of hair sits atop a head still magnificently leonine, with a profile that would arouse the admiration of the

Mount Rushmore sculptors. His nose is classically aristocratic—a broad, imperious beak that juts out from between a pair of flashing eyes and rounds off in a set of generous nostrils that dilate expressively as he warms to his subject.

There are, he said, essentially two parties at work in the Vatican. One is the party of Pericle Felici, Egidio Vagnozzi, and Antonio Samore, whose members are essentially against the present pontificate and would like to return to the time before the Second Vatican Council if they could.[4] These people, Father Adolpho opines, do not have the votes, but they are well organized and sufficiently in command of the *apparat* to perhaps be effective as a veto power in any papal choice. The second party is that of the moderates, at the center of which is Jean Villot, the gentle, weary Frenchman from the Auvergne who is the figurehead secretary of state. (He is without real power, since Archbishop Giovanni Benelli, the pope's man, who is technically undersecretary of state, actually runs the whole show.) This party includes other foreigners who are in the Curia and some of the Northern European cardinals, in particular the French. It is to one or the other of these parties that the various candidates are appealing. Thus the Koenig and Baggio articles praising Opus Dei are a direct pitch to the Felici crowd—who think highly of Opus Dei. The rest of the world's cardinals, having no organization at all, would probably be led around by the nose by the Romans.

Adolpho was somewhat high on Cardinal Sebastiano Baggio. Baggio runs the office that appoints most of the new bishops in the world.[5] Adolpho said he did not think Baggio was a man of much depth, but that he was gentle, kindly, and sophisticated, and at least knew something about what was going on. He's also very clever. For example, Villot, titular secretary of state but excluded from power by his undersecretary Benelli, feels very left out. Most people don't pay much attention to him because they know he's a figurehead. Baggio, when he sees Pope Paul (every week), immediately goes down to see Villot, reports the nature of their conversation, and says, "Do you think I said the right thing?" Which, of course, is a touch of graciousness toward a man who is in an awkward position, but it is also very good politics.

So it would appear, contrary to Carter, that there is actual running going on in the inner circles; that one writes articles that are important and pays visits to important people in order to keep the lines of communication open. Adolpho thinks that Sebastiano Baggio is the most likely next pope at the present moment because he has the support of the only two parties which are organized. Now these two parties, at best, aren't very many of the votes, but they are organized.

The birth control encyclical, *Humanae Vitae*, according to Adolpho, was the turning point for Pope Paul VI. He stood by his conscience, as formed by some of the theologians he listened to, defied the majority on his own birth control commission, defied public opinion, defied the world; and ever since then his regime has been essentially one of opposition—the pope plunging ahead, doing what he thinks is right regardless of what anyone else thinks. Pope Paul is assuming, of course, that the Holy Spirit speaks only through him and not through anyone else. Oscar Cullmann, a French Calvinist theologian, visited Pope Paul after *Humanae Vitae* was issued and said, "I have finally met someone I have looked for all my life, a pure Calvinist; someone who for the sake of his conscience would defy the whole world—would defy public opinion, would defy everything."

As to the nineteen new cardinals, Adolpho said that even if Paul VI knew that creating a mostly Italian curial consistory would offend public opinion (and he says Paul may or may not know it), he would go ahead and do it, because his "conscience" would persuade him that it was the right thing to do.

Adolpho thought that Sergio Pignedoli was not a serious candidate as far as the insiders in the Vatican were concerned; they dismiss him as superficial and something of a clown. But Pignedoli is out campaigning in the world. He said recently he saw no reason why there couldn't be an African cardinal elected to the papacy. This, it was promptly observed in Rome, was a political ploy designed to get him Third World votes, which it may have been, but no more so than Baggio's visits to Villot.

Adolpho felt that the new pope would probably reappoint Villot secretary of state or make another foreigner the secretary of state. In either case, the appointee would have real power, so that it would not be a situation where an Italian like Benelli was in fact running the church no matter who the pope was. Pope Paul has always found it difficult to deal with new people; he makes new contacts poorly, he's shy, and the older he gets the less he wants to deal with new people. So on the one hand, he made the Frenchman Villot his secretary of state; and on the other hand, he has Benelli actually running the church because he would be so ill at ease in dealing with the French cardinal. It's clear to me from Adolpho that the man for me to see is Cardinal Sebastiano Baggio—the nearest thing to a front-runner.

Monday, November 17

One enters the solemn porticos of the Sacred Congregation for Bishops just off St. Peter's Square, in a little square called "The Square of Pius XII, the Savior of the City." Apparently, Pius XII is given some credit for the Allies not bombing the hell out of Rome during the war. (I think Italian voters in New York probably deserve more credit for it.) On the right-hand side as you go down from St. Peter's you go into this place, and there are very important-looking ushers who send you upstairs; and when you get upstairs there are even more ushers—three ushers—sitting at desks doing nothing but ushering. You're shown into a little side cubicle, and Father John Strynkowski, an American Pole from Brooklyn, shows up. He entertains you, and you're brought into another anteroom, where you see people scurrying about in cassocks and red birettas. In Cook County, we'd call it the office of the chairman of the patronage committee; it's where jobs are given out, where they make bishops. Some people are coming in looking happy, others coming in looking sad.

I find that Baggio, as a papal candidate, isn't giving interviews to anybody, so I was very lucky to be able to get in to see the man. In any case, this is where bishops come to get other people made bishops, or to impress Cardinal Baggio with their ability so that he may make them archbishop or someday even cardinal. Finally, I was shown into the room with great massive windows from which one can see St. Peter's Square and the basilica itself, to say nothing of the fifth-floor papal apartment in the Vatican Palace, where Baggio presumably hopes to live someday.

Over in the corner are these rich, red chairs, and on a table behind the chairs is a notebook bound in red leather and a copy of the *Annuario Pontificio*, which has the names and vital statistics of all the bishops in the world. Baggio sits in one chair, I sit in another, and Strynkowski sits in a third, to help with the translation. Baggio understands English pretty well, and can speak it—a lot better than I can speak Italian. I say, "Buon giorno, Signor Cardinale," and he's impressed that I know Italian. I tell him I don't know much.

He's a short man, powerfully built, with square, broad shoulders, a broad face—from the Dolomites in northern Italy, sixty-three years old, glasses kind of perched on his nose, smiling, pleasant. I give him my book about Ireland, and he admires the pictures. "These children must be Italian," he says. I say, "No, they're Irish." "They are so beautiful they must be Italian." And I say, "Both Irish and Italian children are beautiful," and we laugh. Then he laughs some more. He thanks me for the things that have been sent, Bishop Mark Hurley has spoken of me, and I am a very controversial person. That's the opening line.

Now, what are you supposed to do with a line like that? And then he says, "But then, you know, not to be controversial is not to do anything." And that pretty much sets up the tone of the whole conversation. In other words, it was a nothing conversation. Bishop William McManus had spoken about me. "He said you were very important, a very vigorous man, very dangerous in some ways to the hierarchy, critical at times; but it's good to be critical, we need people to be critical, but then we must be careful not to hurt people's feelings." Who is he trying to kid? The only bishop I've ever criticized by name is Cardinal John Cody, who is madcap, and Baggio knows that as well as I do.

I suspect the reason he wanted to get a look at me is that he'd read some of my columns in the *San Francisco Chronicle*. (When I'm not occupied doing sociology or harassing the church, I write a syndicated column.) He'd gotten the sociological material Bishop Mark Hurley had sent to him, and he'd probably heard about my criticizing of Cody, so he wanted to get some kind of idea of what I was like. Well, what he found out about me is about what I found out about him, that I can be charming, pleasant, witty, and say nothing. Vis-à-vis the sociological material: "Yes, it's very important, very interesting, it's very good that the council has been such a success. This negative impact of *Humanae Vitae* is very disturbing, it would say some grave things about the faith of the Catholic people, eh?" Nothing grave about mistakes having been made by the Holy See. "But it would not be very different in Europe." He did not know of any research, but he thought it wouldn't be any different. Damn right, it wouldn't be different!

He said that Chicago is a very interesting city. He had been in it once in 1945, just after the war, in a little town called Oak Park, Illinois (which, I quickly pointed out, was the place where I had been born). "Oh, that is very nice," and we talked about Oak Park and about his relatives in Oak Park, and then we talked about Canada, and then we got back to Chicago and he said, "Oh, it is a very controversial, a very difficult diocese." He feels sorry for Cardinal Cody, he has such a hard time there, but then any man would have a hard time in Chicago. To which I replied that Cody's predecessor Cardinal Albert Meyer liked it.

Now, mind you, Sebastiano Baggio knows about Cody. I know this from other sources. But to give the devil his due, the man is papabile, and the best way to run for pope in that position is not to say or do anything. He is talking to a controversial American journalist and sociologist, and so he's got to be careful, and he's got to be able to say to others that he met me and found me delightful, charming, and able to take good photographs.

Then he comes back to the business of the sociological material and says it is not especially appropriate for the office of creating bishops. He does not know "stateestics." I didn't say to him that Richard J. Daley learned accounting after he became mayor because he thought accounting was necessary for being a good mayor. If you're going to be a pope these days, you damn well ought to learn some statistics and some sociology. I didn't say that.

"Well, . . . this material would be more important if you sent it to the Holy Office, because they are the ones who are interested in matters of faith and morals. Do you know anyone at the Holy Office?" ("The Holy Office"—not its proper name; it is now officially called the Congregation for the Doctrine of the Faith, but everybody here still calls it the Holy Office.)

And that was about it. My summary of Sebastiano is that he will do no great harm to anyone. He is a kindly, pleasant, cheerful man. Oh, he could stick a knife into the back of a Vatican rival, but on the whole he would be very friendly, very charming, and perhaps democratic.

He would never try to put the mass back into Latin, he would never try to reverse anything substantial that has been done, but he would basically have the view of things that is common to a typical enlightened, gentle, pleasant, charming member of the Roman Curia.

With Baggio, you would have a lot of smiling, a lot of charm toward tourist pilgrims. I do not think he would try to put Hans Küng in the bowels of any prison either. He is apparently everybody's favorite candidate around here, the pope's included.[6]

The church is made up of human beings, not angels, and as every Catholic who has got beyond the perspective of the catechism knows, the "human element" in the church is subject to all the weaknesses of any human leadership. Often these weaknesses are shocking and disgraceful; other times they are tragic. A colorful example of the tragedy which afflicts the human element in the church was the hand wringing of the Curia about the "Chicago affair." Everyone knew that something had to be done about it, but no one knew what to do. Cardinals are the top elite in the church structure. While not exactly untouchable, they are treated with great reverence and respect; even when you have decided that for the good of the church it may be necessary to replace one of them, you procrastinate and delay, hoping that the problem will solve itself. You are especially likely to procrastinate when the city involved is American and you know that Americans are quite docile. The Chicago affair is an example of the human political struggles that go on in the Catholic church largely unknown to laymen. It provides a microcosm for the political intrigue that occurs on the world scene among papal candidates.

Though I did not know it at the time of my interview with Cardinal Baggio, both he and the then Archbishop Benelli—rarely in agreement—had already determined to attempt to remove Cardinal Cody.

Sometime in the spring following my visit, the cardinal was offered a Roman position by the pope personally. (The offer was reported by the cardinal to several priests of the archdiocese and confirmed by two of my Roman sources.) The cardinal bluntly refused the offer. Several more attempts would be made during the rest of Paul VI's administration.

After the meeting with Cardinal Baggio, I went back to the area around the Piazza Venezia for lunch with two more sources, one of them American and one Italian. They both said that there is a scheme going on to ensure the election of an Italian as the next pope; a plot that involves the plans for the next consistory (the rumored nineteen new cardinals). Most of the new cardinals will be members of the Curia and former papal diplomats; very few will be residential bishops and none from the United States. The diplomats in Paris, Lisbon, Madrid, Brussels are likely to make cardinal, but of the nineteen or twenty new voters for the next pope, at least two-thirds of them will be either Italian or in the Italians' pockets. The Curia is convinced it has won, the Holy Year enthusiasm persuades them of this even more, and they are now going about business as usual.

The result will be that the church will drift further and further away from its central authority, but they don't know that.

Tuesday, November 18

I am here in my cubicle at the Hotel Michelangelo looking out on a Roman tenement next door, barely visible through the drizzling rain. It's about five o'clock, and unfortunately, the Romans have a terribly uncivilized custom of not eating supper until about seven o'clock.

I stopped by earlier in the afternoon to see an old friend of mine at a certain educational institution here in the city. He was somewhat disheartened both by the changes happening in his own religious order and by the confusion in the church. "There are lots of new things unleashed by the Council," he said; "Pentecostalism, Third Worldism, ecumenism, the reorganization of the Curia; and all these are good things, but they're all so dangerous." He was staring glumly out the window at the rain-drenched piazza, his kindly face lined with worry.

The old bonds, he said, are weakened, and in some cases, almost nonexistent. A lot of people are "letting it all hang out"—doing their own thing. Liberationists, pietists, mystics, Zen-types—everyone scurrying around, while the leaders over at the Vatican are pulling and tugging, desperately trying to deal with the dynamics at work without much notion of what's going on.

I left feeling very disheartened. The man I visited was one of the greats of the Second Vatican Council. He was a little too old to cope with the changes that came after the Council, and he is terribly upset by Rome's inability to maintain some order in the church.

My meeting with Father Micheli certainly confirmed that impression. A short, wiry priest from the West Side of Chicago, he talks in explosive bursts, his thin red lips pushing out the words with machine-gun rapidity. His bushy eyebrows function like semaphore flags, signaling, in gyrating spurts, the gist of the mood or thought he's communicating. A powerfully animated man, he leans into the conversation with his entire body, hacking the air with his gnarled hands, underscoring certain points with a lunge of his shoulders.

In some ways, Micheli is a conservative; he surely doesn't buy liberation theology, for example. On the other hand, he is quite upset by the new papal election reforms because the laity is excluded. Sitting with him in his room watching the rain pour down, I asked him whether anyone was indeed minding the store. The Curia, he replied, his eyebrows arching over his penetrating brown eyes, is utterly cut off from reality. They sit up there on the Vatican hill and make decisions based on the world that they know—that is to say, the world of the diplomatic service, the Italian seminary, and the Italian church. Paul VI's gestures are strangely out of sync with what's going on in the real world. His recent appearance at the University of Rome was pathetic because the motions that he was going through seemed curiously quaint to the students—and not quaint-lovable the way John XXIII was, but *quaint–out–of–it*. He is an old man who grew up in a different kind of world, has no contact with the modern world, and is surrounded by advisors who have no contact with it either.

Micheli told me a chilling story about Montini (Pope Paul) when he was a young monsignor in the Secretariat of State during the war years. The ambassadors to the Holy See of many of the countries who were at war with Italy lived in apartments just on the outskirts of Vatican City as enemy aliens huddling under the protection of Vatican extraterritoriality. It was a strange, artificial, goldfish-bowl experience, but the families of the ambassadors necessarily became very close; and a teenage son of one ambassador and a daughter of another, as young people will, fell in love. One night, hurrying home in the blackout, they paused briefly on Vatican property to exchange what was, by even the standards of their day, a very chaste kiss. Montini happened to see them out the window (he was working late, as he still does) and was horrified. The boy's father was called the next day and severely reprimanded for permitting such profanation of sacred places. Both the kids were forced to go to confession because of their sacrilegious behavior. I record this story not to ridicule the pope (he was, after all, acting according to his own lights), but rather to illustrate how stern and demanding his conscience is.

Many of the decisions that Paul VI has made, the trivial little compromises, the mountains of labor that bring forth a mouse, are a result, not of intellectual deficiency—the pope is a very smart man and is well read, if not deeply read, particularly in French literature—but of a man who, for all his intelligence, is frightened by dynamisms he doesn't understand. Any attempts to view the problems of the papacy in terms of right or left, conservative or liberal, progressive or reactionary, democratic or authoritarian, even Italian or non-Italian, don't come to the heart of the problem. The Vatican is a structure which is not very well organized, where no one is really in charge, and within which people are cut off from any good sources of information. Decisions are being made in an information vacuum; for example, the current attempt to talk Italians out of supporting the Communists in the municipal elections here in Rome—which is going on at a frantic pace—is based on a lack of information on how the Italian electorate reacts. Similarly, the support for the Italian antidivorce referendum that the Vatican was engaged in a couple of years ago was based on a fundamental, deep-seated misunderstanding of what that issue was and how the Italian public was reacting to it. The people who run the Vatican don't know what they are doing.

There is also considerable theological controversy about the nature of the papacy. I thought that one had been settled forever—but I told Micheli about my idea of the pope as the religious leader of humankind, and he responded that a fair number of the more progressive theologians really don't like this role and would much sooner see the pope as merely bishop of Rome and the man who presides over the unity of the rest of the church. They, therefore, argue that the pope should be an Italian because he's primarily bishop of Rome and his basic responsibilities are to Rome. Thus, we have a curious alliance between the right-wingers, who want to keep an Italian papacy because it will maintain their power (and their principles too), and the left-wingers, who want to continue the Italian papacy because they think it makes ecumenical sense. Characteristically, the left gives you no hint of how the centralized, world-ruling Roman Curia is going to be eliminated by an Italian pope.

If the pope is the bishop of Rome, then let him be elected by the clergy of Rome, but if he is elected by the Roman clergy primarily to be bishop of Rome, there's no reason why he should be the ruler of the whole Catholic world. However, if the pope is the head of the whole church, there is no reason why he has to be an Italian, and every reason why he should be elected by representatives of the world.

The pope is not the bishop of Rome in any meaningful sense; other people run Rome for him. He is the head of the Universal Church, and he should be elected by the whole church. However, very progressive churchmen like Yves Congar, a French theologian, want to go to the other route and reduce the pope to being the bishop of Rome, who simply presides over the other bishops but does not govern them. It seems to me that the pope should be the religious leader of the whole world. Where he comes from is less important. The local people are now using this bishop of Rome thing to suit their own purposes, to rig the next papal election. Whether they'll get away with it or not depends on (1) the next consistory (when new cardinals are made) and (2) whether the cardinals outside of Rome, who are the overwhelming majority, can be hoodwinked.

In summary, we have a church that is much less well organized at the top than even I would have thought before I came here. We have a pope and advisors fundamentally out of touch with things, just not understanding the basic realities; we have a church with all kinds of dynamisms and forces and movements whirling around, many of them shallow and superficial; radicals who, for all practical purposes, are not Christian in any sense; conservatives trying to dig in their heels; Pentecostals, and charismatics, and many varieties of other enthusiasts flourishing in every corner.

The result, ten years after the Second Vatican Council, is drift. A stronger pope than Paul, a man of vision, perhaps would have seen us through this chaotic era with somewhat better direction and more confidence. What happened was we had Paul, a weak pope, whose vision became blighted almost when he took office, a man who lacked the administrative strength to tie things together *and* the personal strength to make the kinds of decisions that his own intellect inclined him to. He was weak when we needed strength, and the result has been chaos. The next pope should be strong, and strong does not necessarily mean autocratic; rather, it means confident. He should be a visionary with a sense of direction. It is not likely—from what I've learned in Rome on this sortie—that we will get such a man.

The best way to treat this whole show is as comedy. Somebody remarked to me yesterday that a certain cardinal is a buffoon. That is true; he's a lovable guy and a buffoon. But that doesn't make him unique around this scene. Everybody is a buffoon. The only way you can really grasp this show is to consider it a comedy—men parading around in red robes, white robes, and with fans and banners waving. Mind you, this is all in the name of a church that was founded as a symbol of simplicity. See Pope Paul wringing his hands and whining, claiming to be the vicar of one who came to instill confidence, hope, and joy in humankind. There are characters like Cardinal Felici (and what an ironic name that is!) who cavort about the Vatican trying desperately to cling to power over an institution that is in chaos and whose founder rejected power on a priori grounds. The comings and goings of this isolated aristocracy, which doesn't run the church and, to the extent it attempts to, runs it badly, can be best appreciated as wildly funny.

Wednesday, November 19

My sinuses are completely out of hand, and I seem not to have brought enough sinus pills. I'm going to have to ask the sometime bishop of Manchester what one does for sinuses in this crazy city.

I had lunch today in one of those marvelous little restaurants clustered in the streets off the Piazza Venezia, which served unspeakably good pasta for moderate prices (but won't take American Express credit cards). My companions were an Austrian and an American journalist. They both agreed that the Vatican staff is out of touch with what is going on in the rest of Italy. Many Italians think that the best thing that could happen to the church in Italy would be to get a non-Italian pope, or, alternately, someone like Michele Pellegrino of Turin, the so-called red cardinal, who would clean house at the Curia.

After lunch I decided to take a walk, so I walked by the Holy Office, past the gate you have to get through to go into the Vatican. I strolled across the wet and deserted piazza, down the Via della Conciliazione by the souvenir shops and the old palaces, hotels, and churches down to the Tiber. Then I turned to come back, and, somehow or other, got myself thoroughly lost. All my much-vaunted geographical sense failed me, and I ended up, it turns out, walking in exactly the wrong direction, farther and farther away from St. Peter's and the hotel—which would have been all right except the rain came back and it poured. As a punishment for my pride, I got soaking wet and had to hail a taxi, come back to the hotel, and dry out. The end of a perfect morning.

One of my informants at lunch said that for the Vatican under Paul religion means effectively the relationship between church and state. It means what happens to the church in Spain after Franco? What will come of Archbishop Agostino Casaroli's negotiations with the Poles? What sort of deals will one have to make with the new African governments? This sort of religion is the traditional concern of the Roman Curia; it always has been since the temporal power of the pope began—which was a hell of a long time ago. Religion as such, religion as the answer to fundamental problems of meaning and belonging, is something these folks don't understand and, indeed, shy away from. To speak of the pope as a religious leader, a man who gets up and talks about good and evil, life and death, joy, hope, confidence, the great forward movement of humankind on its pilgrimage, is totally foreign to the curial mentality. They are concerned about politics, administration, and finance.

After this melancholy lunch and walk, I managed to have a flood in my room at the Michelangelo by not keeping an eye on the bathtub that I was trying to fill (the shower doesn't work); I then went to a pharmacy to find some Actifed. To my astonishment, they knew what Actifed was. Some things do work here. Then I went off to supper with an old Roman hand (clergyman).

Since life in the Vatican bureaucracy consists of pushing pens, stamping papers, and dealing with other curialists, I raised the question about what happens sexually under these circumstances. (I think you can practice celibacy if you're ministering in some fashion to people, but if all your work from beginning to end is paper, then the human juices and emotions well up and destroy you.) Apparently, the sex lives of those in the Curia are reasonably presentable. There are some aberrations but not many. My own personal feeling is that they'd be a lot better off with more aberrations. At least they'd be more human.

My friend switched the conversation to Archbishop Benelli. Benelli, unlike most curialists, is tremendously efficient and has probably run the church primarily out of great personal loyalty to Paul VI. If anything has been done efficiently in the Pauline regime, it is because Benelli has done it. Benelli is no great liberal, even though he sent Jean Jadot to the United States as apostolic delegate, but he is not the villain Peter Hebblethwaite, in his article in the *London Observer*, chose to make him. He's a loyal operator who gets things done, and when it comes to personal position, he is more likely to be on our side than the other side.

Thursday, November 20

Today I had lunch with one of Rome's more distinguished British journalists, Peter Nichols of the *Times* of London. At the last two conclaves, he said, the pattern was an Italian pope, acceptable to the outlanders. The French came down both times determined the pope would not be a man from the Curia. It was Angelo Roncalli (John XXIII) the first time because he had saved them from de Gaulle. Then it was Montini (Paul VI) the second time because he had been thrown out by the Curia and because he had maintained cordial relations with the French.

Something like this will happen the next time. The Curia will push one of their candidates, most likely Baggio, at least they'll push him on the second go-around (after Pericle Felici has a shot at it), and then the next step will be an Italian candidate whom the other Europeans and the Third World types could accept and who wouldn't be too offensive to the curialists. Nichols suggested a fellow named Salvatore Pappalardo, the archbishop of Palermo in Sicily. (That's enough for me to favor him, since some of my best friends are Sicilians.) Apparently he's doing a superb job down there—helping the poor, denouncing political corruption, staying out of party politics, open, friendly, a former diplomat who has been in Indonesia. However, he's still quite young for a papal candidate, only fifty-seven.

The Curia types really can't distinguish between the papal mystique, which appeals to all kinds of people (just as does the mystique of the British royal family) and which brings people here during the Holy Year, and the papal policies, which people cheerfully ignore. You can come and shout "Viva il Papa" at St. Peter's because of the symbolic power of the office and still not really take seriously the kind of stuff the pope tries to teach you.

Also, Nichols thought this new theological awareness of the pope as the bishop of Rome was ironic, given the fact that the pope has nothing to do with the diocese of Rome, which is in terrible shape. The papacy has never spoken out about the tremendous urban decay in Rome, the bad transportation, the bad housing, the lack of parks, the pollution. Now all of a sudden, with the threat of a Communist mayor here, the Holy See suddenly gets terribly concerned about Rome, warning people against voting Communist in the election, a tactic which will absolutely guarantee the Communists 500,000 more votes. Thus, we will have the very interesting possibility of the election of the next pope going on in a city with a Communist mayor—a marvelous symbol of the utter failure of Pope Paul to be vicar of Rome in any meaningful or effective way.

I was impressed with the Englishman's strategic design, his idea that the new pope would be a non-curial Italian. But he also added that this time there is no non-curial Italian who is obviously and clearly the candidate the way Roncalli was in 1958 and the way Montini was in 1963.

Later in the afternoon, I had a drink with an American who works in the Curia. His view of the upcoming papal election was somewhat different from those I heard earlier. He does not think the Roman vote is nearly as powerful or as well organized as some of my other sources suggested. There are twenty-five Italian cardinals, and they are badly disorganized. Many would not fit into the Felici party, and they have lots of grudges to settle with the current top brass in the Vatican. There has only been one curial man elected pope in two hundred years, Eugenio Pacelli (Pius XII), who was the overwhelming choice in the late 1930s—because he was competent for the job. The Romans will have to get a lot of votes from the outlanders to guarantee the election for one of their number. The Baggios and the Pignedolis are not exceptional people. So his description reinforces the idea I came here with: there is no clear candidate; it could be that the next election will be a very long papal conclave.

I asked him what he would do if he were a candidate and he said, "Well, the first thing to do would be to get non-Italian support." You do that by traveling, so all of the visible candidates, Pignedoli, Baggio, Johannes Willebrands (not Felici) have been traveling, seeing cardinals around the world. Some of them are also busy being very impressive at the synods when the bishops and cardinals come to Rome for their triennial meeting.

While Baggio can clearly be said to be the winner-book favorite, with some support in the Curia and no really great opposition anywhere, he has by no means got the vote sewed up. What goes on here in those ten days between the arrival of the cardinals after the pope's death and the entering into the election conclave will be very, very interesting.

He told me the usual number of horror stories about how the Curia operates—people being passed over for jobs, people having opponents put under them. The latter was done to Cardinal Paolo Bertoli, head of the Sacred Congregation for the Causes of Saints. So he did the unthinkable and quit the Curia.[7] He is off to Lebanon now as papal delegate, to try to settle things there. Another story was about someone getting into trouble with one of his superiors and being exiled to Portugal for seventeen years and then being exiled further to Indonesia. Cardinal Antonio Samore, who is one of the villains, used to wait on tables and type for Cardinal Tardini when he was secretary of state. He waited on him hand and foot, and that's how he got to be cardinal.

The Curia leaders are still ruthless in their quest for power, absolutely unforgiving to their enemies, and not very trustworthy to their friends. Their motivations are not evil; while some of them might be interested in money (it would be more for their family than for themselves), their basic motivation is the good of the church. Sometimes they are too Christian, they don't sack enough people, they don't get rid of incompetents; Paul, for example, tends to keep incompetent people around. One of the advantages of having Giovanni Benelli as his hatchet man is that Benelli isn't afraid to chew out incompetents.

Tonight, I had supper with a number of Americans and Englishmen who work for a certain agency at the Curia. They do not think Baggio will be the next pope. The situation, they tell me, is very fluid and no predictions can be made. So much depends on what happens in the next consistory, how soon there is a papal death and an election, and how the people from around the world react when they come to Rome.

Some of them thought that the Cardinals from around the world would take leadership from Rome; others thought they would not, that they were stubborn and angry at the mess Rome had made of things. They were hard-pressed, however, when I pushed them to say who might organize the outlanders and, indeed, whose candidacy to organize for. Cardinal Koenig of Vienna, they said, was seventy and perhaps too old; beyond that they had neither a candidate nor a leader, and no thought as to how either might emerge. They were apparently quite willing to accept, more or less passively, the notion that the cardinals would gather here in Rome for the conclave, and in those ten days between the death of the pope and the locking up of the conclave, a natural leader would arise among the outlanders, who would oppose the well-organized Felici crowd. They also said (and this is a new bit of information) that the Italian cardinals meet regularly to discuss among themselves who the next pope will be, despite the prohibition under pain of excommunication for campaigning for a new pope while the old one is still alive. I said suppose we get two million dollars from a foundation to wire the next papal election, how would we go about doing it? Well, they made some funny remarks about bribing Italian cardinals, but clearly they hadn't thought through any of the techniques necessary to organize an election. About all they could say was that anyone who wanted to be pope should do a lot of traveling. Everybody mentioned John Krol, the archbishop of Philadelphia, who does a lot of traveling.

(Incidentally, there's an interesting story about Krol that's worth noting here. When he was in Chicago recently, Tim Lyne, the rector of the Holy Name Cathedral [and no friend of mine, I might add], invited Krol up for a drink, and Krol said, "Well, I'd like to come, but I won't." Lyne said, "Why not?" Krol said, "You probably don't have what I drink." "What do you drink?" "Old Forester." "Six, eight, or twelve years old?" Well, that's putting John Krol in his place.)

Friday, November 21

I picked up today a description of the balloting at the election of Pope John.[8] There were five candidates: Cardinal Roncalli, who became John XXIII; Alfredo Ottaviani, the curial reactionary par excellence; Ruffini, a northern Italian, archbishop of Palermo in Sicily, proved to be very conservative at the Council, but at the time was probably getting some Italian votes by people who viewed him as more progressive than the reactionary Ottaviani; and Gregory Peter Agagianian, an Armenian cardinal, born in the Soviet Union actually, lived his whole life in Rome at the Curia and was a curialist, the favorite of those who thought he might be the first non-Italian pope in many years. The fifth was Masella, a kind of moderate curialist.

Roncalli started out with five solid French votes, and they stuck. The moderates were going for Agagianian, the conservatives for Ruffini. It became clear into the third ballot that neither Agagianian nor Ruffini was going to win; then the conservatives switched from Ruffini to Ottaviani on the fourth ballot and the moderates switched to Roncalli; thus on the fourth ballot Roncalli and Ottaviani were running neck and neck. The fifth ballot was the critical one. Roncalli moved ahead and Ottaviani lost one vote. Apparently some of the Masella people finally switched to Roncalli; he probably picked up one or two votes from them, and when Ottaviani lost one vote, that was the ball game. But it was a near thing, a near thing.

How did Roncalli vote? He voted for Ruffini on the first two ballots. Roncalli got seven votes on both ballots (he wasn't a leading candidate by any means), and probably Ruffini was closest to him ideologically, at least at that stage of his life. On the third ballot, when Roncalli gained a vote, Ruffini lost two, one of which was Roncalli's, who then, sensing that the tide was beginning to turn in his direction, voted on the next two ballots for one Valerio Valeri (the only vote he got). So instead of going to Ottaviani as the other Ruffini people did—or most of them did, in any case—Roncalli began to throw his vote away. On the last two ballots, he voted for Lercaro, the progressive bishop of Bologna, who didn't have a chance. That should have been a hint to one and all what kind of man they were getting. Someone who could move from Ruffini to Lercaro was obviously going to be one hell of a pope.

WILLEBRANDS — too Dutch?

PIGNEDOLI — too volatile?

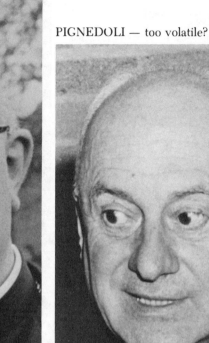

Religious News Service Photo

Religious News Service Photo

Religious News Service Photo

BERTOLI — too stern?

BAGGIO — too curial?

Religious News Service Photo

"COMPROMISE ITALIANS"

URSI — too mercurial?

POLETTI — too close to the Curia?

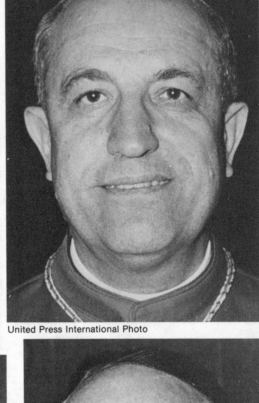

United Press International Photo

Wide World Photos

PAPPALARDO — not interested?

COLOMBO — too old?

"THE THIRD WORLD"

CORDEIRO — the most powerful of the Asians.

LORSCHEIDER — Luciani's candidate to the end.

GANTIN — an African "long shot".

ARNS — the other German "ethnic" from Brazil.

"THE MEN OF THE COUNCIL" — *The Real Winners*

MARTY of Paris
Religious News Service Photo

ALFRINK of Utrecht

Religious News Service Photo

Religious News Service Photo

Religious News Service Photo

KOENIG of Vienna

SUENENS of Mechelen — Brussels

CODY — he was fighting.

JADOT — he wasn't there.

Wide World Photos

Religious News Service Photo

DEARDEN —
he was silent.

Wide World Photos

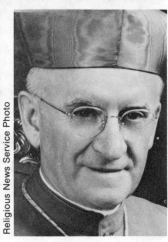

Religious News Service Photo

CARBERRY — he was worried
about his electric razor.

Wide World Photos

KROL — he was pleased.

ENRIQUE Y TARANCÓN — Spanish progressive

HUME — English liberal

Religious News Service Photo

Religious News Service Photo

Religious News Service Photo

PELLEGRINO — Italian Holy Man

Religious News Service Photo

HOEFFNER — German autocrat

Religious News Service Photo

ODDI — would remain "unemployed" as long as Paul VI lived.

VILLOT — secretary of state — too gentle for the job?

Religious News Service Photo

Religious News Service Photo

PIRONIO — of the Congregation of Religious and Secular Institutes, was on Latin American death lists.

Religious News Service Photo

Religious News Service Photo

FELICI — "Supreme Court" leader of the conservatives.

VAGNOZZI — the man to blame for the mess in the United States.

"FINAL CONTENDERS"

WYSZYNSKI and WOJTYLA — the primate of Poland and his counterpart.

United Press International Photo

Wide World Photos

SIRI — He "heard nothing".

United Press International Photo

BENELLI — the "pope maker" who did not make pope.

The important thing to notice in this story is the role of the French, because if they had cast their early votes for Agagianian, Roncalli would only have had one or two and would not have been seriously considered. Agagianian would have ended up with close to twenty votes on the first ballot. At that stage of the game he might have been very hard to stop. But the French held firm for Roncalli, and on the third ballot, Agagianian lost one vote to Roncalli; on the next ballot, four more jumped to Roncalli, and two more on the next ballot.

The French, in other words, came in with a disciplined block of votes and were able to push through the election of their candidate. It was a brilliant political exercise, and the lesson of it for the next papal election is that if you have a really tough, disciplined block of voters who are not likely to lose their nerve, you can have an influence out of all proportion to your size.

Recapitulating the insights of today, the papal election seems to operate on the same political dynamics as any election. In the election for which I have evidence, the Curia types did not want Gregory Peter Agagianian because despite being one of their own he was still an Armenian, and they dug in their heels against him. The French dug in theirs for Roncalli, and there was indeed more support in the body for either a non-Italian or a noncurialist than there was for an Italian curialist; the stubbornness of the French and the discipline of their voting assured victory for their candidate.

The same processes are at work as in American political conventions. It is interesting, incidentally, that even though the election is supposed to be completely secret, this rather detailed account of the balloting is out; the person from whom I got it also knows whom each cardinal voted for, a matter which is supposed to be impossible to learn. But somebody who was in the conclave not only kept track of how many votes everybody got but also noted who voted for whom. (It is alleged that Cardinal Richard Cushing came out of the conclave with the precise totals of each ballot written on his shirt cuff!)

So it is quite easy, despite all the rules and all the emphasis on secrecy, for the electors to know not only how the votes are going, but who is voting for whom, who is likely to change, and what kind of arrangements need to be made.

It was observed to me today (I am being deliberately obscure

43

about this source, even more obscure than I usually am) that the Curia has a tremendous advantage when the cardinals come to town to choose the pope. The Curia is, after all, made up of the people in charge; the cardinals have been pulled away from their work, are weary from jet fatigue and confused about the issues in the election. The curial officials, like the cardinal camerlengo (a kind of an interim pope while the new one is being chosen—currently, Cardinal Jean Villot), know where the washrooms are, where you eat and what time mass will be said, where you should be going on each day, what the proper procedures for the meetings are. Hence, they have far more power than anyone else. Although they no longer have the majority of votes, they control the apparatus and the structure and are ready for the election while everybody else is not ready. Organized and in control of the structure, the Curia starts out being in charge of the process and may dominate it.[9] As one cynic put it, the Holy Spirit gives them a head start.[10]

Saturday, November 22

One of the persons I saw today had some interesting comments about the papal mystique. The papacy has been so sanctified, so deified, he said, that the people around the pope take the papacy so seriously that it becomes impossible for the man to take himself as an ordinary leader and religious administrator. My informant said he has heard people at supper say ecstatically, "I saw the pope twice today." My friend said he was tempted to reply, "So what? He's nothing but a little old Italian man."

Mystique is important, indeed, indispensable in the human condition. People need a sacred leader; but often they turn the sacred leader into someone who thinks himself to be sacred, hence Richard Nixon's comic opera guard around the White House. It's probably not impossible to have both the mystique and a democratic papacy, but it's difficult. And how can you have self-criticism in the midst of all the quasi-sacred environment in the Vatican Palace, such words as "Your Holiness" and "Holy Father," the white robes, and all the traditions and customs? As my friend said, it's sometimes funny to hear Pope Paul begin a talk by saying that he is overjoyed at something or the other, with a face filled with sorrow, anguish, and pain.

Later on I went to one of my informants to get the final details on the whole *Humanae Vitae* story. Pope John XXIII had set up a birth control commission in the early 1960s to advise him about birth control—a commission which met, I gather, in a rather desultory fashion, as a lot of things were likely to be carried out in John's splendid, charismatic, but not always very efficient administration. Paul increased the membership of the commission, put it to work on a systematic basis, and removed from the Vatican Council all discussion of birth control. This was, incidentally, a characteristic action of Paul VI's. He did not trust his brother bishops to handle the question of birth control intelligently in the open; so he had to do it himself secretly.

Nevertheless, everyone in the world knew there was a commission considering the question. Once you think the thing has to be reconsidered, then you admit it's changeable, which was all the Catholics of the world needed. As the Princeton University fertility study shows, American Catholics turned to the birth control pill in enormous numbers in the early 1960s. Pope Paul's commission felt that its mandate was to find out whether the doctrine was indeed changeable, since there would have been no point in convening the commission if the pope hadn't been looking for a way out. After considerable discussion, they concluded that the pill was not the issue, but that artificial contraception was, and that one could find justifications for a change in the position by concluding that as long as a whole marriage relationship was open to procreation, each individual act of intercourse within it did not have to be open. Only a few members of the commission dissented, but those were curialists like Cardinal Ottaviani. Indeed, Cardinal Heenan of England, who was a member of the commission, went back to London to tell some of his marriage and family advisors to prepare for a dramatic change in the church's teachings on birth control and to think about how such change might be explained to the Catholic people.

Meanwhile, back in Rome, Ottaviani and his colleagues began to orchestrate a backstairs campaign against the commission decision, complete with articles in magazines and newspapers, letters from the bishops around the world, and protests from carefully chosen "Catholic married couples." The appeal was to Paul's conscience—he was changing the law of Christ—and to the fact that there was not moral unanimity among authorities on the commission because a few members had opposed the recommendation. Finally, the pope decided he would not accept the commission's report in favor of changing the church's stand. Then the report itself was leaked to the press with tremendous impact on Catholic laypeople. (The press handled the leak responsibly. Great care was given to the translation of the technical Latin documents. It was published simultaneously in full text by the *National Catholic Reporter* in English and *Le Monde* in French.)

In the meantime, some cardinals like Albino Luciani of Venice weighed in with memos of their own to the pope suggesting that nothing be done at the present time, that Paul simply remain silent on the issue. This would have been the easy way out and was probably all the curial opponents wanted in the first place. But given Paul VI's conscience, he had to settle the question by issuing an encyclical reaffirming the traditional teaching, even if his whole papacy would hang in the balance. Note the psychological process: he started the commission's investigation to find a way out and ended up by rejecting the commission's recommendation with a decision that he knew full well could jeopardize his credibility and authority. One may well wonder why he would get himself into such a bind.

His supporters here in the Vatican argue that the *Humanae Vitae* has been misunderstood, that it is really in defense of the sanctity of the family, and that the birth control decision must be seen in that context. But this is beside the point. Rome ought to know that most laypeople don't read encyclicals, all they read are newspaper accounts of the decisions made in the encyclicals. Most Catholic married people do not believe that every act of intercourse has to be open to procreation. The National Opinion Research Center's data show that in the United States 85 percent of married Catholics reject the pope's teaching and that there is no difference between the devout and the undevout in this matter, between those who had sixteen years of Catholic education and those who didn't go to Catholic schools at all, between weekly communicants and those who scarcely go to communion once a year. Furthermore, virtually all of the declining Catholic practice since the late sixties can be accounted for by the unfavorable reaction to the birth control encyclical.

The weakest part of the encyclical was the failure

of the pope to address himself seriously to the reasons his own commission presented to justify the change. He listed them and then dismissed them by saying in effect that the teachings of Jesus required one to continue the ban. But he offered little if any evidence that the teachings of Jesus did indeed require this, other than his own apodictic statement that they did. He crossed out the phrase that had been put in the original draft "with our infallible authority." But apparently he was persuaded the decision was damn near infallible.

This book is not the place to argue the birth control issue, though it is sad to see the glorious tradition of Catholic Christianity, which produced Dante, Michelangelo, Thomas Aquinas, St. Peter's, the Sistine Chapel, John of the Cross, Teresa of Avila, hinge on the mechanics of procreation. The birth control decision rather shows, for the purposes of this report, how the Vatican works: how the Curia isolates and influences the pope, how Pope Paul VI's conscience was repeatedly exploited and manipulated by the curialists around him, and, finally, how nothing can be kept secret despite the elaborate precautions.

Incidentally, I haven't been able to find anyone here in Rome who will answer my question of how you can theologically reconcile the rejection of official papal teaching by the overwhelming majority of the faithful, including the most pious and devout faithful, with what we were taught in the seminary. We were told that the learning church (the laity and their experience) was as infallible as the teaching church (the pope and the bishops); that the Catholic people could not make a mistake in their belief and practice any more than the official authority; and that the "sense of the faithful" was a proper place to discover sound Catholic doctrine. When you have only about 10 percent of your population accepting a papal decision, what has happened to the sense of the faithful?[11]

The man I had lunch with commented that when everything is secret, nothing is secret; and everything here is as secret as the Vatican Press Office can make it. The Vatican Press Office exists essentially to give out whatever news reporters can pry loose. It's not as though they manage the news for the Vatican; rather, they give out the minimum amount of news they can persuade Vatican officials they have to give.

Well, that's the end of my first reconnaissance in Rome. Pope

John was supposed to have been asked once how many people worked in the Vatican, and he said about half. If he had been asked how it worked, a proper answer, I think, would have been, not very well at all.

Scene II

I went back to Rome in the spring of 1976 for a weekend to keep up-to-date. There had been one dramatic change—the pope had appointed twenty new cardinals, and, contrary to the rumors I had picked up and contrary to the advice he received from the Curia, most of them were not Italian and several of them, Paulo Evaristo Arns and Aloisio Lorscheider of Brazil, Bernardin Gantin and Hyacinthe Thiandoum of Africa, Eduardo Pironio of Argentina, Jaime Sin of the Philippines, were men to whom the Curia would be bitterly opposed. Paul VI clearly was trying to tilt the election of his successor in the direction of his own progressive reforms and against his curial enemies. Still, the diffusion of the cardinals around the world made it even more difficult to get a feel in Rome for the direction in which the conclave might go. It seemed to me that the size and the geographic diffusion of the cardinals might make manipulation easy for the Curia. Further, impulse voting by those eager to say they voted for a winner might be inevitable.

Tuesday, June 22, 1976

The rumblings I picked up in the spring were correct. The newly elected cardinals were a severe blow to the members of Roman Curia. They see their power to influence the papal election waning not only because of the kind of men Paul appointed as cardinals, who are not likely to vote for them, but also because there are some men at least who might actively organize a campaign against them—most notably Lorscheider of Brazil. Sebastiano Baggio has apparently given up his candidacy for the papacy, for he attended none of the receptions for the new cardinals—an act of rudeness uncharacteristic of him. (Such papal aides as Benelli and Casaroli made all the receptions.) This was as pointed a way of Baggio's pulling his hat out of the ring as anyone could imagine. Pignedoli made all the receptions, but his reputation as a lightweight has been growing; apparently everybody shares that image of him now. Thus, at the present time, candidates are much less obvious than they were six months ago (and they weren't all that obvious then). The plot thickens.

The new cardinals are Paul VI's choices. Apparently he turned down the list that was presented earlier in the year (about the time when I was there), which had fifteen Italians and three non-Italians. He simply reversed the list. He was also responsible (over Benelli's objections and, I gather, over Baggio's too) for appointing the Benedictine Hume as archbishop of London—a kick in the teeth to the English hierarchy if there ever was one. Hume got the job because the Swiss papal nuncio in London wanted him and because there was tremendous support for him among the well-educated English. Also, an editorial in the London *Tablet*, apparently written by the editor, Tom Burns, greatly influenced everyone's thinking. The ability of a relatively small group of people to bring that kind of pressure to bear in the English church is interesting. Certainly there is nothing like it in the American church—or at least not yet. But then the American church doesn't have anybody who is quite so obvious a candidate and so well qualified as Hume was—with the possible exception of Theodore Hesburgh, the president of the University of Notre Dame.

Since I was last here the Holy Office issued a statement on sexuality which was no prize by any means. I hear it was even worse in its original form, virtually copied out of one of Cardinal Palazzini's textbooks. (Cardinal Pietro Palazzini, the moral theologian and canonist, is thought by many to be one of the most reactionary of the curial archconservatives.) It was rejected by the pope and rewritten hurriedly and in somewhat more benign fashion by the ever-present Benelli. Some of the theologians here make an important distinction between moral theology and pastoral theology. One of the men who drafted the statement stated publicly that while homosexuality is morally wrong, it might be pastorally right to encourage homosexuals to enter sustained relationships with one another. Italian moralists can't understand why the "Nordics" (people like us) find this kind of distinction difficult to understand. For example, obviously, they say, birth control is against moral law, but pastorally one can permit it in most cases.

Pope Paul will surely not resign, according to my Roman informants, because of his fear of schism. He much exaggerates the influence of the Christian traditionalists and Archbishop Marcel Lefebvre, who has organized a traditionalist seminary in Switzerland. In fact he went out of his way at the creation of the last bunch of cardinals to explicitly and by name denounce Lefebvre, a condemnation which he balanced with some vague references to radical aberrations. All of this is quite baffling unless one understands the European cleric's fear of right-wing anticlericalism, which is much better organized and has much more effective resources available in Europe than in the United States. Paul is afraid that if he resigns the right-wingers will still hail him as the pope and deny that his successor in fact has succeeded him. It is all very weird and strange, but I guess if you grow up in northern Italy you think in those categories.

Cardinal Paolo Bertoli, by the way, is not sick, as American rumors reported. He is alive and well and still very much a candidate. He is still unacceptable to his former curial allies despite his mission to Lebanon, which, like all missions to Lebanon, was a waste of time.

I am also told that, despite his recent heavy influence on the appointment of American bishops, Archbishop Jean Jadot continues to have many enemies in Rome who are envious of his success and popularity.

It would be a mistake to exaggerate the importance of the Third World component of the College of Cardinals. There are, after all, only ten Africans and even fewer Asians; they are disorganized and mostly subservient to Rome. The powerful block now is the Latin American and Iberian contingent, which now numbers over thirty. Spaniards, Portuguese, and Latin Americans are potentially well organized and have a number of tough, outspoken leaders. The new Brazilian cardinals—Arns and Lorscheider—are the people the Curia really has to fear.

(Incidentally, the French ambassador, who was about to leave the Vatican and who also had served in Budapest, had this comment to make: "The Vatican runs the same way the Kremlin runs with the single exception that in the Kremlin everyone knows who is in the Politburo; here they don't.")

Wednesday, June 23

On the way back from Rome, I began to wonder, as I looked over my notes, whether I had been too hard these past two trips on Paul VI. He does not have a good world image, in part because he looks so bad on television and because his gestures seem so inappropriate—talking about how joyful he feels when his face betrays what he says. Still, those who know him personally are profoundly impressed by the man. I am doing this research at the end of his administration when the church is grinding to a halt and waiting for a new regime. Nobody looks good under those circumstances. So I decided to dig out some of the history books and try to locate Paul VI against the backdrop of the last century. When one does this, his contribution looks much more impressive.[1]

I went back to Rome in November of 1976 to check with my sources and make some new contacts. Cardinal Eduardo Pironio had come to Rome, and as an Argentinian of Italian origin, he, at first blush, seemed to be a happy solution to the problem of maintaining the Italian papacy. But neither issues nor candidates had really clarified in Rome and the church continued to drift.

Thursday, November 25

Blessedly, the weather isn't like it was last year. It is sunny and crisp instead of rainy. In fact, if the truth be told, I'm rather enjoying the trip, which for me is almost against the rules. To reveal even more, this is the second jaunt to Europe in a row that I have enjoyed. It might become a habit.

On Thursday and Friday, I met with a number of people in various restaurants, tearooms, bars, eateries, street scenes, and other such places. I have come to the conclusion that this trip may not have been necessary, although it may well have been worth the trip to find it out. Most everyone has stopped thinking or talking about the papal election. The psychological dynamics behind that are interesting. A year ago, they really didn't think that Pope Paul VI was going to last much beyond the end of the Holy Year. Well, the Holy Year has ended and Paul VI goes on—mentally more alert than ever. His physical health is not good. Father Carter was telling me that he attended a small meeting of some big-wheel religious leaders and the pope not so long ago, and that the pope talked to them for almost an hour—intelligently, even wittily— without the slightest sign of a mental lapse. He had to be helped out of his chair; he tried to get out of it himself and could not. So, physically, he is weaker than he was, but mentally, if anything, he is stronger.

It would also appear that the influence of Archbishop Giovanni Benelli is somewhat on the wane, especially since the Archbishop Lefebvre case. (Archbishop Lefebvre is the man who is running a new separate church up in Switzerland that goes back to the pre-Vatican days with Latin mass and his own seminary.) The energetic, irrepressible Benelli is apparently the scapegoat for the failure of the Holy See to handle that one rightly. Heaven knows, they blew it badly. So it is said that while Benelli is still the prime minister, he doesn't quite have the power he used to. It hasn't gone to anyone else; it has simply reverted to the pope, who now is running things more himself.

Still it is purported that things happen that the pope himself doesn't know about—though that was alleged to have occurred even when he was in fine physical condition. One doesn't know whether to believe this or not; it may be the usual baloney set up to protect the pope from his own mistakes, or it may actually be the truth. For example, I learned from an American Jesuit, whom I encountered at the Vatican yesterday, that an order went forth from the Congregation for Catholic Education, presided over by Cardinal Garrone, and the Congregation for the Doctrine of the Faith (or the Holy Office, as it is lovingly called), presided over by Cardinal Seper, that all married clergymen teaching in the theological schools in Holland were to be dismissed. Now Cardinal Willebrands, the new, tough-minded archbishop of Utrecht, arrived on the scene here (as he does periodically, because he is still the head of the ecumenical secretariat) and said they really couldn't do this because it was against Dutch law and these people had contracts. The last time it had been tried in Holland (by the Jesuits), the Dutch courts had imposed a $100,000 fine. Well, Garrone, at the Congregation for Catholic Education, said, "Oh, that's too bad. Okay, keep the ones you have, but don't hire any new ones." Seper, at the Holy Office, said, "No, fire them and pay the fine." So then Willebrands went up to see the pope on his ecumenical affairs business and raised the question of the firings. The pope said, "Oh sure. Don't pay the fine, don't fire anybody; just don't hire any new ones." Then the pope is alleged to have added, "Incidentally, send me your copy of that letter. I never saw it."

There is lots of debate around this town as to whether the Curia is servant to the pope or the pope is prisoner of the Curia. Nobody has really been able to answer that one satisfactorily. A lot depends on your own personal ideology and perspective.

There's a meeting going on of the heads of all the pontifical degree-granting institutions throughout the world to discuss the future of the institutions. A number of the people I have chatted with think it's basically a trick by which the Curia wants to impose its control on these institutions and then, after them, on all other Catholic educational institutions in the world. The Americans tell me it won't work, though Rome could make all kinds of harassing rules that would be difficult to get around. This meeting was billed as an absolutely free and open discussion. Those who attended were promised that there would be no preparatory documents. Sure enough, they arrived on the scene and there was a preparatory document, which is supposed to be the thing they will adopt. My contacts say that the meeting is being ineptly and stupidly run, that the people at the Congregation for Catholic Education really don't have the basic intelligence to know how to deal with deans and presidents of theological facilities around the world. They may not be malicious but they are incompetent.

Father Micheli and I had lunch at the L'Eau Vive this afternoon. It's a marvelous French restaurant off the Piazza San Eustacho. You walk in a door in the street wall and you step into another century: soft music, light green walls, pretty tablecloths, and lovely French-speaking women from every continent in the world waiting on tables. It's run by a missionary secular institute which, for reasons that escape me, runs high-class French restaurants all around the world—God bless them for that!

Micheli feels that the last consistory really created a much more obscure situation than ever existed before, because there are now so many cardinals from so many different parts of the world who know relatively little of one another, relatively little of the universal church, and even relatively little of what happens in Rome. Now you have a far more atomized group of electors, most of them scattered around the world and not bound together in any cohesive groups, factions, or parties; the curial party is now so small that it doesn't swing much clout. There really isn't any power structure in the College of Cardinals, and the question of who the pope would be if the election were held tomorrow is quite uncertain. Because it is so uncertain, people are hardly even talking about it—even the Curia. When it does happen, it's going to be a surprise, almost an anticlimax, because subconsciously people are working on the proposition that the pope will not die. The *fin de régime* situation has gone on for so long now that one begins to take it for granted.

Johannes Willebrands is still being mentioned, but now one hears everywhere people saying, "It won't be Willebrands because the cardinals will simply never vote for a Dutchman." (Even if he is doing well in calming the situation in the Netherlands.) Johannes is also in his late sixties, and if Paul VI lasts another couple of years, as he well might, Willebrands will be too old to become a serious candidate. Cardinal Koenig at seventy-one, for example, is now much too old.

The name most frequently being heard around here is Cardinal Pironio—one of the new cardinals, an ethnic; his parents were born in Italy but he's an Argentinian. He's the former bishop of Mar del Plata who was on a couple of assassination lists before they got him out and brought him to Rome to head the Congregation for Religious and Secular Institutes. He is extremely well liked, very progressive, very open. But, I'm told, he is a poor administrator; he thinks the head of the Congregation for Religious and Secular Institutes ought to attend all the general chapters of the religious communities, thus leaving the congregation in charge of those who have always been in charge of it, the Italian curialists; they, therefore, continue on their merry way, laughing behind Pironio's back about how they are still running things.

Pironio's big disadvantage is that he is young; he's in his middle fifties. That's a disadvantage because it means we might have him for twenty-five years, which would be long for a papacy.

Willebrands and Pironio are about the only names one hears mentioned. Sebastiano Baggio, Sergio Pignedoli, and Pericle Felici seem to have slipped into the background. The truth, though, seems to be that nobody really knows. The electorate now is so big, so diffused, so out of communication with one another that almost anything could happen when it assembles in Rome. It means, I guess, that the two or three weeks between the death of Paul and the election will be even more important than I thought.

Saturday, November 27

The young American clergy I encountered last night are all good fellows but are beginning to catch the Roman cynicism.

Working at the Vatican is enough to make anyone cynical. There's not much of a social structure, and lots of antisocial individualism.

Signor Cardinale said tonight that there are five things that happen after an auto accident—nobody hurt, just typical banged up Roman cars: you get out of your car, shake your fingers at the other driver, a crowd gathers and you shake your fingers at them, the police come and you shake your fingers at the police, everybody pulls out their notebooks and writes down numbers, and then everybody goes home. Such is it in the city. A very, very old city. You walk through the streets and someone says, "There's the palace Queen Christina lived in," and, "There's the palace the Doria-Pamphilis have, they had to sell their other palace." After a while all this oldness, and to some extent shabbiness, begins to depress you. I think the most depressing thing of all, though, is the Roman clergy. These characters you see going around, some of them still in cassocks, some in blue berets, some in black suits, some in gray suits—none of them are ever smiling. They won't even smile at one another. A Jesuit took me back to his room at the Gregorian University today after lunch. You walk in, three or four people are walking out and they don't smile; they are presumably colleagues on the faculty, but there is absolutely no exchange of even normal human friendliness of the sort you would get in the National Opinion Research Center.

The Vatican is scared stiff by the Communists. Although they didn't win the last election (in fact, they didn't do as well as most people thought they would), the Vatican is worried about them. God knows why it chooses to be worried now instead of twenty years ago. What's more, it doesn't know what to do. In some Communist cities of the north the squeeze is being put on the church—convent land being turned into parks and other such things. So they know the Communists are for real, but they just don't know how to react to them. It has had a sort of paralyzing influence on the operation of things in the Vatican: a combination of the apparently implacable and unbeatable Communist threat, plus the numbing effect of the prolonged end of the Paul VI regime.

The pope, I am told, is now very much concerned about priests. He is afraid that they have been led astray by all the confusion, and he feels a deep sense of responsibility for it. Therefore, he thinks that before he goes to his reward, the last thing he can do is see that priests get good educations once again. Hence the attempt by the Congregation for Catholic Education to grab control of what happens in the theological faculties. By controlling the universities where the theologians are taught, the pope's wishes may be implemented. The intent is a worthy one; theological education is all fouled up. It is not at all clear that you can straighten it out, though, by having a meeting in Rome and trying to impose universal norms on the rest of the world. I'm not sure just what I would do if I were in the pope's position. I don't know how clerical education can be unfouled except by a new pope who will reestablish the credibility of the central leadership.

Sunday, November 28

It is now Sunday night of a dark and gloomy day. My only effort today was an afternoon lunch with Father Carter and Luigi Barzini, the famous Italian writer and author of the book *The Italians* and now a new book called *O America*, about America in the 1920s. Barzini lives in a villa with a butler and a cook out on the Via Cassia north of the city of Rome. It is very much an Italian haute bourgeoisie sort of place—elaborate library, elegant dining room, overcrowded parlor. He himself is an Etruscan, I think. I hear that his brother has red hair; and while Barzini has a Roman nose, his face and skin color represent something that is almost certainly pre-Roman. He is a very, very clever and sophisticated gentleman—very much the Catholic humanist. He is thoroughly pro-American and also feels that the church has a tremendously important role to play in developing the intellect and defending pluralism in the contemporary world. Carter asked him how it could be that the Jesuits want to jump onto every new fad. Barzini said it was all the fault of Pio Nono (Pius IX), that worthy pope whose *Syllabus of Errors* missed the bus. Since then the Jesuits have been jumping on every bus that comes by the bus stop. An interesting way of putting it. The reason Rome is so obsessed with the Third World, he added, is that it did such a bad job in the First World countries of North America and Europe.

Barzini also gave an interesting way of predicting the next pope. The Italian tradition is that there is an alternation in popes, a politician then a priest, a fat man then a thin one, a man with an "r" in his name then a man without an "r" in his name. Thus, Pio Nono was a fat man, his successor, Leo XIII, Cardinal Pecci, was a thin man, a politician with no "r" in his name. He was succeeded by Pius X, Papa Sarto, an "r" in his name, a fat man, and a priest. In turn, Benedict XV, Cardinal della Chiesa, a thin man, a politician, no "r" in his name. The next one, Pius XI, was Papa Ratti, etc., who was succeeded by Papa Pacelli, thin, no "r," a politician. Then Papa Roncalli (John XXIII), fat, "r," a priest, followed by Papa Montini (Paul VI), etc. If one looks at this (and it's a bit like the twenty-inch rainfall line), there are three likely choices: Corrado Ursi, Salvatore Pappalardo, and Eduardo Pironio (but he would have to put on a few pounds). I wonder what we would think of John Krol or even Joseph Bernardin in such a paradigm. Ah, well . . .

The lunch at Barzini's was very fine. The butler served in a white jacket—elegant silverware, and, would you believe, finger bowls at the end? It's been a long time since I had anything like that. Barzini's son, Andrea, who wants to be a movie director, was there, and we had a splendid talk about the movies, over a strawberry liqueur that would have delighted the most discriminating palate. Barzini is a man I would like to know more of.

Monday, November 29—Noontime

As always, Father Adolpho is extraordinarily candid—not completely candid, of course, but then nobody in this place ever is. He tells me that Cardinal Florit of Florence has resigned—not a very popular man at best, and I guess he made a real mess out of Florence. A new archbishop will be appointed there, as in Munich. These are two critical appointments—both being cardinalatial seats. Possibly there will be a new consistory in which the men who get those places will be made cardinals. Adolpho is, by the way, very high on both Joseph Bernardin and Jean Jadot, and he tells me that Jadot's prestige here is at an all-time high; everybody is simply delighted with the way he is handling the American church. Apparently Jadot's stand against the ordination of women has reassured the people in the Vatican that he is not an out-and-out radical. Anybody else I might suspect of taking that stand for diplomatic purposes; but since he clearly eschews such diplomacy, I guess he must be sincere. Anyhow, one of the rumors is that Giovanni Benelli, the pope's number two man—"his executioner"—may go to Florence; but then again he may not.

Adolpho did not think that Benelli's influence had waned very much, though he said there were always things being done independently of Benelli. For example, the decision to receive Archbishop Lefebvre at Castel Gandolfo was made by the pope and Macchi, the pope's personal secretary, without Benelli's being informed. Also, Benelli's political influence is not what it used to be, because he was closely allied with Fanfani in the Italian Christian Democratic politics. Fanfani is out now and Andreotti is in, so that means that Benelli's political advice is not as impressive as it used to be; hence his clout in the Vatican on the basis of his political connections is weakened. (The link between the Vatican and Italian politics is just utterly destructive, it seems to me—both for the Italian nation and for the Vatican.)

Incidentally, Barzini yesterday remarked that Andreotti was a curious mixture of Machiavelli and saint, who, he said, was probably the only kind of person who could effectively hold the Christian Democratic party together. Father Adolpho said that there was much less talk about the papal election than there was a year ago. He agreed that it was partly due to the psychological numbness caused by the long duration of this end-of-the-regime. Also, he cited a couple of other factors. First of all, as the conclave gets closer, people are less likely to talk about it for fear that they may harm their own candidacies. Nobody wants to take chances because one can never be sure whether he might on any day suddenly be called to assemble in conclave.

Father Adolpho still thinks there is a slight advantage for Italian candidates, but much less than there was even a year ago. He also thinks a curial cardinal would have a slight advantage simply because they are better known to the people out in the boondocks than are other cardinals. Again, the name Pironio arose. He had been with him the day before at the meeting of the superiors general stationed at the Vatican. His opinion seems to be the same as everyone else's—that Pironio is a nice, pious, open man, rather emotional, not an administrator at all but a man of inspiration. We checked his age (fifty-seven), which is getting closer to the age when the cardinals might think of electing him. My guess is that if it goes on for another year or two, Pironio's chances will get very good indeed.

Adolpho also agreed that Willebrands's star is no longer in the ascendant, partly because he's getting older, party because he's not progressive enough for the Dutch but is still too progressive for the curialists. He also noted that the ecumenical secretariat is slipping because Willebrands is not around very much and when he does come to Rome, Holland takes precedence on his agenda over the ecumenical secretariat.

Anyhow, Adolpho says, the lack of any clear leaders and the fact that people are now being cautious have resulted in relatively less conversation about the election.

Sergio Pignedoli's star has declined because of his bungle at Tripoli last year—he signed something that was in Arabic and that he didn't bother to read which turned out to sound like a condemnation of Israel. It cost him all sorts of points and helped confirm the allegation of his enemies that he is shallow.

Sebastiano Baggio is also less talked about, though it would be a mistake, I guess, to write him off either. I asked Adolpho about the Iberians, and he said that Vicente Enrique y Tarancón of Madrid was a very shrewd and able man, quite capable of organizing things, who might well be the leader in the conclave.

The Marcel Lefebvre case is viewed with great concern here. There are many Europeans who are solidly on Lefebvre's side. In fact, Adolpho said, if he had not been disobedient to the pope he would have had even more support. A number of people in the Curia say Lefebvre was right, "We've gone too fast, we've gone too far, we've got to reassure the conservatives." This is absolute nonsense as far as the United States is concerned, but it may actually be a real problem and not a curial myth for Europe.

Another issue, besides Lefebvre, which might come up in the papal conclave is Ostpolitik, that is, relations with the nations in Eastern Europe. There is more concern about Eastern Europe now, particularly with the death of Doepfner in Munich and the rise of the autocratic and conservative Hoeffner in Cologne to the leadership of the German hierarchy. Both Western Europeans and Eastern Europeans are going to become very much concerned about personal freedom in Eastern Europe and throughout the world. In the countries of the Third World there would obviously be concern about justice, especially since many of the archbishops, particularly in Africa, tend to identify with the militant nationalisms of their own countries. Adolpho seemed to think that there would be substantial interest in how the papacy would be used to affect world events in the ten years ahead.

The most basic issue would continue to be how to hold the church together. Unquestionably, centrifugal forces were unleashed by the Second Vatican Council; these forces may be good or not, depending on your viewpoint, but they are there and they are not going away. Now what do you do about them? Paul VI's administration has been one in which you try to counteract them by a highly authoritarian centralization. It is not clear that it has worked all that well; the people who come together will want a strong papacy and a strong united church but a central bureaucracy less likely to interfere in the administering of church problems in various parts of the world. That is something close to a contradiction in terms: a strong pope without a strong papacy.

The final issue, according to Adolpho, is that we desperately need a man of hope, a man of cheerfulness, a man who can give some confidence in the midst of the confusions and the uncertainties of the present world situation. He wished for someone of the same style as Pope John, but perhaps not quite so blithely confident.

Adolpho, who I suspect has had his conflicts with Benelli, also was prepared to defend the hard-driving papal chief of staff. Benelli is in fact the pope's man; his loyalty is basically to the pope and not to his own career, and he is executing what he thinks the pope wants executed. He realizes he is making enemies and hurting his own future in the process.

We talked about the sexuality documents. He said that many of the Third World countries were cheerfully supporting *Humanae Vitae* even though the priests in their own confessional practices would probably agree with what most Americans do with birth control. Even those bishops like Helder Camara of Brazil endorse *Humanae Vitae* because they think that birth control is a First World attempt to impose population limitation on the Third World.

I told him Bill McCready's theory of the two churches: the *official* church (the Holy See, the chancery office, the bishops' conference); and the church of the *parishes*. He said he found the same thing in Kenya, a country very different from the United States. When he was in Nairobi, he went out into the countryside to talk with the clergy, mostly Irish, English, Spanish, and Italian. They were all of different cultural backgrounds, but all said the same thing—that they just didn't care what Rome or the chancery offices said and that they were doing their own work. It had nothing to do with theological perspective—they were quite traditional in theological formulation—it was just pragmatism. What went on in the central bureaucracy was irrelevant to them and they weren't going to be bothered by it.

As I was leaving, Adolpho said he thought the Germans could be very influential because there is so much German money subsidizing the poor in the churches of the world that many of the cardinals coming in from abroad would wait to see which way the Germans went.[2] With the death of Doepfner, that is less clear, especially since we don't know who the new bishop of Munich will be. He said that, as usual, there would be no leadership at all from the American cardinals.

Late Evening

Supper with Father Micheli and Desmond O'Grady.

O'Grady still thinks Sergio Pignedoli has a good chance of being pope. The argument is not implausible. He says, sure, Pignedoli blew things at the Tripoli meeting; but the cardinals outside Rome don't know that, and he is still quite popular with them because of his many wanderings around the world.

After we had dinner and I was walking Father Micheli back to his residence in the cool, crisp early winter air, he made some interesting observations about Italian politics that can be easily transferred to the Vatican administrative style. In Italy, the political parties don't give a hoot about their constituents except at election time. Members of the Chamber of Deputies vote the way the party leadership tells them to vote; they have no constituencies at all in the sense that they have to go back and keep the constituency happy. Italians don't write letters to their senators or deputies. You get into Parliament because you are a loyal member of the party and because you get put on a list—the proportional representational thing; and there isn't much relationship between whether you get elected to Parliament and how well you have served the people in your district who voted for you. The people are voting for the party lists rather than for you as a person. What that means is that the deputies don't feel very responsible to the constituents. Micheli suggests there may be something like this in the Vatican, that while the officials there claim to be an authority of service and assert that the pope is the servant of the servants of God, they don't give much of a damn under ordinary circumstances about what the ordinary people think. They make the decisions and the others follow.

As we were saying goodnight, Micheli ended his monologue by noting that the pope had weakened the power of the curial congregations by centralizing even more power in himself and in the new Secretariat of State. The Curia is weakened but a super-Curia has been established so that Paul's own authoritarian, centralizing, and autocratic tendencies could operate.

I picked up an interesting story earlier today which is symbolic of the Vatican style. The *gabinetti*, that is to say, the bathrooms, behind the stage in the new papal audience hall are divided not into two but into three: one of them has a symbol on it representing a man; another one is hard to figure out because it shows somebody in a long skirtlike affair; you would think that that one is for women until you go to the third one, the symbol on which is clearly of a woman, someone in a short-skirted garment. So you have one bathroom for men, one for women, and one for priests.

Tuesday, November 30

I went over to the Vatican Press Office this morning to try to get accreditation. They wouldn't give it to me, saying they only give it to people who are in Rome for a long time. There are no rules that say they may not give it to people who come back and forth to Rome, but since they don't have anybody like that, their first reaction is to say, "Of course not, no, we can't do it." I will take this up with the appropriate parties when I get back to see if we can't do something about it, just for the sheer sake of pushing the so-and-so's. When you get bullied you bully back, though I didn't bully this morning because the woman was pleasant enough and she couldn't make the decisions anyway.

Afternoon

Traditionally (since 1903) the election of a pope is by a two-thirds majority of cardinals and is signaled by white smoke pouring out of the special chimney over the Sistine Chapel, where the conclaves have been held since the 1870s. The conclaves before 1870 took place in the Quirinale Palace in the heart of Rome, and the cardinals used to walk down the street outdoors to the cheers of the citizenry to cast their ballots. The crowds now wait eagerly in the great piazza of St. Peter's for the first whiff of smoke and then go delirious with joy.

The majority required is two-thirds plus one—to prevent a man's giving himself the decisive vote (even though cardinals are forbidden to vote for themselves). In his reform of the election rules, Pope Paul mentions neither the Sistine Chapel nor the white smoke. The cardinals may choose to meet anywhere within the Vatican and can use the white smoke or not, as they please. But the document carefully insists that the extra vote must be added lest a man invalidate his own election by voting for himself—although since the votes are supposed to be secret, it is not clear how anyone would know about the fatal vote.

The origins of the selection of the pope by the College of Cardinals are shrouded in antiquity. The present format began to emerge in the eleventh century, although as late as 1059 the laity and clergy as well as the chief clerics, the "hinge" (in Latin, *cardo*) of the city of Rome, participated in the election.

It was then decreed that only the cardinals had the right of election but that the clergy and laity should "assent" to the election. However, this rule had little impact for over a hundred years, and the laity and clergy of Rome continued to exercise their ancient and traditional right of selecting their bishop. In 1417, Pope Martin V was elected by a conclave of cardinals and thirty other prelates from an ecumenical council which was then in session.

In its long history the election of the pope by the cardinals has had some wild moments. In one conclave the majority of the cardinals (or a large minority) were teenage boys appointed by their uncle (or father), the last pope. In another, the majority was from the French city of Limoges. In many others the European monarchies meddled shamelessly; in one papal election, Cesare Borgia controlled all but two of the votes by using two techniques to establish his control, bribery and murder; the Austrian emperor vetoed an election in the twentieth century. Some conclaves were held in France, others in Italian castles; some ended in violence; some took as long as two years. The Roman citizens had at one time the pious custom of sacking and robbing the house of the new pope.

The practice of locking the cardinals up was not designed to preserve them from outside influence or to ensure secrecy but simply to put pressure on them to finish the business. In some lengthy conclaves (from the Latin word meaning a lock) the outraged citizenry first curtailed and then cut off food supplies in order to produce a result. On other occasions they slowly demolished brick by brick the castle in which the prolonged deliberations were taking place.

When Paul dies the cardinals must wait until the nine days of official mourning for him are completed. They must allow at least fifteen days for far-flung cardinals to get to Rome and can wait an additional five for stragglers. However, in the jet age such waiting will hardly be necessary. So it is likely that they will decide to have themselves locked up in the Vatican shortly after the mourning period ends.

The day-to-day governance of the church is entrusted to the whole College of Cardinals, which must meet every day in "general congregations" to discuss matters affecting the church and to begin making plans for the conclave. The executive body is made up of the cardinal chamberlain (*camerlengo*) and three others chosen by lot to meet in "particular congregations." Other commissions, some elected, some chosen by lot, make arrangements for the beginning of the election. Active soliciting of votes and the making of "deals" are forbidden, but "consultation" is permitted during this period. However, since the line between "consultation" and "campaigning" is so subtle as to be invisible—especially for Italians—campaigning, and even campaign speeches, are certain to take place.

Paul VI's "reform" of papal elections severely limits the number of people who can accompany the cardinals into conclave. It used to be that each elector was permitted to bring one "conclavist" to act as a secretary or physician. Now, however, special permission is needed for such a companion. A secretary, a sacristan, a few assistants, two confessors, two doctors, two technicians (who will check to see that the conclave is not bugged), and an architect (to make sure the meeting remains sealed) will enter the conclave with the electors.

The actual balloting takes place in the morning and in the late afternoon, with two scrutinies (votes) often taking place each time. Ballots are to be secret and are promptly burned. All male

Catholics in the world are eligible for election, although it has been half a millennium since the cardinals went outside their own number.

The most solemn oaths are taken that everything must remain secret. The obsession with secrecy, however, is a twentieth-century phenomenon. Ways can be found around such promises, of course, and members of the Roman Curia, whose future depends heavily on what occurs, are alleged to have detailed reports on their desks after each vote—even though the ballots were supposedly destroyed.

Wednesday, December 1

I've been here a week. This will be the last entry in this phase of my Roman diary. The rain is pouring, by the way, which is also beginning to be like last year. I think it's a good thing I never had to live in this city for very long, because my sinuses simply couldn't take it.

Briefly summarizing this visit, a disgruntled American source who knows the Vatican very well said to me this afternoon, "Well, nobody over there is doing anything." He meant that even the Vatican is winding down in this period of quasi-interregnum. They're worried about the explosive situation in Europe, they're worried about the unity of the church, they're worried about Lefebvre (strange, they're not apparently worried about Hans Küng anymore); but they really don't know what to do about any of them, and so everybody sits and waits for the next administration with some sense of resignation that it will probably be a long time. There is also no intense speculation about who might head the next administration. The likely candidates of the past, however, like Franz Koenig of Vienna, now seventy-one, are becoming older. Even Johannes Willebrands, at sixty-seven, will be too old if a number of years pass before the vacancy occurs. New candidates have not yet emerged clearly.

The Bertoli clique here in Rome is relatively small and doesn't have a power base. It must be said about Paolo Bertoli that he is somewhat ample, has an "r" in his name, and is more priest than politician.

One of my sources also told me that the Vatican is bugged by five different intelligence services, which is why they are so worried about bugging at the conclave; I gather the five are the KGB, the West German, British, French, and Israeli agencies. This was mostly a waste of the money of the taxpayers of the respective nations, because virtually all information that comes into the Vatican will be leaked out eventually either by the left or the right. Their internal security system is an absolute sieve. My source also said that they are so inundated with paperwork over there that documents not submitted in Italian or French simply do not receive any attention at all.

So more background materials assembled, more Vaticanology learned, more jokes acquired, more materials for the book; but a frustrating and unsatisfactory visit because there isn't anything dramatic happening here. However, I've managed to scrape together some information about the other twentieth-century conclaves which confirms my suspicion that the dynamics of conclave voting are very much like the dynamics of a political convention.[3]

Scene III

In the fall of 1977, a Synod of Bishops of the world was meeting in Rome. The synod was established by Pope Paul to implement the doctrine of collegiality developed at the Second Vatican Council. The pope, it was decreed by the Council, ruled together with the bishops of the world. The synod was supposed to be an in-stitutionalization of this "togetherness"; in fact, it was pretty much under the thumb of Pope Paul and his secretary of state. It could not choose its own topic, issue its own report, or even decide on its own agenda. The members of the Council of the Synod, elected after every meeting (the group meets at three-year intervals), had enormous prestige because they represented the bishops of the world, but had little real power; the permanent secretary general of the synod, Polish Bishop Ladislaw Rubin, was frustrated and unhappy with his impossible task. The progressive bishops of the world insisted repeatedly, though usually off the record, that the most important structural question in the church was whether the Synod of Bishops was subordinate to the Curia or the Curia was subordinate to the Synod of Bishops. Some of the members of the Council of the Synod argued that the role of the synod would be the critical issue in the next conclave. Since more than half of the cardinal electors were also members of the synod and since the pope was now approaching his eighty-first birthday and was speaking frequently about his own death, it seemed to me that the time was ripe for preconclave politicking (the synod's official topic for discussion was religious education).

One major thing had happened in the previous year. Giovanni Benelli had been given the ax and sent to Florence as archbishop. However, Benelli was promptly raised to the cardina-late, so the pope could reassure himself that he had not done the same thing to his second-in-command that had been done to him (Paul) when he was Pius XII's second-in-command. (He was ship-ped off to Milan without the cardinal's hat.) Apparently, the curial officials (this time the Curia of Paul VI) had had it with Benelli's highhanded supervision. Jean Villot and Sebastiano Baggio were among those responsible for sending him off. But now he was a

68

cardinal elector himself and perhaps even a candidate.

With Benelli gone, influence on the day-to-day operation of the pope's office came under the control of his secretary, Macchi, and a clique' of his friends—Levi, the editor of Osservatore, Panciroli of the Vatican Press Office, Marcinkus of Vatican Bank. There was nothing necessarily conspiratorial about this influence. It seems to be an iron law of the papacy that when a pope's health fails power passes not to the established bureaucrats but to those members of the papal household in whom the failing pope has the greatest personal confidence.

"Macchi"—no one ever used his first name—said one curialist to me, "was Montini's equivalent of Pacelli's Madre Pasqualina."

He bawled the pope out when he let himself become morbid or depressed, told him to go to bed when he stayed up too late (which happened often), forced him to make decisions when he hesitated, and kept the church running—insofar as it ran—during the last months of Paul's pontificate. Late at night after he'd finally got the pope to bed, Macchi could be seen not infrequently at a certain restaurant just off the Piazza Gregorio Settimo with Marcinkus or other friends.

How much substantive influence he had on decisions is hard to judge. . .as it is still hard to judge of the role of Madre Pasqualina. It is also debated whether Macchi played a role analogous to that of the German nun in the exiling of Benelli to Florence. Some curialists hint, however, that just as Madre Pasqualina got rid of Montini so Macchi got rid of Benelli.

It should be emphasized that neither confidant was motivated by personal ambition; both knew that their fall from power would be rapid as soon as their patron was dead. The two of them were motivated by loyalty, in both cases a passion which turned out to be far more powerful than ambition. Students at the North American College, where The Papessa worked after Pius XII's death, admired her as a gracious and beautiful woman who put flowers in their rooms on their birthdays. . . .

Tuesday, October 25, 1977

Back in Rome again; I flew in from a happier if somewhat wetter country, the Republic of Ireland, where two women had just been given the Nobel Prize for trying to keep peace. The IRA celebrated that by shooting a twenty-four-year-old woman in bed and trying to shoot her three-year-old child too.

I am not able to get into the Hilton until tomorrow, so I am staying at the Excelsior Hotel on the Via Veneto, which is a posh old Roman hotel. I mean, it is really classy. Great, spacious lobbies, people sitting around sipping tea and sherry, very, very expensive folk drifting in and out. The Via Veneto doesn't seem to be quite as chic as it used to be, but there's no sign of deterioration in the Excelsior Hotel. It would still be, I think, where the beautiful folk would go, unless they want to swim, in which case they go to the Hilton. The rooms are incredibly elegant, though not quite as elegant as Ashford Castle. Everybody is polite and courteous, the sort of behavior you encounter at the top levels of Italian society. That doesn't mean that things ever really get done, but it does mean that they don't get done in a much more efficient way. Thus, there was no telephone book in my room; I had to go downstairs to borrow one, but they found me a telephone book with a great deal of flair. Mind you, they weren't prepared to let me take it back up to the room. The room is done in hangings and fabric walls, and there's an elaborate bathtub.

The weather in Rome is pleasant—coolish but not cold, clear skies. Apparently it rained all last week; maybe I've avoided the rain this time.

If there are economic troubles in this country, and of course there are, it certainly doesn't show up in the way people dress, the cars they drive, the advertisements on the boards, or the materials in the store windows. And, oh yes, despite my weariness and despite a couple of days in the Republic of Ireland, Roman women are still the world's most beautiful.

Back in my parquet-floored, oriental-rugged room on the Via Veneto. When I left the hotel I was accosted by two gentlemen at different points asking me if I wanted to come "to a special night-club." I allowed as how I didn't. I wonder what the hell they thought the Brigid cross in my lapel stood for. Well, in this city, that may not matter.

The discussion with Father Carter this evening was wide-ranging and very informative. (We ate at a very old restaurant. Beneath the floor of the restaurant is the floor of an ancient Roman eating place carefully protected by a glass covering. I wondered how many generations of conspirators had eaten supper in the same place.)

The synod turns out to be a waste of time. The Curia and the secretary of state are rigging the thing. The synod fathers realize that they haven't much to say about what happens in the church. George Basil Hume, the archbishop of Westminster, is said to be furious that he's wasting a month of his time.

There is some very interesting new material on the papal election, however. Carter's feeling is that a lot depends on when the election is going to be. He thinks that Sergio Pignedoli's campaign is futile. Salvatore Pappalardo from Palermo may not be a serious candidate because many of the Italian bishops don't like him because he is a Sicilian and an intellectual. Most Italians don't like Sicilians for reasons that are pretty close to racism (there hasn't been a Sicilian pope for twelve hundred years), but a Sicilian intellectual is simply intolerable. Corrado Ursi of Naples, he felt, was too unstable, and Pignedoli has been branded by the Italians as a lightweight. That puts the Italians in the strange position of narrowing it down to one man, namely, Baggio. Giovanni Benelli is not a papal candidate.

But Carter doesn't think this is the way the thing is going to go. Whether it's now or later, he thinks that the disappointment, not to say the anger, at Paul VI for his refusal to step down is such that the electors are simply going to insist well before the voting starts that there be some kind of commitment to retirement. With that in mind, they could easily go down to people in their fifties and choose one of them for pope, so that a man like Eduardo Pironio would become a very serious candidate even if the election were soon. Hume would also be a very serious candidate. Hume is apparently extremely impressive at the meetings of the synod. People respect his intelligence and his abilities. It is also thought that the real question marks are the Asian and African cardinals; Father Carter thinks they are probably more progressive than they let on to their Roman bosses.

Pironio's strength, he says, continues to grow out of Rome. In Rome, however, his enemies increase; the Curia and the Italians say (and according to Carter, it's quite true) that he is no administrator. Also, his more casual style offends them; they feel it is not appropriate for the papacy. Pironio is a man, they say, who is all heart; and that's not what the Curia folk want.

Father Carter also thinks that a conclave now would be a very long conclave.

One gets the feeling here, at least after the first day's conversation, that there's a lot of uneasiness and restlessness, that the drift has to stop soon, and that there has to be some kind of change.

Tomorrow morning I am going to go off to the Vatican Press Office and see if I can finally extort credentials from those worthy souls. I check out of here, go to the press conference in the afternoon, and see Signor Cardinale tomorrow night. Somewhere in the midst of all this I hope to get a chance to swim at the Rome Hilton. I'm really tired, and it's only been several hours of interviewing. I guess I'm not very good at this intellectual journalism.

Wednesday, October 26

It's hot in Rome today. Apparently it was cold last night, from what people said, but the sun is out now shining brightly and the city is filled with noisy people. It continues to be a depressing and distressing place, however, at least for anybody who has a Catholic religious commitment and gives a hoot about the church.

I went over to the Vatican to pick up my press credentials, and I am now a certified, card-carrying Vatican correspondent.

Rome is filled with tourists, swarming with them. The Via della Conciliazione, the broad street that runs from the Tiber up to St. Peter's, is lined on both sides with tourist buses, so you only get one-lane traffic. I don't know why I am so distressed by the place. It may be the Italian clergymen wandering around in old-fashioned robes, the stern-faced nuns walking down the street, the piety of the good, simple tourists who are being had, or maybe it was simply going to the Vatican Press Office and picking up the documents that have come forth from the synod so far, which are just unspeakably stupid. They show absolutely no relationship either to the personal experience of people in the ministry working with the young or to any empirical evidence. Fortunately, one keeps telling oneself, the strength of the church is not here, it's out there—someplace.

It is now evening time, 6:20, and I'm walking around the Bernini colonnade of St. Peter's, soaking up the atmosphere, such as it is. The sun's already set, just a glow of light in the western sky. The lights are on in the pope's office at the top of the papal palace. People wandering around St. Peter's from tourist buses still here, kids—young people—just sitting, staring at the place.

I went to the American bishops' press conference this afternoon in the USO building where all the great, exciting press conferences were held during the Vatican Council. It was pretty much of a dud. Presiding over it was Russell Shaw, the PR man for the United States Catholic Conference. The two bishops were Archbishop John Whealon of Hartford and Timothy Manning, cardinal archbishop of Los Angeles.

That's when my headache started getting really bad. Whealon went through a brief summary of what the synod was all about that was just worthless. The questions were bad and the answers were bad, all a waste of time. One has the terrible feeling that the Synod of Bishops is reflected accurately by the press conference—lots of people making noise. Manning, Whealon, Raymond Lucker, Joseph Bernardin, and the other American types are decent enough men, kindly, personally devout, even seriously attempting to be open and democratic. Manning tells how he meets once a week with seven priests in a little cursillo group of which he's a part; it's all quite sincere but quite irrelevant. Manning said young people were hungering for spiritual truth, which is doubtless the case. He also said that the church hasn't been able to communicate effectively with them yet. He didn't propose to go into any detail as to why. I almost asked him why but I decided, what the hell, I just better sit there and listen and watch.

In one of their statements to the synod, the American bishops raised the question of the neutron bomb. There were headlines in the Italian papers saying "American Bishops Condemn Neutron Bomb" precisely at the time when the American secretary of defense was in Paris for a meeting of the NATO defense ministers to defend the neutron bomb. Our friends promptly issued statements saying they had been misquoted, that they were saying people ought to consider the morality of the neutron bomb. They didn't realize what could be done with it. So there they are again looking foolish in public. Not, mind you, that the neutron bomb is not an appropriate subject for commentary by ecclesiastical leaders, but if they're going to comment, they should do so deliberately and intelligently, not by mistake. They should carefully weigh the consequences as well as the arguments instead of throwing it in as an obiter dictum.

Father Micheli and I rendezvoused at L'Eau Vive for lunch

today, and he played some variations on his theme that to understand the Vatican one has to understand the Italian culture. Pope Paul VI does not retire because no Italian political leader retires. A good part of the problem in Italian politics is that the government is currently a gerontocracy, with no political leader willing to step down. Once you get power in Italy you don't give it up. It is taken for granted that the patriarch rules the family until he dies. It's also important, according to Father Micheli, to look where in Italy a given curialist comes from. For example, he says that you can only understand the undisciplined ruthlessness of the late Dino Staffa in terms of the fact that he was a Calabrian. Calabria is a region of southern Italy which has lost one-half of its population in the last fifty years. This means that even with the natural increase there has been a tremendous emigration of its citizenry, mostly to the United States. Crime is a way of life in Calabria; there is in this small area at least a murder every day, also a fire. Forest lands are burned down by the shepherds who want the land for grazing. The Italian government has poured in money for reforestation, but trees never grow because the people are afraid that if you actually reforest, the money will stop coming. Also, whenever anyone becomes a successful farmer, he is instantly the object of blackmail, his well is poisoned, his orchard burned down, his animals die. Success is negatively sanctioned; although the government has poured $50 billion into Calabria and other parts of southern Italy since the war, there is virtually no social progress. The culture resists or exploits those attempts at social progress that are made. Thus there is a big, government-built auto plant in Naples in which the absenteeism is tremendously high because nobody really thinks of it as a place to make automobiles. The local citizenry view it as a government payoff, kind of a superwelfare proposition. One has a job there and gets paid, but it doesn't matter whether he shows up for work or not, because he still gets paid. One holds other jobs too. You also can't get the local folks to work the night shift because they're afraid that their women will be carrying on with others, so northerners have to be brought in to work the night shift. Some cars do get built apparently. Such is southern Italy and its economic problems. When one stops to think of the large number of southern Italians who are on the Vatican staff . . .

Friday, October 28

Today, I got my usual salute from the Swiss Guard as the big black car dropped me in the courtyard from which I ascend the staircase to Father Adolpho's office. He guessed that the conclave would now be likely within the next twelve months. There was no specific illness which seemed to affect the pope other than arthritis and general old age. Still, Adolpho thought his illness last summer, though temporarily healed, represented a major turning point in the pope's condition. "We will see," he said, "what happens next summer at Castel Gandolfo." He did not see Benelli as a papal candidate; however, because of the man's experience here and the sheer force of his personality he would be one of the great electors, thus notably diminishing Pericle Felici's power even within the Italian hierarchy. Felici, he said, would command at most a few extremely conservative votes, while Benelli would command a moderate or realistically conservative bloc of votes. He said Benelli's power would increase with time, as memories faded of how ruthless he was here and people remembered only his drive and efficiency. The only other notable change that he saw was the appointment of Hume to London; he was very impressed with Hume and thought that under proper circumstances he could easily become a papal candidate. One hears that around here repeatedly.

Eduardo Pironio is in trouble. The word about his administrative inefficiency is all around and is being pushed very hard by the Romans who don't like him. They sandbagged Sergio Pignedoli on the grounds that he was superficial; Pironio, they say, is a "lovely man, saintly, but not terribly efficient." Baggio remains a candidate, of course, kind of the least-possible-evil candidate from the point of view of a number of folks.

Adolpho saw the distinct possibility of a long, difficult conclave out of which would emerge some kind of elderly compromise candidate, like Franz Koenig from Vienna or Jean Villot, the secretary of state, both of whom are seventy-three years old. The church lucked out once this century with an elderly compromise candidate (John XXIII); another such attempt might not be so fortunate.

I asked him about Carter's notion (without attributing it to him, of course) that there might be a confrontation at the beginning of the conclave in which some stands were taken on retirement by the pope. He seemed less persuaded than Carter that such a thing could occur, but did think there might be a fairly open discussion about a job description, or at least a list of the kind of qualities the pope should have.

Adolpho remarked that it was indeed curious that while everyone knows a conclave isn't really too far off, there is absolutely no discussion of it. The pope and the Curia are feared. There may be conversations going on, but they are very discreet and private.

So much, according to Adolpho, depends on who the great electors are, the vigorous, decisive, precinct-type people. Unfortunately, there don't seem to be that many around. Benelli would certainly be one, and George Hume in the English-speaking world; John Krol of Philadelphia, oddly enough, might be a bridge between Eastern Europe and the rest of the world—at least he will try to play that role. But Joseph Bernardin, the natural leader of the Americans, and Roger Etchegaray, the natural leader of the French, are not yet cardinals. Also, Anastasio Ballestrero, the new archbishop of Turin, is not yet a cardinal.

One of the things to watch will be the twelve men who are elected to the permanent advisory council of the synod. Adolpho said that might be a signal as to how the cardinals would vote for pope. That's something we'll have to check on after the synod is over and after I get home—who they elect as the permanent members of the council. (*Aloisio Lorscheider and Joseph Bernardin were elected on the first ballot. The first European to be elected was Karol Wojtyla of Cracow.*)

I had lunch with Father Micheli. He talked about the degeneration of the Jesuits. The dilemma of contemporary Jesuits must be thought of as a problem that arises from their turning away from that which was once their greatest tradition, a tradition of concern about ideas and competence. They are now emphasizing egalitarianism to such an extent that competence is not only not important but frowned on. Feelings, emotion, romanticism are stressed to such an extent that their old contribution of rationalism and ideas is no longer viewed as important. He said that instead of the Jesuits saving the church, as it used to be said, it now looks like the church will have to save the Jesuits.

A fittingly melancholy ending to a melancholy couple of days here. Nothing seems to be working right in this church, and the prospects of things getting any better in the proximate future don't look good. The synod is a mess, a disaster. There is virtually no serious preparation for a papal election, and maybe the best prognosis for a papal election is that we will get an old man who will serve as a transition. A transition from what to what remains to be seen.

I decided to go to the English-language press briefing tomorrow, presided over by Jimmy Roache, and abandon my policy of not saying anything. Those of you who know me and love me will realize that having exercised this policy for two press briefings, I have earned great merit, notably diminished my allotted time in purgatory, and literally astonished everyone. The fact that a synod on education would completely ignore all of the empirical evidence about young people and about education is enough to make anyone sick. What's going on in the synod hall in the Vatican this week is worldwide tragedy.

Catholics should be angry, as angry as Ken Woodward of *Newsweek* was this afternoon. He's trying to raise three kids to be Catholics in a church where the bishops of the world come together to talk about raising Catholics without even looking at the empirical evidence or talking with parents or catechetics teachers, or catechetics writers, or researchers, or anybody who knows anything about the real world in which young people live.

Saturday, October 29

It's now Saturday afternoon, and I'll tell you one thing. You can scratch Cardinal Lorscheider from your list of those to elect pope; he didn't show up for his interview with me. Or rather, I showed up for the interview and he was nowhere to be found. What's more, the people at the Brazilian college didn't know where he was. So I hung around for a half-hour, and I said to hell with it. For McGeorge Bundy I will wait half an hour, and, under the proper circumstances, for almost any governmental funding agency; but I'll be damned if I'll wait for any cardinal.

This is the guy who's supposed to be efficient, mind you. He's the one great organizer in the present College of Cardinals—and he doesn't keep appointments. Well, he's a busy man, I suppose, but, still, he didn't show. It was another melancholy event in a melancholy experience. I'm willing to sell this project to the nearest bidder.

Then on to the press conference at which Jimmy Roache produced one Derek Worlock, the archbishop of Liverpool. He read through the summaries of the small-group discussions, *circulus minores* they call them here. It was all unmitigated nonsense. He made a number of assertions about what young people wanted. Finally, I broke my silence and asked how he knew what young people wanted, and he said, well, there's been lots of consultation with young people and that he and some of his priests had gone to a pop festival once.

The synod, if anybody cares, will lumber on trying to prepare some final document, although some more elaborate document will probably come down from the pope after the synod. It is reasonably clear from the thirty-one speeches that were given today that an awful lot of folks are dissatisfied, but that they're muttering their dissatisfaction in very low-keyed tones.

Midnight, Monday, October 31

I leave tomorrow for Amsterdam and home. I guess as I become either a more experienced traveler or a more cranky one I like to make quick, smooth getaways—bills paid, clothes packed, alarm set, breakfast programmed, right downstairs to the bus, right out to the airport, quick check-in, through the passport business, and onto the plane. Unfortunately, the world, particularly this part of the world, isn't organized to facilitate that sort of thing, so I find myself looking forward with dread to the escape tomorrow. The departure the next day from Amsterdam, of course, should be a lot smoother.

I like the central organization of the Roman Catholic church even less this trip than I have during the previous reconnaissance expeditions. There is a world of young people out there open to the possibilities of religion, and many of the young are quite consciously and quite explicitly looking for some faith to give order to their lives and some community to make life more intimate and supportive. Bishops of the world come together through their elected representatives here and make noise for several weeks but are absolutely precluded, because of the absence of prior investigation and the controlling apparatus which dominates their meeting, from addressing themselves to the problems of young people or even being aware that there are problems. Religious education is discussed ad nauseam without any reference to the fact that human beings are sexual creatures. One would think that the race is continued by some sort of parthenogenesis. An almost complete conspiracy of silence veils the subject of sexuality.

I knew the Curia was rigid and incompetent. I'm even more disillusioned to learn that the bishops of the world, brilliant though some of them may be as individuals, can dither so ineffectively on a subject of critical importance. It is fashionable to say that we get the leaders we deserve, but I can't believe we deserve leadership as bad as we presently have.

Scene IV

Friday, May 12, 1978

I'm sitting in the *trattoria* of the Rome Hilton. It's four-thirty in the afternoon, but my poor stomach, confused by the jet lag, thinks it's noontime and is avidly demanding lunch. Well, I'll do penance when I get home.

I suppose I shouldn't be eating at five o'clock, because I am going to have supper with Signor Cardinale tonight at seven. Tomorrow I see Des O'Grady and Father Micheli at lunch, and Father Adolpho at supper.

My feelings driving into Rome today were mixed, more sharply ambivalent than they've been at any other time here. It was a lovely day, robin's-egg blue sky, soft sunlight, green fields. Weather in the high sixties. The country between Fiumicino and Rome (once doubtless part of the Mediterranean sea bed) is flat and kind of nice looking, and the city glows in the distance. It is one of the loveliest cities, I think, in the whole world. There is a vitality in the pulse of its life and an attractiveness in its people that make the heart beat faster whenever one comes back. I don't pretend to understand it; maybe it's a couple of thousand years of history, maybe just the sunlight. Still, *O Roma felix* is one of the world's greats.

On the other hand, they buried Aldo Moro yesterday, as much a martyr to the Christian Democratic party's coalition with the Communists as a martyr to the Red Brigades. Coming in from the airport there were various places where there were roadblocks of cops, with machine guns at the ready, though whatever earthly good they were doing, I can't fathom. For anyone with any experience of this country at all, it's not surprising they couldn't find Moro or his kidnappers. Indeed, what's surprising is that anything works here at all. It's a country where everybody is slightly paranoid and social trust rarely extends beyond the family and immediate friendship links, and even the latter aren't all that strong, witness the way the Christian Democratic leadership betrayed Aldo Moro. I don't mean that they should have released some of the Red Brigade types, but they should have negotiated,

negotiated, negotiated, stalled, and done all in their power to keep Moro alive until they found him or until all hope of finding him was lost. Their Communist allies wouldn't let them do it, because the Red Brigades are more of a threat to the Communists than to anyone else, operating mainly to the left of the Communists, and thus, according to the best Marxist ideology, occupying an extremely strategic position.

Attractive people, the Romans, but also, if one is to believe people like Luigi Barzini and some of the recent studies of Italian sex life, a frustrated, lonely, and unhappy people, the gaiety covering despair.

Then there's the Holy Roman Catholic church, this year busy celebrating the twentieth anniversary of the convocation of the Second Vatican Council, the fifteenth anniversary of Paul VI, and the tenth anniversary of *Humanae Vitae*. Talk about a downhill slope!

It's pretty clear from *L'Osservatore Romano*, from Archbishop John Quinn's (from San Francisco, the new president of the American Conference of Catholic Bishops) speech at the bishops' meeting, and the various celebrations of *Humanae Vitae* that are being planned around the world, that the Roman authorities have sent out word that they want celebrations of the encyclical. It seems to me to make as much sense as celebrating the sinking of the Titanic, the Johnstown flood, or the Chicago fire. Still, Pope Paul clings to the papacy, apparently too weak now to see any visiting bishops, and the church drifts even more aimlessly than it was drifting three years ago when this project was launched.

It would be a mistake to underestimate the amount of spontaneous paranoia to be found in Italy. The typical Italian driver, for example, believes firmly that the things going on on the highway around him are part of an organized conspiracy. "They" are out to get him, and their behavior on the highway only confirms his suspicions. Thus the young cabdriver who brought me in from the airport today would gesture expressively with his hands every time a motorcyclist would cut in front of him, a truck driver would slow down, or a car would change lanes dangerously close—events which transpire on an Italian highway about every fifteen seconds or so. (The young man had a lot of handwaving to do.) The sense of the gesture is "See, I told you it was a conspiracy. I told you that they were out to get me. Look, doesn't that motorcyclist prove it?

Doesn't someone have to be absolutely against me to drive that way?" It is something of a self-fulfilling prophecy, of course, because if everyone is out to get you, you've got to get them first. So you cut in front of them, switch lanes on them before they can do it to you. The same thing goes on in the Vatican. The thought of a well-organized curial conspiracy is something that can only be dreamed up by quasi-fiction writers like Malachi Martin. There's not enough trust in the Curia to generate a systematic plot. A curial scheme to reverse the effects of the Vatican Council is as much fiction as is organized crime in the United States. The effects are the same as if there were a plot, but there is no "grand conspiracy" and no evil genius behind it. There does not have to be, you see.

Friday Night, 11:00 P.M.

I just got back to the Hilton after supper with Signor Cardinale. He is in much better shape than he was in October. According to his aide, he continues to improve. Dinner was at 7:00 instead of 6:00, as it was my last visit, and he did not seem visibly tired when I left at 10:00.

Saturday, May 13

Foggy, misty morning, not exactly what one expects in May. Indeed, if this is the way Europe will be in the next several days, I'm going to have a hard time making my way around. I'm having lunch with Father Micheli at a French restaurant on the Piazza San Eustachio, which, all of you Roman types will remember, is the place where instead of a cross on the steeple they have a stag's head, an interesting regression to paganism, if I ever saw one. I also find myself in the awkward position of having to buy detergent. I wonder what the Italian word for detergent is? Would it be "detergento" or "sopso"? In this whole week there isn't going to be a single place I'll be long enough to get laundry done. I'm going to have to do it myself. I wonder if they have a laundromatto, or would it be laundromatico, here? Well, I'm not going to wander out to try to find out.

The state funeral for Aldo Moro is this morning. I learned last night that the Moro family was going to send one representative to the funeral, apparently at the instigation of the papal household.

My friend Adolpho is over there this morning; I wasn't able to talk to him on the phone. I did manage to struggle through a conversation in Italian with his secretary. I don't think it would take much practice for me now to become fairly proficient in the language. Heaven knows, though, I'd never get the pronunciation right.

I had supper with a weary and discouraged Father Adolpho tonight. He feels that if we have five, six, or seven articles— particularly articles—about what the new pope should be, we can sell them to *Panorama* and *Espresso* in Italy, *Paris-Match* in France, and *Der Spiegel* in Germany. We would have the College of Cardinals in our hip pockets. The idea is that someone should contact each of these journals and tell them about the study (especially about the American sociologist who has been studying the papal election for three years) and make available to them at a very reasonable charge (beforehand, so that their journals will have them in their files) a series of articles which can appear in the issue of the magazine that will show up between the vacancy and the conclave. The Germans will read *Der Spiegel*, the French will read *Match*, everybody in Rome will read *Panorama*, and if we can get into the *Rome Daily American*, and possibly deal with the *International Herald Tribune* in Paris, we will also get it to most of the English speakers. Since everybody reads either French, German, Italian, or English, we can inundate Rome in that critical week with our perspective on the election. According to Adolpho, they may get mad at us, they may not like what we say, but we'll be there and no one else will be.

Paul VI has been slipping badly week after week. Adolpho says he does not see how he can last another year. This is the same Adolpho who said last fall that Paul could go on for four or five years. He says the Moro kidnapping, death, and funeral were a tremendous strain on the pope, since he and Moro were close friends and since the family is a little mad at the pope, quite a bit mad, because the pope's plea that Moro be released *without condition* was in effect the Christian Democratic party line. The pope was apparently quite unsteady and very uncertain at the Moro funeral mass this afternoon, though he is still sharp on occasion. For example, the plea he gave for Moro when he was still captive was brilliantly done, as was the recent conversation with Edward Gierek, the Polish prime minister. He is an old, old man, growing more feeble, but still capable of producing intelligent, if not brilliant and profound, performances under pressure. The real decline, according to Adolpho, began last summer when he went to Castel Gandolfo in July, sort of the phenomenon of retirement: when a man stops working he begins to deteriorate. When Paul VI begins to rest, his physical condition goes down rapidly. It is for this reason that he hypothesized the final deterioration will begin this summer and may well reach the final phase sometime during the month of September. I think we'll all have to keep very careful watch on the newspapers.

The Vatican, Adolpho tells me, has ground to a halt. Decisions don't get made. In Pope Pius XII's declining days, Madre Pasqualina, the German nun, was running the church. With Benelli now in Florence, nobody is running the church. The secretary, Macchi, is concerned about the Vatican library and the Vatican museum; Villot, the secretary of state, is ineffective. It used to be said that Villot had no power because Benelli had it all; it now turns out, according to Adolpho, that Benelli had all the power because Villot was incapable of exercising power. Giuseppe Caprio, who is Benelli's replacement and the only one who sees the pope every day besides Macchi, is a pleasant and well-meaning fellow, not terribly intelligent, and certainly not motivated to make any hard decisions. Everybody is waiting, biding their time.

Adolpho had complimentary things to say about Il Signor Cardinale's management of his congregation. He said he's the only one who really runs an efficient congregation in the Curia. He also said he's a very shrewd man, and he wanted to know what the cardinal thought about the election. I mentioned that Corrado Ursi was the cardinal's candidate, and Adolpho said he and Ursi were close personal friends, that Ursi is a nice man but terribly, terribly sensitive and easily goes off into rages over hurt feelings. Albino Luciani, the patriarch of Venice, whom my friends of this afternoon thought the Romans were pushing, would be a nice, pleasant man but very unconfident. I jotted down in my notebook what he said about the papal job description: "It is the image of the pope that's important. What kind of man he will be, what kind of symbol he will be, what kind of reactions he will create among ordinary folk. Will he have the ability to be confident in dealing with the concrete problems of ordinary people?" Paul VI, Adolpho says, is the last pope who could pretend to control everything. The next pope will have to be someone who will choose the big problems on which to concentrate, choose the right kinds of people to work with him, and then, through the exercise of teamwork, begin to move in the direction of solutions to the problems. Paul VI, he says, is the last of those who could do everything himself.

Adolpho feels, as I do, that this election is of absolutely decisive importance, and that much can still be done to influence the outcome. But it is now going to be done in the last desperate few days. The whole trouble is, of course, that there are no candidates. He said we ought to put together a conspiracy as the people in England did to get Hume made archbishop of Westminster. Well and good, except they had a candidate, and you can't beat nobody with nobody, which is precisely the state we are in now. At least we can give them something to think about before they go into conclave. The way Adolpho put it, "They'll not put together a job description themselves, but if somebody else puts it together for them, then they might take it seriously simply because it fills the vacuum."

At lunch, Father Micheli showed me some raw data files from a curial office (which apparently are being passed around to everyone in Rome) containing the most vile accusations against one of the candidates, accusing him of cronyism, corruption, venality, and greed. I have had some slight confirmation of these charges from a hint given to me by an American bishop, but it would be irresponsible to set down even in these notes the charges or the candidate's name. To provide some idea, though, of the nature of the charges, one of the women who is supporting this cardinal's candidacy for the papacy in Rome is described as the "slut of priests," that is to say, someone who is readily available, even though she is married, to supply affection to various curial cardinals who need affection. Lots of juicy, raw meat, but thank you, no, I don't want any.

Micheli thought that there might well be another consistory, though Adolpho this evening was less sanguine about that. There is a cardinalatial vacancy in Turin. Anastasio Ballestrero, O'Grady thinks, would have a good shot at the papacy if he were cardinal. He's a Carmelite, by the way, very religious. The big question, as Adolpho said tonight, about another consistory is whether Joseph Bernardin and Roger Etchegaray would be appointed to the college, and presumably Jean Jadot too. A conclave with Bernardin, Etchegaray, and Lorscheider drifting around on the inside would be something else altogether.

Well, that ends the first day's notes. Obviously, the two interviews give somewhat different messages: Micheli thinks that there will be a long delay before the pope dies, that the new pope may not even be a cardinal, and that there might be another consistory; Adolpho feels it will be a rather short time and that there will not be another consistory. Adolpho also lamented the drift of the church, which is now a very serious one, far worse than it was even when Benelli was in charge, far worse than it was even in the synod, when Paul VI still had some vigor. It is like the last six months of Pope Pius XII's reign, except there is no Madre Pasqualina running the show. I am sure that Micheli's position is far more common in Rome than Adolpho's. However, those folks don't get a look at the pope every week.

After dinner at Casseti's, Adolpho drove me back to the Hilton and then came up to the roof bar, the first time I've been up there in all my times here. I had a Coke, he had a Scotch, and we sat there looking over the city. Here is one of the most gifted men of the church, a man who has turned out more intelligent, sensible documents, dealt with more difficult problems, arranged more happy solutions to annoying issues, a man who really ought to and still probably will be a cardinal, feeling very glum, of course, about the Moro affair and feeling even more glum about the terrible last ten years. *Humanae Vitae*, he said, was the catalyst. After that, it's been all downhill, and everyone in the church, from parish priest–sociologist on up to would–be cardinals and cardinals, has been judged by his response to that encyclical. I am reminded of the dictum that things always get darkest before they are totally black. They look pretty dark to us now here in Rome.

Sunday, May 14

I spent an hour and a half talking with Pat Kelly, member of the staff of one of the lesser Roman agencies set up since the Vatican Council to go through the motions of honoring the council and still not make any trouble for anybody in the real Curia. Kelly confirmed that Sebastiano Baggio is making a vigorous power play right now for the papacy. He wants it so bad he can taste it. (Incidentally, in Rome he's known as "Viaggio Baggio," a Roman pun meaning "Baggio the traveler.")

Kelly also confirms the hatred of the Secretariat of State for Baggio. The people in the secretary's office are doing everything they can to blacken his name, so if there is so much being expended in Rome to destroy the cardinals who are likely candidates, Adolpho may very well be right. The curialists smell a conclave and are getting ready for it by attacking their opposition. You get told over here that the Curia is factionalized, and you begin to believe it when you hear stories of the sort that I've been hearing the last couple of days about the character assassinations.

I'll be heading back tomorrow with the conviction that the conclave is near and with the idea that a papal job description from a sociological viewpoint might not be a complete mistake.

CHICAGO

Tuesday, June 1

After thinking about Adolpho's suggestion for a job description I have worked one out. By putting yourself in the position of a non-Christian sociologist looking at the papacy, it's not hard to write such a description. I feel an urgency to focus my own thinking because of Adolpho's prediction that Pope Paul will die before September. My guess is that the job description isn't going to have any effect because, despite Adolpho's enthusiasm, the cardinals are not likely to listen to me or, for that matter, to anyone else. However, if this does get broad exposure in the press and if a copy is given to each cardinal, it may fill the vacuum that Adolpho sees present. So here's my profile of the perfect papal candidate.[1]

A Hopeful Holy Man Who Can Smile.

"Interesting work, guaranteed income, residence comes with position. Protection from proven security organization. Apply College of Cardinals, Vatican City."

A careful sociological study of the top leadership position in the Roman Catholic church suggests that the qualities to be sought in a new pope are not so much characteristics of training or background as they are characteristics of personality and style.

The job description for the papacy is a job description for a man who not only wants to lead the world's largest religious denomination, but who is far and away the most important religious leader on earth.

Given the nature of the position, a good job description must focus on what characteristics are essential in the man who is to be the world's most visible and most influential religious leader.

From this sociological perspective, most of the characteristics discussed frequently as being essential for the man to be chosen by the next conclave appear to be irrelevant.

It does not matter whether he is a curial cardinal nor a non-curial cardinal; nor whether he is Italian or not, nor whether he is of the First, Second, or Third World; nor whether he is an intellectual or nonintellectual; nor whether he is a diplomat or a pastor, progressive or moderate, efficient administrator or lacking in administrative experience; nor whether he is a "liberation" theologian or a traditional theologian; nor what stands he takes or has taken on political issues facing the world.

Doubtless, someone in the papal entourage must be an efficient administrator, someone must be a theologian, someone must be a diplomat, someone must be a pastor, someone must understand Italy, someone must be sensitive to the Third World, someone must know how the Roman Curia runs and how it can be brought under control; but it is not necessary for the pope himself to have any of these abilities.

At the present critical time in its history, faced with the most acute crisis, perhaps, since the Reformation and dealing with a world in which both faith and community are desperately sought, the papacy requires a man of holiness, a man of hope, a man of joy. A sociologically oriented job description of the pope, in other words, must conclude that the Catholic church needs as its leader a holy man who can smile.

There are, it would seem, six principal characteristics that must be included in a job description of the pope:

(1) As the world's most visible and influential religious leader, the pope must be able to speak not only to Catholics but to the whole world with confidence and clarity. He must understand the aspirations, the needs, the longings of the human race and be able to respond, not necessarily with clear and precise answers, but with warm, sympathetic hopefulness.

(2) It is not necessary that the pope be a saint, but he must be a "holy" man. He must reflect in his own personal life the conviction he preaches; his goodness must be transparent; that is, it must shine before men. It is not necessary that he live or have lived in abject poverty, that he be totally without personal ambition, that

he be innocent and naive about political realities; but he must be totally free of the slightest taint of financial and organizational wheeling and dealing.

(3) In addition to being a hopeful holy man, the new man must also smile. He need not possess the jolly, bouncy good humor of John XXIII; he certainly must be the kind of man whose faith makes him happy and whose hope makes him joyful. A grim, stern, pessimistic, solemn-faced pope will not appeal to the world as a man who is really possessed by the "good news" he claims to be teaching. Quite simply, the more the pope laughs, the more effective he will be.

(4) Since it is no longer possible for the pope to make all the decisions himself, to run everything in the church himself, and to devote his attention to every problem, the new pope must be shrewd in his selection of subordinates and must preside over his "team" of subordinates in such a way as to release rather than inhibit the best of their talents.

(5) A leader of the Roman Catholic Church must have an instinct for the strategically important problems that should occupy his time and energy, and the ability to focus on those problems and to delegate responsibility for other problems to subordinates.

(6) The new pope must trust others—his own staff, his brother bishops throughout the world, Catholic scholars, the ordinary Catholic laity, the leaders of other religious denominations. He cannot do everything himself; he cannot take charge of every part of the world, of every parish, of every family.

Hope, holiness, self-confidence, maturity, trust, the ability to delegate power and responsibility, personal security—these are the qualities the new pope must have, and they are qualities which, while they may also be dictated by religious considerations, are demanded by a purely secular sociological analysis of the role of the papacy.

Friday, August 4

Sebastiano Baggio has been in our city. In a secret stop on his way to a meeting in Latin America, he visited Cardinal Cody with a "request" from the pope that he yield power. The cardinal is already telling people about the visit. I hear that there was a fierce shouting match most of one night at the cardinal's villa on the grounds of the seminary at Mundelein, with the cardinal adamantly refusing to go along with the request. This is Rome's most recent attempt to act on the dossier of charges which have been collected against the cardinal.

The following reasons were repeated frequently in Rome for the concern of both the Congregation for Bishops and the Secretariat of State:

(1) Racism. The arbitrary and seemingly capricious closing of schools serving blacks in the inner city of Chicago (many of them non-Catholics) gave the church an appearance of racism, to which Roman authorities are very sensitive. In fact, the cardinal is hardly a racist but closed the schools because he does not believe that the church has any mission to educate non-Catholics (to provide an alternative to public schools for middle-class blacks). However, the Romans were correct in thinking that annual public conflict about closing of inner city schools had given the appearance of racism to the archdiocese of Chicago. An American black bishop from a diocese where Cody was archbishop (New Orleans) has publicly called Cody a "classic example of an unconscious racist."

(2) Financial maladministration. Roman sources told me that it was generally known in the Curia that after his term as treasurer of the American bishops was over, but before he turned the money and books over to his successor, the cardinal had unwisely invested several million dollars in Penn Central commercial paper a few days before that railroad went bankrupt. I have documented this in a column which appeared in the Chicago Tribune *in 1976. In addition there are allegations that sixty million dollars of parish funds are on deposit at the Chicago chancery, and no accounting has been made either to the diocese or to Rome as to the investment of these funds. (It is a fact that no public audits of these funds have been released.) Finally, while closing inner city schools because of the allegedly impoverished finances of the diocese, the cardinal has poured millions of dollars into a TV network which operates only in rectories and schools. Added to his rumored proclivity for lavish gifts to curial bureaucrats, these facts and rumors made Roman authorities uneasy about the finances of what is generally thought to be the world's most affluent archdiocese. "How come he doesn't have the money for schools, when Cardinal Terence Cooke in New York does?" one Roman official asked me. It is possible that*

ecclesiastical authorities have more detailed information about the finances of the archdiocese of Chicago—reported by present or former staff members troubled in conscience about what was going on. "For Baggio to be going after him," I was told, "he's got to have more information on Cody than you can imagine."

(3) Poor administration. Many American bishops, including some of those who had been auxiliaries in Chicago, have complained to Rome about the arbitrary, highhanded, and frequently inefficient administration of the diocese. The cardinal concentrates all power in himself, Rome was told, delegates no decisions, and consults no one; hence major decisions and appointments get put off for months or even years. The Association of Chicago Priests has complained of most of these matters publicly and bitterly for several years. There has also been complaint to the Congregation for Catholic Education about the lack of a coherent seminary policy. "It's the worst disaster in the history of American Catholicism," one angry bishop told me, "and all we do is stand by silently and fume."

(4) Conflict with the clergy. There is always some tension between priests and bishop, but Roman authorities know that most of the Chicago clergy, normally respectful, have lost all regard for the cardinal. He has been told in public at meetings of the Association of Chicago Priests that he lies to them habitually. This charge was made by three Chicago priests in a UPI story in the summer of 1978. The Romans have some confirmation of this charge in the cardinal's public statements that he has requested auxiliary bishops when in fact no such requests have been made. Protests at the apostolic delegation in Washington and in Rome come not from fringe clergy, but from the most respectable and responsible priests in the archdiocese. Rome's inclination to take these protests very seriously is reinforced by the fact that the cardinal often does not respond to letters from the various Roman congregations and in one case did not respond for several months to a handwritten personal letter from Pope Paul VI (he bragged to others about ignoring this letter, saying that "Baggio made the pope write it"). A senior priest with excellent reputation and a responsible position has said publicly, "It will take a half century to undo the harm." Rome never sees things quite that apocalyptically, but there is more urgency than one normally encounters in their anxiety about Chicago.

(5) Unpopularity with the laity. While Vatican officials would not take seriously a public opinion poll sponsored and conducted by the Chicago Tribune *which showed that the cardinal was no more popular with the laity of Chicago than Richard Nixon was with the American people the year before he resigned, they are upset by the steady flow of protest letters received both at the apostolic delegate's office and in Rome. "They're not nuts," I was told by one informant. "The letters are neatly typed on impressive stationery by important and influential laity. The stack is a couple of feet high."*

(6) Extraordinary personal habits. Rome is also upset about the rumors of the cardinal's personal behavior—tales of his involvement in complex political and military machinations, obsession with keeping track of every outside priest who comes to Chicago, vindictiveness against those who disagree, a passion for secrecy and mystery, allegations of spy networks in the diocese, reported refusal to make annual spiritual "retreats." While it does not have the resources to sort out fact from fiction in these rumors, Rome operates on the assumption that where there is so much smoke, there must be some fire.

As one Roman said to me, "Any bishop on whom they had all that material would have been a chaplain in an old people's home five years ago." But Rome is reluctant to move against a cardinal, no matter how bad the case and how great the potential scandal.

So Paul VI approached his final days knowing that he had a major unsolved problem in Chicago and that one of the men likely to vote for his successor was a man on whom a huge negative dossier had been prepared by staff members who were normally anything but squeamish about the aberrations of highly placed ecclesiastics. Most human leaders are prone to the temptation to ignore unpleasant issues if they possibly can. No one should be shocked that popes do the same thing. Those who care about Chicago, however, might be pardoned for being angry.

Act One

Scene I

The pope was worn out even before he went to Castel Gandolfo on July 14. He'd been seriously ill twice before in the course of the year—the previous August at Castel Gandolfo, and in April. Though these illnesses had never been officially reported, rumors of them leaked out. During the fifteen-mile ride to Castel Gandolfo, he said to his staff, "We are leaving but we do not know if we will return or how we will return." On Friday, August 4, he did not feel well, and his doctor, seventy-year-old Mario Fontana, diagnosed the ailment as a return of the bladder infection which had recurred several times since his prostate operation.

As a precaution, Fontana ordered the pope to bed in his damask-walled room overlooking the castle gardens. Fontana checked with the urologist in Rome and began treating the infection, uneasy because of the pope's age and generally weakened condition, but not yet seriously worried. Monsignor Macchi, the pope's secretary, urged him to announce on Saturday the cancellation of his noonday Angelus blessing on Sunday. The bladder infection worsened on Saturday; Sunday his fever continued to be moderately high, but he was awake and alert, and the doctors were not unduly alarmed. Monsignor Macchi began mass for the pope at 6:00 Sunday evening in the chapel next to his bedroom. Father Magee (his other secretary, Irish born), a doctor, and a few other members of the household were present at mass. Just before communion, the pope became extremely agitated but pulled himself together to receive communion and then lapsed into semiconsciousness. His blood pressure now began to vary greatly, first high, then low, then high again. The doctor diagnosed the seizure during mass as a heart attack. The pope was put into an oxygen tent and Cardinal Villot, the secretary of state and the camerlengo (the man who would be acting pope during the interregnum), was summoned from Rome. The pope's brother, Senator Luigi Montini, was also called. The heart attack was announced to the world, but the pope was still conscious when Villot arrived. Villot spoke to him privately for five or six minutes. Then his breathing grew more labored and he said, "We have arrived at the end. We thank . . ."—using the formal "we" almost to the end. A little later, *he said simply, "Pray for me." Now everyone was present who should have been there—Villot, Caprio, Macchi, Mario Fontana, Magee, the pope's nephew, Marco Montini, and four sisters who cared for the papal household at Castel Gandolfo. At 9:40 P.M. Sunday, August 6, 1978—quietly, almost as though he were falling asleep, Giovanni Battista Montini, Pope Paul VI, came to the end of his life.*

(Later there would be criticism of the medical procedures. The pope, several doctors argued, should have been placed in intensive-care treatment either in a hospital or in a mobile intensive-care unit which could have been brought from Rome in less than an hour. Popes don't go to hospitals, a custom dating to a past when royal personages were cared for in their homes because one received much better care in those days in the home than in the hospital. When Fontana had operated on Paul VI ten years previously, the makeshift operating room had been set up in the papal apartment because protocol forbade an operation in a hospital for the Supreme Pontiff. Perhaps the intensive-care mobile unit was not summoned early in his final sickness because the sickness was not thought to be serious enough and there was fear of unduly alarming the populace of the village. Then, when the pope had his heart attack, it was perhaps thought that it was too late. Still, if the mobile intensive-care unit had been summoned, it would have been there at least an hour before the pope died. The Vatican medical staff never responded to the criticism.)

GRAND BEACH

Sunday, August 6

At 2:45 in the afternoon, Chicago time, only five minutes after the pope's death, CBS News called me at Grand Beach—having alerted me about an hour before to the pope's heart attack. The crew would fly across Lake Michigan to interview me later in the afternoon. It was a beautiful August day, with multicolored sailboats in the lake, young people waterskiing, and a crowd of guests in the dunes to celebrate Bill McCready's birthday (as well as that of his father, Dr. Robert McCready). Mass must be said, interview given, dinner served, the birthday celebrated, and the trip to

Rome planned. I would leave for Rome the next evening from Chicago. Jim Andrews and John McMeel would meet me at the airport to head for Rome and set up the Universal Press Syndicate task force which had been preplanned to cover the funeral and conclave. CBS showed up at the homily of the mass I was saying outside the garden in the front of the Blessed Mother's statue. There was a pause in the mass while the TV cameras rolled for the interview—much to the delight of the score of small-fry crowded around hoping that they would be seen on the evening news.[1]

I felt no reaction at all; neither sorrow at the pope's death, nor eagerness for the upcoming excitement in Rome, not even much disappointment at being torn away from an August at Grand Beach. The social science and journalistic professional in me took over completely, snuffing out emotional response. I worried briefly about this. Anyone who cares about the papacy and the church as much as I do ought to be able to feel more emotion. There are sentiments which professional restraints ought not to inhibit. There was little time to think such things, however; time enough later for emotions after the job was done.

Monday, August 7—Chicago—Morning

In the midst of collecting airplane tickets, cashing checks, and trying to say something not too unintelligent for the TV cameras, I've been trying to think my way through the tragedy of Pope Paul VI. There are fulsome tributes in the papers and on television from religious and civic leaders, such things that people in positions of power and responsibility have to say at the time of a death. But apart from what is required, a list of the man's contributions is enormous: completion of the Second Vatican Council, reform of the Curia, the founding of the Synod of Bishops, the breaking down of centuries-old barriers with other churches, the trips to all the continents of the world; what more, one wonders, could a man do to earn the title of "great." Later, in St. Peter's, a young woman from Chicago would say to a reporter, "Let's face it, he was an unpopular man." Another, who had hoped to have an audience with the pope, remarked, "He died on me." Strange epitaphs for a man who made the reforms of John XXIII and the Vatican Council virtually irrevocable.

Afternoon

All in all, the historians may say Paul VI's papacy was a dramatic turning point in the history of the Roman Catholic church.

But then they may not say that at all. They may be forced to say that all the brave beginnings Pope Paul essayed finally came to naught; and in great part because Paul VI did not have the ability to make his reforms stick. Whether Paul VI will be hailed as one of the great popes or an unmitigated disaster depends now on his successor. If the man to be selected in Rome in the next weeks is vigorous enough—and wily enough—to seize on the openings Paul has left him, then Paul will look very good indeed in years to come. It will be said of him that he prepared the way for the great work of his successors.

One suspects that was all he wanted in his last years. His repeated pleas for joy and hope were an expression of his own terrible worry that he might have made a mess of things. Surely he died a man badly disappointed. He came to office with everyone, himself included, expecting a brilliant and successful reign. In retrospect, both he and the Catholic world had to be content with a question mark.

The critics will not lack for material. The world trips were often little more than public relations jaunts, and his speeches were often badly thought out and sometimes counterproductive. For all the ecumenical gestures, the thrust toward church unity had weakened considerably by the end of his administration. The Synod of Bishops has never been anything more than a puppet show rigged by curial bureaucrats—and incredibly frustrating to many of the participants, who knew they were being manipulated. The national hierarchies had very little real power. The infrastaff of the Curia, almost entirely Italian, retained effective control of that body.

Scholars and innovators were still subject to persecution; most notably, Hans Küng and Ivan Illich were subject to constant harassment. No really effective Catholic political voice was heard in the world despite many papal statements and interventions. The vital Dutch church was torn apart by Roman misunderstanding and incompetence. Colorless administrators were appointed to critical positions instead of leaders with broad vision—most notably in the

United States, where, according to one historian, the hierarchy has never been as undistinguished as it is now.

Most seriously of all, perhaps, the papacy lost its credibility among vast numbers of laity and junior clergy because of the long-delayed decision on the birth control issue, a decision which, when it did come, as previously mentioned, brusquely rejected the recommendations of the pope's own commission of experts which had been set up to advise him on the problem.

In the wake of the frustrations, disappointments, and disillusionment after the birth control decision in 1968, much of the élan of the Vatican Council was lost. Church attendance and religious vocations fell precipitously in the North Atlantic world, and massive resignations from the priesthood and the religious life began.

The papacy itself suffered a tremendous blow to its credibility, and from the height of influence during the time of John XXIII has plunged to the lowest level in over a century. Pope Paul lived out his last years knowing that the great opportunities had slipped through his fingers.

Pope Paul began his life as a priest in a student chaplaincy, and with more claim to intellectualism than most Vatican diplomats. He was part of the aristocratic northern Italian "liberal wing" of the hierarchy in his younger days. He was greatly influenced by French Catholic thinkers in the years immediately after the war (men like Jacques Maritain and Jean Danielou—many of whom turned reactionary in their old age, Danielou dying both as a French cardinal and in a scandalous manner—he was found dead in a Paris house of prostitution). Early in his religious career, his pronouncements as archbishop of Milan gave every indication of a man who was courageously open to the possibilities of his time. Yet as pope he turned cautious, indecisive, and melancholy—a phenomenon which produced in many Catholics a reaction not unlike the sense of betrayal felt by Americans who had voted for Lyndon Johnson because of their fear that Senator Goldwater would get us into a deep war in Vietnam.

The years of constant strife in the vicious and faction-ridden Roman Curia doubtless took their toll. He was also certainly shattered when his enemies finally "got" him and persuaded Pius XII to replace him as acting secretary of state and send him into "exile" in Milan—without the red hat. To spend his entire papacy in the shadow of the legendary Pope John—whose picture still can be seen in Roman taxis and can be purchased at any Roman souvenir stand—was surely a trial. One had the impression that Pope Paul began his pontificate with a smooth and serene program for moving the church into the modern world, but never had a chance to set the program in motion. Events got out of control, and he was never quite able to catch up.

He was alleged to vacillate, to be open to the influence of the last person he talked to. Surely there were long delays and indecision after hopes had been raised high by false starts and promises which led to disappointment. The typical Pauline compromises— the reform of the Curia which did not reform it, the modification of the rules for papal election which modified very little—produced dismay and disillusion. Better, it seemed to many, that he do nothing rather than raise expectations and then do so little.

But once he made up his mind, once he was locked into a decision of conscience, there was no changing him. He was indeed the first real Calvinist since John Calvin, as Oscar Cullmann said. He put his conscience against the opinion of the whole world. The birth control problem was not even open for discussion among Catholic theologians, and loyalty to the decision was a sine qua non for promotion. In some cases, it seemed the only criterion.

In his last years, cheered by the large turnout at the 1975 Holy Year ceremonies, Pope Paul often seemed to think of himself as a modern St. Athanasius, standing virtually alone against a heretical and infidel world. It was a stance that Vatican reactionaries did nothing to discourage.

Conservative Catholics will think of him as the great defender of the traditional faith in a time of peril and uncertainty, a man who firmly and bravely resisted the pernicious trends of the time—not enthusiastically or completely enough, perhaps, but still effectively. Liberal Catholics will shake their heads in dismay at a man who was elected on a platform of fulfilling the promise of the Vatican Council and then, perhaps unintentionally, turned against its spirit.

All our lives are tragedies, but all our tragedies are different. The tragedy of Paul VI may be that he wanted neither the praise of the conservatives nor the scorn of the liberals and ended by receiving both.

If Pope Paul VI had been elected in 1958 instead of 1963, he would have had a much easier time of it, I suspect. For the change in the church, to which he was as much committed as anyone, would have come more slowly and gradually, and would have been under his sensitive, tactful control. But he inherited the whirlwind that swept through the house of the church when Pope John opened his famous window, and he never managed to quite catch up with the wind. He also inherited the Pope John myth, which no man could have hoped to duplicate.

Enough. Perhaps it is a mistake to care as much about any public office as a lot of us have come to care about the papacy. The church did well for centuries when the pope was only a distant figure in Rome with little impact on the lives of ordinary Christians. Right now, could we not try to return to such an era and de-emphasize the papacy? The answer is, of course, that we can't, not in the world of the mass media, not in the world where inevitably the pope is the most important religious leader of humankind. Like it or not, that's who the cardinals are going to be electing next week. Small wonder that I'm leaving for O'Hare in a few minutes with a knot of fear in the bottom of my stomach.

ROME

Tuesday, August 8

Rome is almost a deserted city. It's *ferragosto* in Rome—that means the city is virtually deserted. Everyone, as someone said to me, was away on vacation when the pope died, even the pope. There were apparently only four cardinals in Rome; now all the cardinals are hustling from all over the world. The funeral won't be until Saturday—a seven-day wake, too much even by Irish standards. They are going to bring the pope's body down from Castel Gandolfo tomorrow evening. The first service will be at St. John Lateran, on the other side of the Tiber, which is technically the cathedral church of Rome, and then move on to St. Peter's Basilica.

The Italian papers are already filled with speculation about who the next pope will be. They are talking about Villot, who is seventy-three years old; Benelli, who is fifty-seven; Baggio, who is sixty-five; Pironio, who is fifty-seven; Willebrands, who is sixty-nine; Pignedoli, who is sixty-eight; and Koenig, who is seventy-three. Koenig himself, however, has said, in effect, that he does not choose to run and that the next pope should be a young man and non-Italian.[2]

101

The first day here has been a dizzy, jet-fatigued whirl. McMeel and Andrews are here as representatives of the Committee for the Responsible Election of the Pope as well as to set up the UPS task force. They have been wheeling and dealing as befits successful Notre Dame graduates, hiring reporters, searching for translators, meeting other journalists, staying up half the night talking, enjoying the thrill and excitement of the early days of a great adventure (though Jim was uncomfortable that he wasn't in Russia with his wife, Kathleen, and sons, Hugh and Jimmy). Their energy wears me out. I sit in my room and pound out dispatches, some from previous notes to provide readers with background and others based on quick interviews with my sources—though a lot of them, like everyone else, are away for the August vacation weeks. *Ferragosto* has turned Rome into a very quiet city—it's hard to find a place to break your diet rules with pasta.

I'll snap out of it eventually, but right now I'm a tangle of confused emotions—excitement, sorrow, weariness, and confusion. I'm also uneasy about the press conference with the papal job description that I've done for Jim and John. It's going to be misunderstood no matter how hard we try. Those folks don't like Americans. But since when have I cared about things like that?

The Italian magazines, with remarkable speed, have got out special editions on the pope's death, with cover pictures, inside stories, and color photographs, obviously things they have had in their files. *Gente* has a marvelous color centerfold of "Paolo VI, Papa della Pace e dell'Amore" (Paul VI, Pope of Peace and Love). Inside was a second centerfold, three color pictures of a famous singer, minimally clad to say the least. *Epocha* paralleled a special coverage of the pope with pictures of an actress playing Marilyn Monroe. *Oggi*, not to be outdone, had a smiling Paul on the cover with an article by a lover of Marilyn Monroe inside, complete with the necessary pictures, another article listing a nudist's speeches in Europe and a third advocating extramarital affairs during August vacations. *Panorama* managed to have pictures about autoeroticism a few pages away from its coverage of the pope. Like I say, it's a real accomplishment to get out special editions on the papal death just a couple of days after it happened!

The cardinals are starting to arrive in Rome. They really have so little time. They know, relatively speaking, so little of one another. They are being pulled away from vacations. It's likely to be hot here in Rome (though the weather has been lovely today and is already cooling off this evening). The requirements of secrecy, prohibitions against explicit campaigning, the protocol which forbids the cardinals to admit their real differences of opinion—all of these are going to restrict and inhibit the wisdom of their decision even more.

Only eleven men have been in the conclave before, and only three of them were at the conclave which elected Pope John: Siri, Wyszynski, and Léger (Gracias, the Indian cardinal, is apparently too sick to come). Wyszynski and Léger probably voted for John; Siri certainly voted against him. Inexperienced men without the time or the preparation or the freedom of discussion are going to make perhaps the most critical choice that a group of cardinals has made in the last half of a millennium. I have the knot of fear in my stomach once again.[3]

Wednesday, August 9

A pope's death does not stop a city. Rome continues to function despite *ferragosto*. St. Peter's Square is filled with tourists. They are putting up barriers down the Via della Conciliazione around St. Peter's, presumably to contain the crowds which are going to be there tonight. It is hot again today, but not unbearably hot. The sky is blue with only a few lacy clouds. The dome of St. Peter's rears up against the sky; there are tourists everywhere.

There's no reason why the tourist business should stop; indeed, there is no way that it can. Yet, as I stand in the shadow of the Bernini columns and look out over the piazza, it somehow seems strange that there is no mood of mourning. The piazza is as festive as it usually is in the summertime—tourists with their flight bags and cameras winding in and out, kids chasing the pigeons and feeding them, young people in shorts and slacks, halters and Fruit-of-the-Loom shirts—not a sign other than the barriers that anything unusual has happened. Perhaps by this evening there will be a mood of reverence and sorrow.

At the door of St. Peter's they are turning away people in shorts, men and women alike. Apparently, the guards are able to make some decisions as to what kind of sundresses get you into St. Peter's and what kind of sundresses keep you out. I'd be interested in knowing what the principles are.

The Associated Press said this morning that Paul VI achieved in death the popularity he did not have in life. Throughout his reign, more Pope John artifacts, the report says, were purchased in Rome in religious stores than Pope Paul artifacts—symbolizing, I guess, one of Pope Paul's principal problems: how do you follow the Pope John act?

Now the Associated Press says that people are snapping up Pope Paul artifacts in the stores as souvenirs and this is evidence that he has achieved popularity. I doubt it, but then you have to file copy every day, and with Rome still caught in its *ferragosto* lethargy, you've got to say something.

Later in the day

The pope's body was brought back tonight. I'm sure the papers tomorrow will speak of the large crowds of people— "Throngs Mourn Pope," the headlines will say. But there weren't throngs, there was only a thin line of people along the barriers and several thousand clustered up in the front of St. Peter's, where a brief service took place. There's no way to sort out how much of this is indifference to the papacy, how much of it is indifference to Paul VI, and how much of it is simply August. However, despite the vacations, there are still a lot of people in Rome, and the sidewalk cafés in the streets a few blocks away from St. Peter's seem to be filled with people, and there are young folk going in and out of the movie houses. Of course, what else should they do on a cool, lovely summer night? Still, I can't escape the feeling that there ought to have been more people in front of St. Peter's.

There is a meeting tonight on the Via della Conciliazione long after darkness between the Brazilian cardinal Agnelo Rossi (who works in the Curia) and the ineffable Pericle Felici. Rossi has come as a delegate of Sergio Pignedoli, who proposes an alliance with Felici to protect Pope Paul's status quo. Two men, clad in black cassocks so that they will not be recognized, talk briefly as they walk along the sidewalk close to the walls of the buildings that line the street. Felici dismisses the proposal out of hand. Pignedoli is a lightweight; he wants no part of him.

There will be no such deal. Rossi nods noncommittally and says that he will convey Felici's refusal to Pignedoli. Felici returns to his apartment near the Vatican and relaxes on his favorite couch and continues to make phone calls. There is no real support, he is convinced, either for Baggio or Pignedoli among the foreign cardinals. He and his allies in the Curia trust neither of the men. They can easily be stopped. But who then to nominate–Bertoli, the seventy-year-old former diplomat who has been on Paul VI's shelf? A difficult and contentious man, too rigid in his principles, but at least not a lightweight like Pignedoli or an unpredictable opportunist like Baggio. There must be support for Siri on the first ballot of course, for old times' sake, but Siri cannot win. Felici thinks briefly of Albino Luciani, his good friend from Venice. The dean of the College of Cardinals, Carlo Confalonieri, who will not be able to vote because he is over eighty, has also spoken of Luciani as a good and gentle man. Luciani's holiness would doubtless be attractive to foreigners: since he has gone to Venice he has proved quite responsive to curial instructions. Doubtless he could easily be persuaded to see to the promulgation of a new code of canon law to which Felici has devoted so much of his time in the last decade. Yes, Luciani might be a good compromise candidate. Perhaps Felici briefly thinks of his own chances and then dismisses them. The foreigners are too unpredictable. There is no way of knowing what they will want.[4]

Thursday, August 10

Today is the first day of the papal wake in Rome (there having already been three days of it up in Castel Gandolfo). The Via della Conciliazione buzzes with people. Clerics in various garb scuttle up and down the street—some in gray suits with Roman collars, some in black suits with Roman collars, some in cassocks, the traditional cassock—thin Roman coat, round hat—occasionally somebody with purple or even red buttons. None of them is smiling, but that's not because there's a wake going on over in St. Peter's; rather, it's because Roman clerics don't smile on the streets no matter what day of the year it is, a result, I suppose, of the old hostility between the clergy and the laity in this city, dating back to the time when the pope was the absolute temporal as well as spiritual ruler of Rome.

But the area of St. Peter's Square continues to have a festival atmosphere. Sidewalk cafes are filled, with journalists taking the place of the regulars who are away on vacation (I guess at least five hundred reporters are already here). Tourist buses line the streets and tourists with their cameras and flight bags are streaming up toward St. Peter's, the young people often arm in arm. There is a crowd, about eight across, passing through a narrow set of barriers going to the basilica, not a very thick crowd and not a very slow-moving one either. It almost seems as if there are more people out on the Conciliazione than are going into the basilica. Even if it is *ferragosto*, I think that the Vatican authorities ought to worry if the line doesn't get much longer by the time of the funeral Saturday night.

The cardinals continue to arrive. Franz Koenig has repeated his idea that the next pope ought to be a young man and non-Italian, possibly non-European. Leo Suenens has suggested that it might be a good idea to have four popes, one for each part of the world. The Third Worlders are being very discreet but sounding tough. Joseph Cordeiro of Pakistan, for example, observed that it would be all right if it were an Italian pope, so long as he was chosen by the Third World cardinals. Half of the American cardinals are here; the other four, including John Cody, are arriving today. The American reporters are trying to get an answer from our cardinals as to why everything has to be in secret. The cardinals are trying to answer, but the only real answer is that the secrecy is intended to keep the influence of the Austrian emperor out of the election. At least that's the official *historical* explanation, but no cardinal will dare say that because it makes the secrecy sound as absurd as it is! Indeed, the cardinals do not know where the other cardinals will be; nobody provides them with an address list. If you want to find out where someone else is staying so you can invite him to supper, you just have to ask around and find out.

The London bookies are giving odds on the election, with Sergio Pignedoli as a front-runner. Their own man, George Basil Hume, is somewhere around fifty-to-one, which strikes me as being a not unreasonable estimate of his chances.

I'm now in the line for the wake, having overcome my untypically Irish reluctance to attend. There are many different languages being spoken by the people in line with me, but very little Italian. I have the impression that the pope's body has become a tourist attraction. Inside the basilica everybody is talking. Not only a tourist attraction, but a kind of museum.

There are a couple of fellows going up and down the aisle trying to push people into two separate files. As soon as the crowd is separated, the lines promptly close together again with the Italians in the crowd using the empty space between the two files to sneak ahead.

Near the catafalque, I can see that the pope is wearing a red vestment over his white garments and that he looks very purple and pasty and corpselike. There's an Easter candle lighted behind him. The Swiss Guards in their brilliant uniforms are statue-still, cameras are going off all over the place. The crowd moves very quickly by the catafalque; some of them go out, others linger about watching from a distance. The tourist guides are giving their instructions and their lectures as usual. There are some folks in here with yarmulkes on.

I'm sorry, but the whole thing reminds me of the King Tut exhibit in Chicago. Though, unlike the King Tut viewing, you move quickly in and out of this one. There's lots of curiosity, but no sign of mourning or grief. The people at the door have now clearly abandoned the usual Vatican standards about shorts and sundresses. Anybody who wants to get in can come in.

The Northern European cardinals, by the way, are taking their sweet time coming down here. Either they are very confident about their ability to organize things in a few days, or they haven't thought about organizing. If the former is the case, then they are presumptuous; if the latter, they're irresponsible. No wonder people are saying thet Felici is in a euphoric mood. No wonder Cardinal Agnelo Rossi vigorously denounced the collaborators and staff of Paul VI. The absence of any organization among the foreigners or the progressives is enabling the local right-wingers to feel their oats. They may think they've already got things sewn up. Lord, what a disaster for the church that would be.

I can't quite get over how bad that scene was inside St. Peter's. Paul VI deserved better. Hell, anyone deserves better than a wake like that. I am feeling very depressed and discouraged. It is a rotten wake. People are not interested in the death of the pope.

I confess that I feel ambivalent about the involved and musty rituals—the strange dress, the ancient language, the ceremonials that are relics of another age. Are non-Catholics put off by such "mummery"? This stuff is accidental to the church; maybe the man who is crowned pope before August is over could abolish it all with a stroke of the pen; nothing essential in Catholicism would be changed.

I'm embarrassed by the bafflement of my non-Catholic colleagues over the ancient customs, ceremonies, and rites. Why does it have to be nine days of mourning? Why the almost compulsive secrecy of the conclave—which no one here thinks can be maintained? Why the triple crown? Why the change of name when a man becomes pope?

Yet, on the other hand, non-Catholics seem to be fascinated. There is something to be said for the power of mystery and antiquity, particularly when it doesn't get in the way. Before I came to Rome, people stopped me in the corridors of my research center and on the street to offer condolences over the pope's death, a sympathy which was genuine and sincere, if perhaps a little mystified. They knew that the man and the office were important to me, they knew that the role is the most important religious leadership position in the modern world. They were intrigued by the colorful pictures that accompanied Winston Burdette's commentary from Rome on Sunday evening (you really can't have a papal death and election without him, can you?). The drama of these days may mean more to many than it does to me—sweltering in the vile Roman August.

The cardinals and their assistants are shuttling around the city now in their black cars, discreetly ducking in and out of colleges and seminaries, not campaigning, since that is not permitted, but "consulting"—all things here must be done with elegance and grace. Right now the really best guess is no guess at all. No one knows with any degree of confidence who will don the triple crown in a few days.

But one thing can be said with confidence—the winner will be a compromise candidate. The fact is built into one critically important mechanism of the election: the two-thirds-plus-one majority required to elect.

Those of us with either memory or history of American politics can recall that until 1940 the Democratic party needed a two-thirds majority to nominate a president, and hence had long and dramatic conventions, including the famous 103 ballots in 1924. The reason for that rule was simple—the Democrats were a disparate coalition which had to keep all its major components happy to win an election. Indeed, the Democrats only began to lose the South in presidential elections when they dropped the two-thirds rule.

The idea behind such rules is that some things—like amending the Constitution—are of such great importance that you've got to have more than a simple majority. A disgruntled minority of close to half would mean the possibility of a dangerous split. If you have a large majority—concurrent majority, John C. Calhoun would have called it—you've got a choice which most everyone can live with.

Hence the bias in the conclave—as in all two-thirds-rule voting—is towards compromise, coalition, consensus. You want the kind of man of whom, when the voting on the last ballot comes close to acclamation (as in Democratic conventions), the acceptance will be more or less sincere. The electors will be able to go home with a sigh of relief, not merely for escaping the Roman heat, but because they feel that at least they will have held the enterprise together.

My hunch at this stage of the proceedings is that they will have a hard time arriving at a candidate who can get the required seventy-five votes (two-thirds of 111 plus one). Cardinal Pironio, for example, will certainly get many Hispanic and Third World votes on early ballots, but it is doubtful he could command the necessary number. Similarly, the curial conservatives might, through some quick coup, be able to elect one of their candidates by a simple majority. But it is most unlikely that, let us say, Cardinal Felici could round up seventy-five votes.

The electors will not want a deadlock; they will want to get out of the Roman heat as quickly as possible. They will not want to worry the world by the appearance of conflict. Hence, they will be powerfully motivated to begin searching early for a kind of compromise candidate. In the end, they may have to settle for some elderly interim candidate who will reign for a few years until a new consensus leader appears. A good guess would have been Vienna's Cardinal Koenig, if he had not done his Calvin Coolidge refusal. However, he may have to be talked out of it. Another interim possibility is Cardinal Villot, the secretary of state, though many here are not happy with his hesitancy as an administrator. Hence, no one should expect dramatic change out of this papal election, though there may be important stylistic changes.

I'm afraid I'm going to pieces. I've lost my glasses, I've walked out of the hotel without my wallet, I've forgotten phone numbers, and am in mortal terror of missing appointments. I don't know whether I'll be able to pull myself together before the press conference on Sunday when the Committee for the Responsible Election of the Pope releases my papal job description.

I hear from my sources that so far the cardinals who are here are talking in generalities in their formal sessions in the morning, trying to hammer out some kind of a job description of their own, and then in the afternoons and evenings at their informal sessions, they are very discreetly, very elegantly, and very informally trying to fit people to the description. The news is that some of the Orthodox prelates who are coming for the funeral are going to drop subtle words to their friends among the cardinals about the kind of pope they would like to have. Wouldn't it be marvelous to invite some of the Orthodox and Anglican and Protestant leaders into the election, if not as voters, then at least as observers? Well, they can't do that this time.

Pignedoli, whose cooks, two Canadian nuns, are said to be superb—the best pasta in Rome, one hears—is already tooling his campaign up by having people over for dinner. He is running like mad. Some people here who basically support his position think he's hurting himself by being too obvious in his candidacy. Right now, as I look over the list of people whose names turn up in the Italian papers, I can't find anybody to get enthusiastic about nor can I think of any favorite I would like to add to the list myself. Just now I wish I were back in Grand Beach.

Friday, August 11

In one of the most bizarre events in the history of papal elections, the process of the "making of the pope" has ground to an unexpected halt. The cardinals will not go into conclave until August 26 and will not start voting until August 27, three weeks after the death of Pope Paul VI. Some cardinals are actually leaving Rome to go home in the interim, others are dispersing to the countryside. The hundreds of members of the world press who flocked to the Vatican are trying to figure out what to do, while their editors wonder about expenses, news value, and what craziness is going on in Rome.

Consider the differences: in the era before transatlantic jets,

Pius XII was buried four days after he died, the cardinals went into conclave sixteen days after his death, and a new pope (John XXIII) was elected nineteen days after Pius XII's death. Pope John was in his tomb two days after his death and succeeded by the new pope (Paul VI) eighteen days after his death. The funeral of Paul VI, on the other hand, occurred almost a week after he died, and the electors will start to vote after a period of time longer than it took to elect the last two popes. It took nineteen days to elect a successor to Pius, eighteen days to elect a successor to John, but there will be a delay of twenty-one days before they even begin to vote on a successor to Paul.

It is the longest delay in modern history—a ten-day wait occurred before the conclave which elected Leo XIII in 1878, the same period for the Pius X conclave, twelve days to the beginning of the Benedict XV conclave, eighteen days for Pius XI.

As one wag here put it, "Too bad the Wright brothers couldn't make that thing fly."

And a bitter Roman official commented, "The man is as difficult in death as he was in life."

Such a statement is unfair to Pope Paul, save that he was the man who appointed the camerlengo (chamberlain or acting pope), Cardinal Jean Villot, whom Vatican observers are blaming for the disgracefully long wait for the funeral and the delay of the beginning of the conclave.

Some reporters are attributing the delay to a shrewd move on the part of the cardinals, who, it is alleged, realize that they have a potential deadlock on their hands and want more time to consult before they get locked up. But this is typical of the temptation of the press to read into Vatican behavior meanings which are appropriate for North American politics but which have no relevance here. (Another example: the call of Brussels's Cardinal Leo Suenens for four mini-popes around the world was falsely interpreted as a statement in behalf of twenty "liberal" cardinals—as though the liberals were organized, which they are not, and as though they would choose Suenens for their spokesman if they were, which they would not.)

Some Vatican experts see the delay as a curial plot to give the Italian cardinals more time to manipulate the foreign cardinals. One can never tell about curial conniving, but the delay also gives a non-Italian—particularly such charismatic types as Aloisio

Lorscheider, Jaime Sin, and George Basil Hume—time to put together a coalition.

In fact, the decision to delay was made by only thirty-two cardinals (the ones present at the meeting in which the date of the beginning of the conclave was set)—and mostly because of the inability of the camerlengo, Cardinal Jean Villot, to impose any order on discussion and debate. Villot is also blamed for the long delay before the funeral, which spread out the crowds and made each day seem poorly attended. One Vatican type told me, "Whatever chances Villot had to be elected went down the drain in those decisions." But don't bet on it. In the wonderland which is the Vatican, anything can happen.

There's another explanation, of course, and that is maybe the most interesting of all. The reason for the delay is that the Vatican workers are all off on vacation and are not about to come back to wall up the apostolic palace and the Sistine Chapel, so the three-week delay between the death of the pope and the beginning of the election of a new one is necessary to ensure that there will be enough workers around to seal the cardinals in properly. That makes as much sense as anything.

Felici is not the only one who can use the telephone. Already the church leaders in the Low Countries, France, Spain, Austria, and Germany, as well as some in Italy, are talking to each other discreetly on the telephone. They ignore the foolish speculations in the Italian newspapers and agree that neither the Baggio nor the Pignedoli candidacies are satisfactory to them; they begin to sense in one another the desire to have a pope who is pastoral in his orientation, an "experienced pastor," and has nothing to do with the Curia. Anti-curial feelings among the Europeans are strong, and at least some of them know from their travels that many of their non-European colleagues share the same feelings.

No organization, church or other, ought to arrange its affairs to suit the convenience of the media. But neither can any human community be unaware of the impact of the media and the importance of timing. In addition to the possible negative effects the long delay might have on the outcome of the conclave, it has turned the papal election from high drama into almost comic anticlimax, thus adding one more unnecessary burden to the task of the pope who is finally elected.

My job description is coming out Sunday, and on Monday *Time* magazine will have the parallel job description written by Hans Küng (notably changing the first draft I did). There are posters all over the Via della Conciliazione from various groups mourning the death of the pope implicitly or explicitly setting out a description of what the new one should be. One outfit called Christian Civilization is demanding a Catholic pope, by which they mean one substantially to the right of Paul VI. Nobody, however, seems to be insisting on any particular candidate. If anybody should ask me at the press conference who my own candidate is in view of the job description, I can honestly say that I don't have any.

Saturday, August 12

Today is the day of the pope's funeral. Rosalynn Carter showed up last night and got considerable notice on Italian television, but not nearly as much notice as Senator Edward Kennedy did. You'd almost think, from the crowds following him, that Teddy was running for president of Italy.

They released Pope Paul's will yesterday. It was a heart-rending little affair, giving some clue to why some people found him personally attractive, but also revealing the anguish which seems to have marked his whole life. Two pages added in 1972 and 1973 were especially interesting. He insisted on a simple funeral, which they are going to give him, with a plain wooden box, and also asked pardons from all those he had harmed.

A number of American cardinals are being quoted in the press these days; their statements are profound. New York's Terence Cooke says we want the best possible man, and Boston's Humberto Medeiros says we want a pope just like Paul VI. The current betting odds in London are five-to-two on Pignedoli, seven-to-two on Baggio, seven-to-two on Poletti, four-to-one on Benelli, eight-to-one on Willebrands, twelve-to-one on Pironio, sixteen-to-one on Koenig, twenty-five–to–one on Hume, thirty-three–to–one on Cordeiro, thirty-three–to–one on Lorscheider, and thirty-three–to–one on Suenens. I wouldn't bet on any of them at this stage of the game.

Late Afternoon

They are getting ready for the funeral mass in a couple of hours in the piazza. Today is the hottest day yet. It's a good thing they scheduled the funeral at 6:00, when Rome begins to cool off. The souvenir shops are all open. Though the vendors have been chased out of the piazza, they are still hassling people up and down the street. There are actually fewer people on the Conciliazione today than there were earlier in the week—possibly because many of the tourists have gone home. There's a fair number of Italian security police–types around in khaki uniforms with automatic weapons. The crowds going into the wake are smaller than they were yesterday and still seem to be composed mainly of tourists. Even on Saturday, there are few Italians going into the basilica to view the remains. As far as I can see, the security cops are mostly interested in talking to pretty girls in sidewalk cafes. I hope the Red Brigades don't have anything in mind for the evening. They could arrive with automatic weapons and knock out many of the world's leaders in one fell swoop. There are people sitting already in the front chairs near the altar, and most of them seem to be tourists. Despite the beautiful blue sky, the piazza today is a profoundly depressing place.

Along the Borgo Pio, the street just beyond the wall running from the Vatican on down to the Castel Sant'Angelo, there is a large contingent of Italian security police, army troops, and other people in brown and green uniforms. Buses all along the wall are filled with police and soldiers. They don't look especially competent or especially interested.

John McMeel and Jim Andrews went over to watch the funeral mass in person. I'm going to see it on television because you can get a much closer view of people's faces that way. The choreography is superb, the music magnificent. It is a simple funeral all right, but one done with elegance and beauty; old Carlo Confalonieri is dignified and reverent at the altar, the Sistine choir is marvelous, the movements of the various ministers of the mass are precise, yet reverent and relaxed, the artistic genius of Catholicism is here for the whole world to see. Unfortunately, the genius that produced the ritual and the music is half a millennium old. It has no counterpart in the church today.

The piazza was half empty during the funeral mass. Indeed,

more than half empty, because many of the chairs they had set up in the front were unoccupied. Most of the congregation—if one can call it that—showed no signs of reverence or grief or mourning. Indeed, I was able to see on the television screen some of the members chatting with one another.

McMeel and Andrews just came back. They said that at the fringes of the crowd, there was a festival, with people talking, laughing, eating ice cream, drinking Coke; the souvenir shops on the Via della Conciliazione were open and doing land office business.

I keep trying to tell myself that my depression is a combination of anxiety and fatigue, yet, when I hear that people are eating ice cream, drinking Coke, and laughing at the fringe of a papal funeral mass, I think that there are plenty of objective reasons to feel depressed. The knot in my stomach is getting bigger and harder.

Sunday, August 13

The job description press conference was today. Jim and John were delighted by the outcome of the conference, but I am convinced the Italian press will murder us tomorrow, and so, for that matter, will the English. However, it doesn't make much difference.

Things started out quite badly. The week caught up with me last night and I slept through two alarms, waking up at 10:32 for a press conference that was at 11:00. Putting an electric razor in one pocket and contact lenses in another, I managed to arrive with a few minutes to spare. Describe the press conference? Well, the operation was successful and the patient died.

There's something to be said for having a press conference in the Columbus Hotel here in Rome—once.

The Columbus is a fading, distinguished gentlewoman about halfway down the Via della Conciliazione from St. Peter's, the scene of many conferences, compromises, and connivings during the Vatican Council. Squint your eyes a lot in the Veranda Room and you can fool yourself into thinking you're in the Sistine Chapel.

The hotel has been around so long that you expect it was built by the grandmother of the admiral who bore the same name. You wonder about all the secrets it could tell if the Vatican would let it.

First, Jim Andrews explained the purpose of the Committee

for the Responsible Election of the Pope (CREP), a group composed mainly of North American journalists who had become convinced that the secrecy shrouding papal elections was irresponsible in view of the importance of the office. Their objective at this point was merely to provide information about the cardinals—not to push a specific candidate. To this end they had commissioned a book of dossiers of all the cardinals which had been published a month before Pope Paul died. The book, *The Inner Elite*, by Gary MacEoin, made quite an impact and sold out immediately. All the journalists in Rome were begging copies.

Jim explained that because the committee had been in existence for only a short time before the death of Paul, there was little consensus among its members concerning individual candidates and that CREP thought my job description would be a contribution of significance to the church and to the cardinal electors.

I explained quite carefully to the assembled folk (a couple of hundred reporters, I guess, and maybe a half-dozen people with TV cameras) that I was not a member of the Committee for the Responsible Election of the Pope because I was engaged in a study of the papal election process and I thought there would be some conflict of interest between the two. My description, I insisted, was an objective sociological exercise which the committee had requested. This did not prevent Peter Hebblethwaite from asking if there was not some contradiction between my job description and some of the things said in Gary MacEoin's *The Inner Elite*. I said yes, of course there were contradictions, because I didn't agree with everything MacEoin said. Anyhow, I plunged on with the observation that the pope was the most influential leader in the world, that he could serve as a moral and religious beacon for humankind, that he would be in the homes of millions of the world's families a few days after he was elected. Therefore, I mildly suggested, the cardinals ought to seek out a man whose faith and hope and trust and confidence and goodness and love could appropriately incarnate the Catholic faith. The other skills—administration, diplomacy, and the like—are important, I told them. But sanctity was the most essential requirement; even a pagan sociologist would say exactly the same thing.

You'd think I'd told a dirty joke from the high altar of St. Peter's—or thrown mud on the *Pietà*.

I was attacking the church, one angry Italian journalist informed me. Wasn't I trying to merchandise the pope? an American asked. How do you merchandise sanctity? I wondered. Who was the candidate this description was slanted to support? I didn't know all of the candidates well enough to say. Weren't *all* the cardinals holy men? Are you kidding? I replied.

Wasn't it all public relations, a mass-media manipulation trick? Try sustaining phony holiness on TV. Wasn't administration more important than holiness? No way; both are required, but one is more important than the other, at least if you believe in Christianity. Isn't sociology an anti-Catholic discipline? Like all science, it is religiously neutral. Who would I vote for myself? Senator Pat Moynihan (none of the creeps even laughed). How did I dare to submit such documents if the cardinals didn't ask for them? They didn't have to read them if they didn't want to. How much impact did I think the documents were going to have? Not much. Why bother then? You have to do what you can.

Should I not leave everything to the Holy Spirit? Orthodox Catholic theology says the Holy Spirit works indirectly through human agents; God is not likely to send a lightning bolt down on the Sistine Chapel. Was I trying to make the church a democracy? A man once said that the only proper way to elect a bishop was by the vote of the clergy and the laity. He was the bishop in this city once, his name was Pope Leo I; anyhow, a job description was a long way from a popular election.

Finally, one wild-eyed young Italian woman, who had Catholic Action written all over her, screamed at me that I was evil and that I had sexual problems. I replied that our data on sexual attitudes came from a national sample research, not personal experience (I didn't add that having sexual problems is part of the human condition, but at least she would never cause me any).

So it went, an exercise in fending off pietists and paranoids. It was fun, and in Rome these days you get your kicks where you can. God forgive me for it: I still think the pope ought to be a man of holiness and hope who smiles often. Despite my "friends" at the conference, most of the rest of the Catholic world would be delighted by such a choice. Don't count on their getting it, though.

Anyhow, to get the bad taste out of my mind, I came back to my room here at the Visconti Palace just off the Piazza Cavour, turned on the air conditioner, and tried to think through who the great electors might be. It was mostly an a priori exercise, but it at least provided a list of people to watch.

Just as there are few clear favorites in the conclave, so there is a remarkable shortage of great electors, to use the name traditionally given the most influential cardinals.

Still, a few of the cardinals are clearly men of great influence.

(1) Aloisio Lorscheider, archbishop of Fortaleza, Brazil, is one of the two most popular bishops in the world (the other is Cincinnati's Joseph Bernardin, who is not a cardinal, but who would surely be a great elector if he were). Lorscheider was elected on the first ballot to the permanent council at the last Synod of Bishops.

He is a Brazilian of German ancestry, member of the Franciscan religious order, a moderate-progressive and an extraordinarily shrewd, hard-working, effective leader, who radiates personal charm and holiness. Lorscheider himself would be a likely candidate for the papacy if he were not so young (still in his middle fifties) and so progressive. Apparently, he is the victim of a mild heart condition. The power of his personality is such that he will influence not only his fellow Latin Americans but others from the Third World. The North Americans and the Europeans will also take him seriously. Aloisio Lorscheider is the kind of man to whom you simply cannot refuse to listen.

(2) Vicente Enrique y Tarancón, the archbishop of Madrid, is in his early seventies, the principal figure in the revival of Spanish Catholicism in the transition between the end of the Franco regime and the beginning of a new democratic government. A shrewd, adroit, open-minded, and vigorous man, Tarancón will be the unquestioned leader of the Spanish cardinals and of many of the Latin Americans too. An alliance between Lorscheider and Tarancón and their respective followers is potentially the most effective block in the conclave, a strong counterbalance to the weight of the Roman Curia and an effective veto power to the election of a reactionary pope.

(3) Karol Wojtyla is in his late fifties, the archbishop of Cracow in Poland, and second in command to Warsaw's aging but redoubtable Cardinal Wyszynski.

He is a supporter of the Catholic intellectual group called *Znak*, which argues mildly for liberalization within both the church and the regime in Poland. Wojtyla is something of a progressive by the standards of the Second World cardinals. Unlike Wyszynski, he strongly supports the Vatican Council changes. Most of the Second World cardinals may well look to him for leadership. But he sees the problems of the church from the perspective of a part of the world where one can deal with authoritarian governments only by having an authoritarian church.

(4) Bernardin Gantin is a cardinal from the African country of Benin. Forced into exile by the Marxist government of Benin, Gantin is technically a member of the Curia and is chairman of the Commission for Justice and Peace. A charming, gentle, and intelligent man, he is probably the model for the Cardinal Azendi in Malachi Martin's meretricious *The Final Conclave*. Most of the African cardinals will look to him for leadership, as will some of the Asian cardinals. He is unfailingly considerate of Third World visitors who travel to Rome—and who are often treated rudely when they come to the congregation which deals with the missionary priests. Gantin's courage under persecution in his native land, his personal holiness and charm, and his openness would make him a possible long-shot candidate for the papacy if he were not "too young" (in his late fifties). His soft, melodious African voice will be listened to with respect in the conclave.

(5) Jaime Sin, the young (just fifty), progressive, and courageous archbishop of Manila, is a Chinese ethnic, the son of a convert father, and one of the most impressive human beings in the College of Cardinals. He is a vigorous campaigner for human rights and social justice in a country whose regime and culture show little concern for either. Sin inherits from his Chinese ancestors a dedication to hard work and an extremely sophisticated political sense. While not all of the Asian cardinals will look to him for leadership, many will. Just as Lorscheider and Tarancón represent the potential block of Iberian votes, so do Sin and Gantin represent the potential of a block of Afro-Asian votes. It must be emphasized, however, that these four men of such extraordinary abilities and talents are far more enlightened and progressive than most of their potential followers, and, like ward committeemen everywhere, they will have to placate the timid and the uncertain within their constituencies.

It is not difficult to choose the five great electors from the Second and Third Worlds. It is much more difficult to judge who will emerge as influential from the First World.

Only Detroit's Cardinal John Dearden has the respect required to emerge as a great elector from America (the role Cardinal Spellman played in the past); but Dearden has consistently refused throughout most of his career to exercise the influence of which he is capable. His close friends doubt that he will be anything but a passive participant in the conclave.

Philadelphia's John Krol will wheel and deal for sheer love of the game and may influence one or two other Americans. The other American cardinals are totally without influence. One of the jokes in Rome is that if the conclave can keep Chicago's John Cody locked up for more than a day or two, it will accomplish what no one else has been able to accomplish for twenty years.

Besides the Spanish Tarancón, who will be the European great electors? In a long conclave certain powerful personalities are likely to emerge with considerable influence. Giovanni Benelli is one. Johannes Willebrands of Utrecht, the canny ecumenist who brought peace to the troubled Dutch church, is a man who knows when to speak and when to be silent, and is a possible long-shot candidate for the papacy himself.

Another would be Joseph Hoeffner, the archbishop of Cologne, a ruthless, domineering archconservative, a leader of the persecution of the Swiss theologian Hans Küng, and an arrogantly self-confident authoritarian, the kind of man around whom the timid and fearful from many countries might rally in a last-ditch attempt to completely undo the effects of the Vatican Council. Pericle Felici, a tough Roman curialist and chairman of the commission which has made a mess of the reform of church law, will be influential. The Curia itself is badly divided and deeply resents Benelli; out of desperation they may look to Felici for leadership. A curious entente made up of Felici, Hoeffner, Berlin's Cardinal Alfred Bengsch, and a few of the more reactionary French cardinals could become a conservative power block in the conclave. Presumably, many of the electors from North America would go along with this group.

England's Cardinal Basil Hume made a great impression at the last Synod of Bishops. Hume is anything but naive politically and can be counted on to be a very persuasive insider and perhaps a coalition-builder when the going gets rough in an extended conclave.

It is unlikely that Belgium's Cardinal Leo Suenens will exercise much influence in the conclave. The Curia succeeded in isolating him when he expressed criticisms of Pope Paul a number of years ago. He has been subjected to intense criticism within the Belgian church and is viewed with some suspicion because of his enthusiasm for the charismatic movement in recent years. Nevertheless, Suenens's intelligence and graciousness may gain him some impact among the electors.

There are, then, no likely North American great electors, and with the exception of Tarancón and the unpleasant possible exception of Hoeffner, few Western Europeans will be great electors.

I was obviously wrong in this assessment. The French, Belgian, and Dutch cardinals would prove enormously influential, and Leo Suenens would be a great elector for a second, and even later, for a third time in his life. Indeed, among the many heroes in the year of the two conclaves, Suenens deserves to be at the top of the list. Nor did I appreciate the influence of Koenig, who even at this time was supporting Wojtyla.

Suenens appeared to leave for Brussels after the papal funeral sometime during the day on Sunday. He did not go to Brussels at all, but rather to the mountains of northern Italy, just outside Florence, where he could be in constant touch with his good friend Giovanni Benelli—a friendship which managed to survive the attacks on Suenens by the Curia after he mildly criticized Pope Paul's administration for not having enough "coresponsibility" (power sharing). Benelli, of course, had nothing to do with the attacks on Suenens. They remained close friends even after Suenens became more and more involved in the charismatic movement, a movement viewed with amused disdain in the Vatican. Suenens would be a key link in an emerging alliance between Benelli and the Latin American cardinals led by the Brazilians Paulo Arns (whom I also underestimated) and Lorscheider. With his links to Benelli, to the Brazilians (Arns and he also are close personal friends), and to the European cardinals, particularly the French and the Dutch, who respected him despite the Roman whispering campaign against him, Suenens would prove to be the linchpin in the emerging majority coalition.

Monday, August 14

Well, as I suspected, the Italian newspapers made a meal of

us. A couple of people wrote about the press conference who weren't even there. One reporter called Jim a "hard-eyed American businessman," which gave us all a lot of laughs. They played up my answer to a question that somebody posed about the possibility of a woman pope—"Why not?" That seemed to offend a lot of Italian journalists.

I had a dream last night. I was in the Sistine Chapel with all the other cardinals. I had a card in my hand, on which was printed "Eligo in summum pontificem" (I choose as pope). Unable to control my dream, I found my hand writing the words "Daniel Patricius Cardinalem Moynihan." I walked up to the altar, where the somber faces of the Cardinal Scrutineers (vote counters) were watching me glumly, and dropped my folded card into the chalice, taking an oath that this was the one I thought should be elected. At that point, Michelangelo's *Last Judgment* fell in on me.

I told one of my friends about voting for Senator Moynihan and he said, "You've been here too long—but we could do worse."

The Vatican employees get an extra month's pay to mark the death of the pope—"spoilation pay." In the old days, when a pope was elected, the locals would sack his house and steal all his belongings on the grounds that he wouldn't need them anymore. (A kind of playful "trick or treat" custom.) To stop such playfulness, it was decreed that if there was no sacking, an extra month's pay would be awarded—a useful solution.

I finally got a chance to see Adolpho today. He told me that the Vatican information services were preparing biographies for thirty-four cardinals, each one of them a possible winner—things are that uncertain. The curial strategy is apparently putting Siri first, then Felici, then Bertoli, and Baggio after Bertoli. Baggio is quite low on the list—though the Curia might ultimately settle for him. However, the whispering campaign against him has been especially vicious—he is described as a lover of jewelry and expensive clothes. Pignedoli is still not taken seriously here, and it is thought that his friends from the Third World will desert him after the first couple of ballots. That's the Monday morning line, at least in Adolpho's view of things. He is for Paolo Bertoli, who he thinks would be all right, a moderate-to-conservative man, but certainly sympathetic to the Vatican Council (unlike Siri) and not the kind of person who would try to turn the clock back.

Adolpho observed that most of the men who have been

elected pope in this century have grown notably in the papal office—Benedict XV, Pius XII, John XXIII especially, and even Paul VI. He thought that most of the men who are discussed as possible candidates (though not a weary, worn-out man like Jean Villot) were sufficiently open that they would grow notably should they be elected pope. That is, I suppose, a somewhat reassuring thought.

Finally, there was no evidence yet, said Adolpho, of any attempt on the part of the non-Italians to build a coalition. I said that it seemed to me that one of the mistakes made at the last conclave was that the supporters of Lercaro, with no fall-back candidate to turn to when he did not get enough votes, drifted to Montini for want of another strategy. He responded that it was possible that somebody like Lorscheider or perhaps even Suenens (for whom Montini was the fall-back strategy) might have one this time too. But it is certainly not evident. Of course, the curial strategies are printed every day in the Italian papers, since that's where the correspondents have their sources.

Adolpho also told me, with some amusement, that one of the comments he heard from people in the Vatican who had seen our job description was that well, yes, there was something very important in it, we see now that the papacy can be a basis for evangelization. I would have thought that that was self-evident, but apparently in the Roman Curia it is not.

The whispering campaigns continue to be intense and almost all of them are started by people in the Curia. Some examples: Cardinal Koenig was in an auto accident last year and has not been able to work for a sustained period of time since then; Lorscheider's health is even worse than is publicly admitted; Cardinal So-and-so is not emotionally stable; Cardinal Such-and-such has close women friends, etc., etc. Apparently, most of these rumors originate in the office of the secretary of state, Cardinal Villot, though that gentle little man has nothing to do with the rumors and may even be unaware that they are being spread.

Despite the meal that the Italian and the British press made of our job description on the pope, there are at least two cardinals who seem to be thinking along the same lines. Cordeiro, the Pakistani, said in an interview today that the pope ought to be a man of hopefulness, both spiritual and social hopefulness. "Enough of political popes," he said. The pope ought to be a man who is capable of stirring up optimism and invigorating once again the faith of people both in the church and in the world. He ought to be a sign to all nations of wisdom and of pastoral hope; he should have a stable personality, good health, and a wide knowledge of languages. Pironio seems to have said much the same thing.

The Pironio and Cordeiro interviews received little notice at the time, but in retrospect they obviously represent the ongoing process of clarification that was taking place among many of the non-Italian cardinals. They were slowly developing a job description not unlike the one we had prepared.

Tuesday, August 15

Still the papal election is a horse race, with a large number of front-runners bunched together. It may be a very long race.

No one here wants a deadlocked conclave; the cardinals, the massive press corps, the citizens of Rome—everyone wants to get back to the last precious days of August vacation. A long conclave is therefore unlikely. Yet, no one minimizes the difficulties the cardinals face as they busily "consult" with one another and prepare to be locked up in the Vatican Palace.

Felici discreetly raises the name of his friend Luciani with some of the foreign cardinals. So does Carlo Confalonieri, forbidden by age to enter into the conclave but permitted to attend the general congregations. The name at first seems to stir little interest. Most of the foreign cardinals do not know him. He is thought not to have traveled widely. For a day, some of the Italian newspapers mention his name, and rumors about him percolate around the Vatican Press Office. But then Felici and Confalonieri seem to drop the idea. In fact, Luciani has traveled to both Uganda and Brazil, where his diocese has missions, and has paid frequent visits to Paris and Vienna and the Low Countries. Arns and Lorscheider were greatly taken with him during his trip to Brazil. Suenens and the French are delighted by his charm, his wit, and his broad cultural background. Many ecumenical meetings are held in Venice; this is because Luciani is always extremely friendly and hospitable, inviting the visiting churchmen to his house for dinner or visiting them in their meetings with several bottles of wine in his hands. Philip Potter, the secretary general of the World Council of Churches, says to Willebrands at one of these meetings that Luciani would make a superb pope, and Willebrands agrees. Luciani is not as unknown as he at first appears. The non-Italian cardinals are not organized yet; they are busy trying to elaborate their own job description. The Luciani trial balloon is reported by Benelli loyalists in the Secretariat of State to Florence, where Benelli is amused to discover that he and his bitter enemy Felici are supporting the same candidate. Benelli consults with Suenens and finds him in agreement about Luciani.

Wednesday, August 16

The weather continues absolutely perfect: clear skies, not too hot in the day, pleasantly cool at night. The only trouble is that with *ferragosto* it's hard to know what restaurants are going to be open. There will be a lot of penitential struggle against the effects of pasta when I get home.

Someone asked me today if I knew that Anwar Sadat had proclaimed a week of mourning in Egypt for the death of Paul VI. I didn't know it, but I guess it proves my point about the importance of the papacy in a world shaped by instantaneous communication. There aren't all that many Copts in Egypt and not all of them are Catholic, though they play a disproportionate role in the economic life of the country and are among Sadat's strongest supporters; but I don't think he proclaimed the week of mourning just to keep the Copts in the population happy. He did it because, shrewd man that he is, he realizes that the pope is the most important religious leader in the world. And the Vatican folks are surprised to discover that it is a platform for evangelization!

Cardinal Paul Yu Pin, the exiled Chinese-born archbishop of Nanking, died today. He had collapsed at the papal funeral with a heart attack the other night. Yu Pin was out of China in 1950 when the Nationalists' defenses collapsed and was forbidden by Pius XII to return. He lived in the United States for several years and was condemned to death in absentia by the Communists as a war criminal. Since 1960, he had been president of the Catholic University in Taipei on the island of Taiwan. One forgets until one reads of something of this sort how much so many of these men have suffered. It's easy for an American to take it for granted that cardinals are honored and to forget that they may be killed, as in the Congo, or condemned to death as war criminals, as in China.

Early in the game, leaders of the emerging coalition decide that there is nothing they can do about the eight American votes. Some of those who are in Rome tentatively approached Dearden at the congregations and found that he listens patiently and sympathetically but simply does not respond.

The campaigning is subtle, occasionally blunt, and once in a while ruthless. It's hard to find out the details of the campaign because it's all done in secret. The language used is generally indirect and often convoluted.

There are times when it reminds me of the way the Cook County regular Democratic organization chooses its chairman. All appearances of conflict are avoided; decisions are made often by what is not said rather than what is said; understandings are implicit; commitments, such as they are, are at most gentlemen's agreements; loyalty to friends and allies is taken for granted; and occasionally someone says something vigorous to the press, just to keep the pot boiling.

Thus most cardinals endorse the continuation of Pope Paul's policy and the reinforcement of the work of the Vatican Council. But Cologne's arrogant and tyrannical Cardinal Joseph Hoeffner told reporters on his arrival that it was not the work of a specific pope but the good of the church which ought to be considered, perhaps indicating that he was signing up with the Curia reactionaries—headed by Cardinals Silvio Oddi and Pericle Felici—who thought Pope Paul too radical and who are counting on thirty-five votes on the first ballot.

But such public salvos are rare. Most of the debate goes on in indirect generalities at the daily meetings of the cardinals about the direction in which the church ought to go or the needs the church has.

Such comments, only somewhat less direct, take place at the dinner and late evening meetings of small groups of cardinals. The conversations continue even in the conclave bedrooms (there is not likely to be public debate on the floor of the conclave itself—not even indirect debate).

Thus, if a man says, "The church must be deeply concerned about the needs of the small countries of the world and must have leaders who speak many languages," he is indicating his support for a multilingual pope (thus endorsing men like Salvatore Pappalardo of Palermo, Paolo Bertoli of the Curia, Sebastiano Baggio, and Sergio Pignedoli, who have traveled widely, and indicating opposition to men like Corrado Ursi of Naples or Ugo Poletti of Rome, who speak only Italian).

If a man says, "We must be vigilant in our fight against Communism," he is warning against Cardinal Koenig of Vienna, who has dealt diplomatically with the Communist countries. Or, a comment like Koenig's in favor of a younger man could mean he was supporting Eduardo Pironio or Giovanni Benelli or Basil Hume.

Thursday, August 17

With a few exceptions, everybody seems to be saying that the next pope will be Italian—but if the Curia people keep chopping one another to pieces, they may destroy all the Italian candidates. What will happen then?

I must confess that I am beginning to feel that the Italian monopoly has to be broken. I think a lot of cardinals feel that way too, though they are not saying so publicly. Unless I miss my guess, the code words are: "Nationality is not an important issue." Many of the cardinals are saying that in the interviews they give to the papers. The usual interpretation of such a statement is that if nationality isn't important, then fine, the next pope should be an Italian. But I suspect the more accurate interpretation might be, "If we can't find an Italian who meets our standards, then we are going to look for a non-Italian." There is no evidence, up to the present at any rate, that the non-Italian cardinals, most of whose leaders have gone back to their dioceses because of this long period before the conclave, are capable of putting together a coalition around a candidate or a number of candidates who might measure up to their idea of what a pope should be, regardless of his nationality.

Little was done during the latter half of this week to promote the development of the coalition partly because the European leaders were still in their dioceses and partly because some of them (certainly Suenens) were urging restraint. The Latin American cardinals in particular must be given time to develop and crystallize their own ideas about the papacy. For the rest of this week, curialists sent up trial balloons only to have them shot down by other curialists. The non-Europeans stayed out of Rome; the Latin Americans talked discreetly among themselves; and Cardinal Sergio Pignedoli gave great dinner parties.

One of the best arguments for a non-Italian cardinal is that it would be much easier for such a man to decentralize the church administration, an effort which would require a kind of drastic rethinking of the papal role that might be psychologically difficult for an Italian.

The cardinals are administrators and pastors, not scholars. One prominent candidate hasn't read a book in twenty years. But some of the electors have scholars on their staffs and have come to Rome with memos summarizing the latest historical and theological research on, to use the fashionable phrase, "the Petrine function" (which means the role of the pope as the head of the church).

It is not too likely that these memos will be taken seriously in the present election, but they portend a future revolution.

The famous Swiss theologian, Hans Küng, got into all kinds of trouble with the Vatican by his criticism of the doctrine of papal infallibility. But more of Küng's problem can be attributed to his personal popularity and success—and the resulting envy of Vatican officials and theological colleagues. Other scholars have been reevaluating the papacy much more quietly—and have said far more radical things than Küng.

Much of the new Catholic thinking has emerged from ecumenical dialogue with Protestants after the Second Vatican Council. Both sides have been willing to reexamine their thinking, and many of the Protestants have come to see that the "Petrine function" in the church is essential to the unity of Christians and that Rome has a preeminent historical and theological part to play in that function. As Protestant scholars and leaders have tried to crystallize the kind of papal ministry they could accept in practice, Catholics, on their side, have had to ask whether there is any theological reason why such papal practice is not possible. The conclusion has been that the present highly centralized, juridical, legalistic, and authoritarian papacy is by no means either necessary or normal, and that the convergence between the kind of papal leadership Protestants would accept and even welcome and the kind Catholic theology could live with and even find desirable is very great.

Pope Paul once said that he was well aware that he was the principal obstacle to church unity. The Catholic scholars—all well within the bonds of orthodoxy—who have been reappraising the papacy would agree that the present *style* of papal leadership is an obstacle, but they disagree that such a style is essential to the papacy. On the contrary, they would argue that while the development of a centralized authoritarian bureaucracy may be historically understandable, it is not typical of the papacy.

Some add that historians of the future will be appalled by this era, when the Renaissance ideal of absolute monarchy was combined with modern transportation and communication to make the pope a "super bishop." By "super bishop" they mean a man who governs not only his own diocese but every diocese in the world through a local bishop, one who is not viewed so much as the head of the church in his city as the agent of the pope.

One historian remarked to me, "The practical view of the role of the local church that the Roman Curia holds is dangerously close to heresy. They think all power is in Rome, but the whole history of Christianity has emphasized the importance of the local church."

Before 1850 (and the invention of the steamship and the transatlantic cable) the local church necessarily enjoyed a great deal of freedom; papal control over national hierarchies was quite loose. The Catholic ethical principle of "subsidiarity" argues that "nothing should be done at a higher level which can be done as well at a lower level." For most of the history of the church this ethical principle was also a practical necessity, because obstacles to transportation and communication gave great latitude to the local church and the national hierarchies. The first archbishop of Baltimore, John Carroll, needed more time to get to his home in Rock Creek (in present-day Washington) than his successor needs to get to Rome.

So both the principle of subsidiarity and the theology of the local church suggest that a return to the historical relationship between the pope and his brother bishops would be much more in keeping with the Catholic tradition. The pope would preside over communication among the various local churches throughout the world, promote unity among them, and coordinate international activities, but would rarely interfere with them and would certainly not assume international administration or supervisory responsibility. Such a papacy would fit the traditional model and would be acceptable to many Protestants. Nor would it be unacceptable either to Catholic theology or Catholic history, which now recognizes that the role of the pope emerged only very slowly and has been exercised in many different ways through the two thousand years since Peter.

Such a change in style would be revolutionary, however desirable it might be. It would mean the end of the immense bureaucratic power of the centralized and authoritarian Roman Curia. Most curialists don't care about theology or history or ecumenism; they have a very simple, old-fashioned, and quite unchangeable model of the nature of papal authority. They would cheerfully admit that the pope is a "super bishop" and argue that they share his power; they have every intention of continuing to do so.

No candidate who disagrees with the curial model of the papacy—Renaissance absolutism combined with instant communication and overnight transportation—has a ghost of a chance of being elected. The cardinals are in the interesting position of having to speak very softly about theories concerning which there is virtually no disagreement among competent experts. In the closing years of Pope Paul's pontificate, the papacy became more centralized and more authoritarian than it has been—and probably more out of touch with the development of Catholic thought outside the Vatican than ever before.

There is a good deal of irony in such a situation. The great influence and prestige of Pope John showed that the pope could easily be the most important religious leader in the world if he yielded the style of the authoritarian Roman superbureaucrat. Pope Paul, however, zealously restored that style on the grounds that it was the essence of the papacy—a claim that no one but his own staff would now support.

To protect an untraditional theory of the papacy Pope Paul destroyed much of its prestige. The time is now ripe for a return to the traditional decentralized papacy. Such a return would recapture much lost influence among Catholics and would be a major step toward church unity with Protestants. It would not conflict with Catholic doctrine but would, on the contrary, be more in harmony with it.

When I read over these lines I find myself growing discouraged again. The contrast between the compulsive secrecy of the conclave and the idea of an open, outgoing papacy, which is theoretically possible and which would have much more influence in the world than the closed curial papacy, is depressing. The chances of our getting an open papacy are so thin I feel like I want to pack up and go home. Maybe I've been reading Italian newspapers too much.

Scene II

Luciani drove to Rome with Don Diego Lorenzi, his thirty-nine-year-old secretary, in his Lancia 2000—a somewhat more modest car than most cardinals drive. They parked the car at a service station in Via Gregorio VII just off the Via Aurelia and took up quarters in the Augustinian college nearby. Luciani was within a five-minute walk of the Vatican. Cardinal Reginald Delargey, from New Zealand, was one of his neighbors (it was said of Delargey that he would vote against an Italian pope even if every cardinal voted for one, but Delargey had no trouble supporting his neighbor Luciani).

Luciani, the patriarch of Venice, had come to Rome convinced that it was time to give up the Italian hold on the papacy. Indeed, he was committed to voting for Cardinal Aloisio Lorscheider of Brazil. Luciani was the only Italian to commit to the young, vigorous, and progressive Lorscheider as the next pope. When reporters asked Luciani about his chances of being pope, he laughed them off. "Oh, I'm only on the C-list," he said, dismissing their speculation with a smile. Reading the newspapers like everyone else, he was aware that he had been suggested as a possible curial candidate but that the trial balloon had never got off the ground. He also knew that his impetuous friend Giovanni Benelli thought that he ought to be pope. Even though he received an occasional phone call from Benelli to make sure of his position on an issue like papal retirement, he did not think of himself as a candidate and refused to engage in anything even remotely resembling a campaign. He noticed with growing unease, however, that at the congregations each morning an increasing number of non-Italian cardinals would chat with him and occasionally ask the probing question. Still, he remained convinced that he was on the C-list.

Luciani was born in the Dolomites, a mountainous region in northern Italy between Venice and Austria. It is one of the few regions in Italy where Catholic religious practice is still intense. Indeed, the best way to understand the Dolomites is to think of the region as a place like Ireland, where the faith is in the soil, in the crisp, clear morning air, on the roads, and in the fields—a place where strong, masculine piety is taken for granted.

Pope Paul VI — shortly before his
coronation at St. Peter's Basilica,
Rome, June 28, 1963.

Thousands of persons jammed St. Peter's
Square to witness the crowning of the 261st
successor of St. Peter. It was the first time
in almost a century that a papal coronation
had been held in the square.

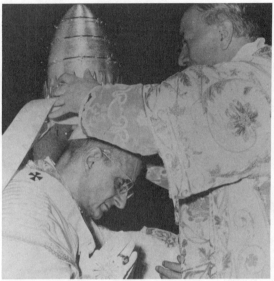

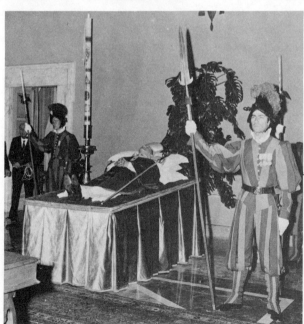

Pope Paul VI in state in his
residence at Castel Gandolfo.
At 9:40 P.M. Sunday, August
6, 1978, Pope Paul had
suffered a massive heart
attack.

The cardinals begin the search for a successor.

Casting the ballot

Religious News Service Photo

Wide World Photos

Locking the door

Religious News Service Photo

Counting the votes

Wide World Photos

Praying to the Holy Spirit

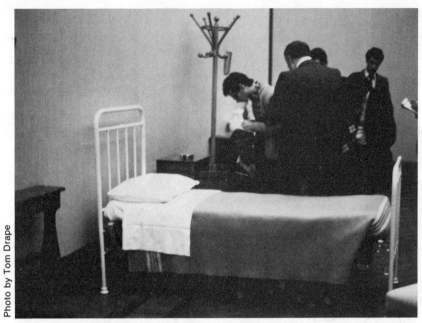

Journalists tour the spare quarters close to the Sistine Chapel used by the cardinals. The Rome Hilton it was not.

Samples of the china, crystal, and silver provided for the cardinals. Carberry, though, brought his own Hershey bars.

Hastily constructed tables and rigid, high-back chairs were placed before the main altar of the Sistine Chapel.

The drama begins: Of the 111 cardinals eligible to vote for the new pope, 100 had been appointed by the late Pope Paul VI.

A "general congregation."

Pope Paul's successor, Albino Luciani, at age of three. "Albino *who?*"

Albino Luciani as a fifteen-year-old student, in Belluno, Italy.

New pope elected — white smoke billows around the chimney atop the Sistine Chapel — Albino Luciani of Venice — John Paul I.

The September Smile

Pope John Paul I greets Rome's communist mayor, Giulio Carlo Argan.

A "hopeful holy man who smiled."
Pope John Paul I on the way to his
first general audience.

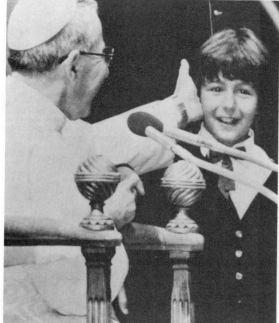

Pope John Paul I pats the face of
Daniele Bravo, the Roman fifth-
grader who, at what would be the
pontiff's last audience, said he
wanted to stay in the fifth grade,
"so that I don't have to change
teachers."

Mary Catherine Whelan Burd, one of the last Americans to see John Paul I, spoke for many on why she would not go into the wake: *"I saw him in the audience Wednesday and prefer to see him smiling. I loved Rome when I came a week ago; now I want to go home."*

Photo by Tom Drape

Photo by Tom Drape

The funeral of Pope John Paul I: a day of rain.

Canale d'Agordo is a town of a thousand or so people, high up in the hills and founded in the fourteenth century. Giovanni Luciani, father of Albino, was a migrant worker seeking employment in Austria, Switzerland, and even in Argentina. His mother was a scullery maid. His father went into exile in Switzerland during World War I, a couple of years after Albino's birth in 1912. But he came back in 1915 and sired three more children. Two earlier children, both daughters, died early in life.

The father continued to be a migratory worker, leaving Canale d'Agordo in March and returning in September, working now in Switzerland and now in France. He was a socialist. Rumors (probably false) said that he burned crucifixes in the family stove. He did not understand why his son, at the age of twelve, had to go off to a seminary, but socialist or not, he believed in freedom for his children.

Twelve years later, on the seventh of July in 1935, Luciani was ordained a priest. For six years, he worked in the mountain valleys of Canale d'Agordo and in 1941 was sent by his bishop to the Gregorian University in Rome for theological training. However, he sought and obtained a dispensation from attending classes in Rome and, after private study, passed his preliminary examinations with the highest possible marks. In 1946, after spending merely a couple of weeks in Rome, he submitted his doctoral thesis on Antonio Rosmini, the great nineteenth-century religious leader from northern Italy and one of the prophets from nineteenth-century liberal Catholicism. The doctorate was awarded magna cum laude.

Don Albino was a popular seminary professor because he oriented his teaching toward the practical work of parish priests and particularly towards religious education. In 1949, he published a little book, Catechism Crumbs, *containing very simple religious instructions for children. Cardinal Roncalli (later John XXIII) met him a couple of times in his term as patriarch of Venice and apparently was impressed. When John asked a bishop friend to suggest some candidates for the small diocese of Vittorio Veneto, the bishop mentioned "a little priest, a certain Luciani, who is all over the place, one moment here, one moment there." Aha, I know him, I know him, beamed Roncalli. So Don Albino became the first bishop that Papa Roncalli would appoint, and the first he would ordain in St. Peter's Basilica in December, 1958. The ten years he spent in Vittorio Veneto seem to have been the happiest in Don Albino's life. The town was not large, and the bishop could easily know all of his priests and many of his people. He lived simply, worked hard, taught catechism whenever he could, and frequently pedaled around town on his own bicycle. He was a masterful teacher, carefully preparing everything he said, committing it quickly to memory—then with his ready smile and his quick wit, delivering what appeared to be an easy, spontaneous lesson during which he and the young people seemed to laugh at least half the time. One of the reasons he told so many jokes and stories was that he realized his high-pitched voice was a distraction to those who heard him and stories helped the audiences to forget about his voice.*

In 1969, he was promoted to Venice, where he was much less comfortable than in Vittorio Veneto. For the first time he came into contact with the paganism that marks much of Italian and, indeed, much of European life. He continued to live simply, dispensing with pomp, giving away precious jewelry, walking on foot through snowdrifts in the mountain villages near Venice to visit the parishes in those villages, where he felt much more at home than he did on the Grand Canal.

Some of his friends noticed a change in his personality after the transfer to Venice. He still smiled, he still told stories for children, but the city was too sophisticated and too unreligious for this proletarian priest. Gloomily he wondered whether anything could be done to win the city back to the church; he plunged ahead even more vigorously in his efforts to catechize the children. Eventually the haughty Venetians came to love their country patriarch, who walked the streets of the city or rode on the vaporetti like a simple citizen. His smile and personal goodness eventually won them over, but he was still priest of the countryside, the son of a rural proletarian. Most Venetians agreed with him when he went to Rome that he was at best on the C-list for pope. Luciani was skillful at presenting the appearance of a simple, unsophisticated man. His book Illustrissimi *would be written off later by a French newspaper as "Reader's Digest Catholicism." In fact, however, the letters to "famous men" had the simplicity which only very sophisticated and complex men can produce.*

Saturday, August 19

The Third World people are beginning to agree on the kind of pope they want. Cardinal Parecattil from India, in an interview today, insisted that the new pope must be a spiritual man, and nothing else mattered—even whether he was a good administrator. These folks are busy enunciating a description of their ideal pope which the folks at the Curia aren't hearing. Hope, optimism, spirituality, closeness to the problems of ordinary people, a holy man who hopes and understands the problems of the people in the pews, particularly when they are poor. There are four or five people who have spoken that way this week. I suspect the Curia crowd is simply dismissing these comments as official pieties. If the Third-Worlders mean them, there may be a confrontation between the political and administrative concerns of the one-third of the cardinals who are curial and the religious-human concerns of the one-third of the cardinals who come from the Southern Hemisphere. That could make for a very interesting conclave.

The places where the various cardinals are meeting to sit down and talk informally are now pretty well known to me. The French meet in Jean Villot's office in the Vatican; the Germans at the Collegio Germanico just off the Piazza Navona; the Africans meet in Gantin's office in the Commission for Justice and Peace in the Piazza San Calisto; the curialists, of course, meet in their Vatican offices. All the Americans live out at the Villa Stritch, but they seem to be sitting around waiting for the Holy Spirit to tell them for whom to vote. Most of the cardinals who are not living in their own national colleges are living in the religious order houses, a triangle bounded on the south by the Janiculum hill, on the north by the Borgo Pio, and on the west by the Piazzale Gregorio VII, a rather small district in which it is fairly easy to move in a car or on foot by side streets and hardly be noticed. So if you want to consult with a cardinal who is a friend or who thinks like you do, you can talk to him on the telephone, scurry down a side street, or make a very quick automobile ride. At these informal gatherings of two, three, four, or five cardinals, after an exchange of generalities about the needs of the church, the participants get down to brass tacks and begin to discuss specific candidates. We know whom they are discussing in the Curia because there are pipelines from the curial

135

offices to the Italian press, but whom are they discussing at the religious houses near the Vatican or at the Piazza San Calisto or in Cardinal Villot's apartment? About that, as yet, there isn't the slightest hint.

On Saturday, Evaristo Arns and Aloisio Lorscheider decide that they have delayed long enough and that it is a time for a larger meeting to hammer out a clearer description of the characteristics the new pope should possess. Phone calls are made, and a meeting is arranged for Sunday afternoon.

Since there is nothing much else doing here, I decided to try to figure out some of the demographics and the mathematics of the conclave.

To begin with, all the electors are men. Their average age is 68.78 years. The youngest is the remarkable Cardinal Jaime Sin. The oldest at seventy-nine is Cardinal Trin-nhu-Khuê of Hanoi. Twenty-two of them are under sixty, thirty-nine are between sixty and seventy, and fifty-five between seventy and eighty. More than half are old enough to have been retired in most of the countries of the world.

How is it that this gerontocracy will elect the next pope? An unelected group at that. Is such aristocratic government unjust? Can they get away with it by repeating that the Catholic church is not a democracy? Let us listen to a legal dictum: "Qui praesidet super omnes, ab omnibus eligatur"—the one who presides over all should be chosen by all. Thomas Jefferson? Blackstone? Hans Küng? Some flaming "radical"? No, the words were written by a man named Leo I, who was a pope and a saint. Another ancient pope said much the same thing: "That which is likely to have an effect on everyone should be decided by everyone." Other medieval popes said it was gravely sinful to choose a bishop by any other means than free election by the laity and clergy.

One may or may not approve of the election of the leader of 700 million Roman Catholics by a group of elderly men who represent no one but themselves. However, if Leo I or his ancient colleagues and successors should show up in the Piazza San Pietro in the next couple of days and be told what was going on, they would on the basis of their own stated principles unquestionably denounce it in no uncertain terms as immoral and gravely sinful.

Sunday, August 20

I've finally figured out why I am depressed. I want badly to have a pope of whom we can all be proud, and I'm afraid that I am going to be disappointed. I am deliberately taking a pessimistic view to prepare myself for the letdown. That's a very Irish way to approach reality.

The critical meeting took place Sunday afternoon at the Brazilian college on the Via Aurelia (where Lorscheider had stood me up last year during the synod). Arns, the more "evangelical" of the two Franciscan cardinals from Brazil, presided over the meeting, the charismatic Lorscheider choosing to stay somewhat in the background. The cardinals worked out a detailed description of the kind of pope they wanted, heavily emphasizing a pastoral orientation, personal holiness, openness to the poor, along with an ability to exercise a worldwide appeal and a commitment to more collegiality in the church. The final document is stated in very general terms and will be distributed the next day to all the other cardinals. They do not decide to endorse a specific candidate, since the leadership feels that it is too early to attempt such a tactic and fears it will lose some of its potential coalition members. It will line up support for a candidate short of the last minute. Privately, at least some of them have designed a strategy in which they will support Arns on the first ballot and then Pironio on subsequent ballots—as a show of strength to counter the curialists and perhaps to impose a compromise candidate of their choosing and not of the Curia's choosing. The Sunday afternoon group is virtually unanimous in its implicit rejection of any candidate who has been a curial cardinal. Thus, Baggio and Pignedoli have lost their support on the left and are already vetoed on the right. After Sunday afternoon, their candidacies cease to be important, even though the Italian news magazines coming early in the week will still describe them as being contenders. Bertoli's chances aren't very good either, because of his curial background.

Peter Hebblethwaite has more courage than I do. He has predicted Bertoli will be elected. I wouldn't dare crawl out on a limb now and predict a winner, not in the public record in any case. I'll play games with Ernest Primeau and Jim Roache (Primeau is predicting Luciani), but that's fun and guesswork and not a serious prediction. If Hebblethwaite is right, he is going to look very good; but if he's wrong, a lot of people aren't going to let him forget it.

Is the patriarch of Venice a liberal or a conservative? On matters of church doctrine, he is something of a conservative. He's not going to let people deny either the incarnation or the church's commitment to the world. On the other hand, he wrote Hans Küng congratulating him on his book, On Being a Christian, and sent him a copy of Illustrissimi, something that, heavens knows, the German cardinals would not like if they knew it. On matters of ecclesiastical discipline, he is also a conservative, in the sense that he expects people to go along with decisions that have been made. But in the making of decisions, he is a liberal, having said that he would never veto a decision of his priest-senate because he believes that the Holy Spirit speaks through the freely elected representatives of his diocese. As far as openness to modern culture goes, he's also a liberal, having read more books by modern writers in more languages than most of the other members of the college, and being a strong disciple of Antonio Rosmini, the nineteenth-century liberal theologian; he is convinced there is no opposition between the church and modern culture.

However, in the final analysis, the Luciani personality escapes classification. When Louise Brown, the English test-tube baby, was born, a Rome newspaper asked the patriarch of Venice for a comment. Unlike most church spokesmen, who quickly and eagerly condemned the test-tube baby, Luciani's approach was quite different. "I send the most heartfelt congratulations to the English baby girl whose conception took place artificially. As far as her parents are concerned, I have no right to condemn them. If they acted with honest intentions and in good faith, they could even be deserving of merit before God for what they wanted and asked the doctors to carry out."

Having begun with that warm, sensitive, and very shrewd congratulations, he went on to express some reservations about the dangers in such experimentation and to note that while progress may be a good thing, it is not necessarily always a good thing, since progress has led to such things as atomic weapons and biological and chemical warfare. Finally, he concluded that he had yet to find the reason to modify the teaching laid down by Pius XII on artifi-

cial insemination. He did not suggest that no reasons could be found, nor did he reject the argument of some moral theologians that perhaps some kinds of artificial fertilization might even be approved under Pius XII's principles. He simply expressed his own personal opinion and left the matter open. The important thing about his statement is that his reservation and his cautiously nuanced opinions followed the beautiful human touch of congratulating the new child and her parents. Warmth, followed by intelligence . . . Luciani's statement probably had extraordinary impact on the cardinal electors who saw it. Here, they said to themselves, is a man who combines intelligence with pastoral sensitivity.

Late in the Evening

I've just learned from one of my sources that the anti-Bertoli sentiments are picking up steam. He is said sometimes to grow so angry that he must stay in his room for several days to calm his temper so that he will not blow up in public. I wonder who's spreading this rumor. Perhaps Benelli or Benelli's allies in Rome. Since there is no love lost between those two, if there is anything to Bertoli's temper, Benelli certainly would have had a chance to watch it in Paris, where they were once assigned together. The trouble with a campaign by character assassination is that sometimes the stories may be true and sometimes they are not; you have no real way of telling the difference, even if you are a cardinal, since you are not really likely ever to have seen Bertoli under strain.

Benelli learns of the meeting at the Brazilian college when he returns to his house in Florence. Even before he gets the letter, he knows what's in it. He also knows from his friends at the Secretariat of State how the draft speech for the new pope is emerging, a more precise summary of the cardinals' thinking than any of the rest of them have available. He is now convinced that Luciani can be elected. He is a candidate who has something for everyone: collegial with his priests, simple in his personal life, a man of the poor, a whole life of pastoral work, a charming personality—all of that will appeal to the progressives and the foreigners. Solid in doctrine, loyal on church discipline, firmly anti-Communist—that will appeal to the conservatives. Has not Felici already suggested him? Anyone who can win both Felici and Benelli's support must be a saint after all. But the stranieri do not know him well enough. So a dossier must be prepared of some of his recent statements, to be distributed, not to all the cardinals, but to some of the key leaders, emphasizing his intelligence and his "fit" with the model prepared at the Brazilian college. Benelli places phone calls to some of his younger protégés in Rome. They will begin speaking with key cardinals in the next couple of days, showing them a Luciani dossier. His recent statement on the test-tube baby must be in that dossier. Everyone will be charmed by his congratulations of the parents and the new child. The coalition is beginning to fit into place.

The next day, Suenens speaks with the Brazilians, the Dutch, and the French and discovers that they are becoming more and more sympathetic to the Luciani candidacy. The secret is well kept, and the forces have now been set definitely in motion which will lead to next Saturday's quick conclave. Three spokes go out from Suenens: one to the Low Countries and France, eight votes; one to Arns and Lorscheider and the Third World progressives, perhaps twenty votes; and one to Benelli, Pappalardo, and some of the other Italian residential bishops, six or seven votes. Something like thirty-five votes for Luciani on the second ballot—almost, though not quite, in the bag. Benelli and Suenens do not push their respective constituencies. There is still time. Besides, Felici can be counted on to deliver half a dozen more votes, taking them away from whoever the curial candidate may be (unless it is he himself) when Luciani gains momentum.[1]

Monday, August 21

This is not an easy day to be proud to be an American. Three American cardinals gave a press conference today at the USO. They said very little that was newsworthy, but the stories will go out of here anyhow quoting Cardinal Terence Cooke as saying that there are no formal discussions among the cardinals about the next conclave and that the cardinals are meeting in a "brotherly, friendly atmosphere." Cardinal Timothy Manning added that they haven't organized special luncheons with other cardinals to pull everything together. Cardinal Humberto Medeiros said that the outcome of the conclave ought to be left in the hands of the Holy

Spirit.

There was a meeting at the Brazilian college yesterday afternoon of about twenty cardinals, doubtless led by Lorscheider and
Arns, to devise a strategy, a program, and a candidate profile for
the conclave. The American cardinals weren't invited to that and
probably wouldn't have gone if they had been invited—they may
even be unaware that such meetings occur. Perhaps they are
telling the truth when they say that there are no meetings because
the meetings that occur they simply don't know about. The secrecy
requirements that Paul VI imposed on the cardinals are indeed
rigid, as are the requirements against campaigning, but he certainly did not forbid meetings and conversations. The American
cardinals seem to be content with putting the strictest possible
interpretation on the rules of Paul VI, and thus avoiding all conversation even amongst themselves as to what will happen when the
conclave begins Friday night. The Italian journalists are already
making fun of what the American cardinals said. Many American
reporters were equally skeptical. One non-Catholic reporter said
to me glumly, "They're lying; they can't expect us to believe that
baloney."

He was wrong. In their pious conviction that they ought not to
prepare for the conclave by active discussion, the Americans are
being their honest, sincere, and, I must confess, likable selves.
They are decent men, fair, kind, and dedicated. Unfortunately,
they believe that everyone else, including the frantically campaigning Italian curialists, is playing by the same rules. They also
believe that the inspiration of the Holy Spirit works most effectively, not when you've prepared to the hilt, but when you're not
prepared at all.

Like so many other cardinals here, they are lambs being led to
the curial slaughter.

Cardinal Manning commented at the press conference that he
was as excited as a new boy would be at the first day of school and
would cheer for the winner.

Two of the three Americans had not heard of the book on the
cardinals called *The Inner Elite*, of which every reporter involved
seems to have a copy. When asked what the most serious problem
in the American church was, they seemed to agree that it was the
influx of Hispanic immigrants, not perceiving that almost any kind
of religious care is more than these immigrants would get in their

country of origin.

Eighty-five percent of your people reject the church's birth control teaching, two-thirds turn their backs on its divorce doctrine, Catholics and Protestants show virtually no difference in abortion attitudes, vocations are less than a third of what they were a decade and a half ago, less than two-fifths believe in papal infallibility, less than half go to church on Sundays, a new wave of virulent anti-Catholicism is sweeping the country—and your biggest problem is immigration!

Still, one cannot help but like the men and admire their sincerity. Would that piety and sincerity were all that was required of leaders and papal electors.

So, while other men are out on the streets this week trying to organize the conclave (in the good sense of the word "organize"), the Americans are waiting and praying. Many people here regret that they are not *organizing* and praying. (When asked by a St. Louis television station what his principal concern was going into the conclave, Cardinal Carberry said that his main worry was whether he could find a plug for his electric razor.)

How do the Americans compare with their three Canadian counterparts: George Flahiff, Paul Léger, and Maurice Roy?

The contrast could not be more striking. The Canadians are ready for the conclave. They have consulted with one another and with other Canadian bishops. While they may not vote as a bloc, they will keep in close touch with one another. They have evolved a precise job description of the man they want to see elected. They are deeply involved in the "campaigning" that is going on. The Canadians see their voting as a public responsibility; the Americans as a private privilege.

Lorscheider gave an interview today which stands in stark contrast to the American performance. The new pope, he said, must be a man of hope with a positive attitude toward the world. He must not seek to impose Christian solutions on non-Christians. He must be sensitive to social problems and must be open to dialogue and committed to the search for unity. Above all, he must be a good pastor, a good shepherd in the way Jesus was, ruling with patience, a commitment to dialogue, and an eagerness for contact with others. He must be especially committed to promoting episcopal collegiality and to working closely with the national bishops' conferences. He must stabilize frequent communication between the conferences and the pope. He must use the Synod of Bishops as a means of strengthening his global vision. He must even be open to finding a new solution to birth control, which, while it would not contradict *Humanae Vitae*, would go beyond it.

The contrast between Lorscheider and the American cardinals was humiliating. He has a very clear idea of the kind of man he wants for pope and is even willing to speak tentatively on the subject of the birth control issue (he's the only one that I've heard mention it during these weeks in Rome). You know with certainty when you read his words that he is a man who is going to play a major role in selecting the next leader of the church. And you know with equal certainty when you hear the Americans babble piously about the Holy Spirit that they are out of it and not going to have any influence at all.

Tuesday, August 22

I saw Adolpho this morning. In a deadlock situation, he observed, just watch Benelli become the kingmaker, supporting some relatively unknown Italian cardinal like Colombo or Luciani, and then emerge himself as the power behind the throne.

Adolpho was right. Benelli did have a compromise candidate, but rather than waiting for a deadlock, he had anticipated it. The coalition was growing. Its existence was still absolutely secret. Not a single Italian newspaper got wind of it.

There were enough paradoxes in the Luciani choice to fill several cases of empty Roman wine bottles. The coalition candidate was an Italian who had come prepared to vote for a non-Italian (Lorscheider). He was thought to be a right-winger but had the massive support of the progressives. The anti-Roncalli, anti-Montini curialists first mentioned him, but Benelli, a man who was forced into exile by these folks, was now his strongest supporter. He was being presented as a simple, holy, pastoral man, but he was, in fact, a complex, cultivated, and well-read thinker, who had once said that if he were not a bishop, he would be a journalist, and that St. Paul, if he were alive, would probably be the head of Reuters or AP. He was a long shot (he put himself on the C-list), but he went into the conclave as the candidate of a (although silent and un-self-conscious) majority consensus.

143

Wednesday, August 23—Inside the Apostolic Palace

A conclave is a nice place to visit, but you wouldn't want to live there. It's not quite as crowded as the enlisted men's section on an aircraft carrier, but if you have any liking for fresh air or breathing space, stay away from the Vatican Palace. All the windows are sealed and either painted over or draped. The plastic chairs in the dining room in the Sale Borgia look like a discount store bargain sale. The rugs they put in the Sistine Chapel (floor raised eighty centimeters above the usual level) are of cheap felt and will be filthy after the first group of cardinals walks down the aisle to vote.

Each cardinal is issued one roll of toilet paper (Danau Star), two ballpoint pens that barely work, and maybe ten sheets of writing paper in a reprocessed folder. Each also gets a plastic wastebasket out of a dime store, a washbowl and pitcher, a red plastic glass, a tiny bed lamp, one hard-backed chair, and an even harder-looking kneeler. To make it clear that he ought to get out in a hurry, he gets only one bar of soap and two very tiny towels, which will drive the Americans up the wall.

A second-class *pensione* it is not.

The beds are the worst thing I've seen since the seminary, and they ought to be because they were borrowed from a seminary. The beds are very narrow, with thin, hard mattresses over wire mesh. Some of the floors are parquet, but most are slippery marble. All have tiny rugs with exactly the same flower design on each, some red and some brown. There is, it would seem, about one toilet for every five or six voters, and I couldn't find many showers at all, which is probably the reason for the small towels.

A comfortable Boy Scout camp, where you could at least get some fresh air, it is not. Save for an occasional walk in a tiny courtyard, the electors are going to have to live in a hot, stuffy, dense atmosphere until they send up the white smoke. If you are inclined to the slightest bit of claustrophobia, the conclave will drive you right up the old brick walls of the fortress, even with the Michelangelo or Raphael paintings on the wall.

There are traffic signs at various intersections in the conclave area showing the way down the narrow corridors to the dining hall, the Sistine Chapel, and the various bedrooms. But it is easy to get lost, as I did (and was almost locked up in the conclave by mistake!).

If you want to find a colleague for a "discussion" (one doesn't conspire in conclaves), it's likely to take a bit of doing.

You're going to have to wander down some corridors and climb some steep staircases, and heaven only knows what other wandering "discussers" you are going to meet slipping discreetly down the corridors, quite possibly lost, too.

Given the sealed windows, smoke-filled rooms are inevitable. But since each contains one bed and one chair, the other discussers in a particular smoke-filled room are going to have to sit on the floor.

The Sistine Chapel is crowded too. Only about half of it is used for the cardinals, and they are crowded together on hard chairs pushed up against equally uncompromising tables. If you really want your ballot to be secret, you're going to have to hide what you write.

I don't think I want to be a cardinal after all. The whole enterprise is designed to get them in and get them out, but considering their average age (68.7 years), there is almost a cruelty in the harshness of conclave living (I bet the food isn't much either). Existence in a conclave is confusing, tense, uncomfortable, hot, stuffy, and cramped. It may not be the best set of circumstances in which to make a wise decision, especially since the most attractive decision is to get out as quickly as you possibly can.

By Thursday night, Felici and Confalonieri have persuaded a number of Italian curialists that after a complimentary vote to Siri on the first and perhaps the second ballot, they ought to shift to Luciani. All things considered, it was the best you could possibly expect. News of this decision reached Benelli by Friday morning. In the course of Friday, there is a communication between Arns and Benelli through Suenens confirming that after a complimentary vote on the first ballot, a substantial number of Third World cardinals would vote for the patriarch of Venice. The French and the Lowlanders and Koenig have already more or less committed themselves. Benelli could afford a momentary sigh of relief. Everything had gone according to plan. Perhaps thirty-five votes on the second ballot, forty to forty-five on the third, into the fifties on the fourth ballot, and election before noon on Sunday.

Siri and Benelli both give interviews on Thursday. Siri, reaching for some votes from the center, is convinced as always of the correctness of his stand that it is necessary to continue the work of Paul VI without interruption or reversal. The positive and great accomplishments of the Paul VI era must be continued with courage.

While speaking to the **Gazzetta del Popolo,** *Benelli insists that it is absolutely essential that collegiality be promoted among the bishops of the church and that the power of the Synod of Bishops be increased. Paul VI did a fine thing in initiating the synod, but the next pope must push forward even further the development of the synod and institutionalize the relationships between the pope and the bishops in the ordinary government of the church. Benelli clearly is promoting the Synod of Bishops as an agency which must have greater power over the Curia than the Curia has over it. Some observers interpret this as Benelli's campaign address paralleling that of Siri. Benelli knows they will, but he does not care. One of the arguments that is being used in support of Luciani is his support of collegiality. He never overturned a decision, for example, of his priest-senate. Those who know will perceive that Benelli is endorsing not himself but his candidate Luciani.*

Thursday, August 24

Vatican finances are in a much worse state than I would have thought possible.

People who know about such things in this city tell you that the expenses for the funeral of Paul VI and the conclave to select his successor are going to push the Vatican one step closer to insolvency. It is estimated that the expenses for the month of August are going to run between four and five million dollars beyond the ordinary August budget. Since the Holy See is already operating at a deficit, these insiders admit that they don't know where the money is going to come from. It will have to be borrowed from somewhere or taken out of capital. The Holy See's credit presumably is good, but if a death and a conclave, which everybody knew would happen sooner or later, create a financial crisis for the Vatican, one has to wonder what has happened to all the fabled Vatican wealth.

The truth seems to be that the Vatican's financial position is neither fabled nor wealthy.

Why do a funeral and a conclave cost so much?

First of all, each of the three thousand Vatican employees can expect a two-months' bonus, one to mark the death of the old pope and the other to mark the election of the new pope. This is the so-called spoilation pay, which the employees are given lest they sack the house of the newly elected pope. You will have noticed that most Vatican employees seem to be the sort who could or would, at best, sack a small candy store, but it was not always thus. Such extra pay may seem a foolish indulgence until one pauses to consider that the average income of Vatican employees is about $6,000; from $825 a month for a cardinal down to $250 a month for clerks, nuns, and Swiss Guards—scarcely princely salaries for anyone.[2]

So about half the cost of a papal funeral-conclave comes from extra salaries for Vatican employees. The rest of the money seems to go to overtime for security forces, for the workmen who convert the Sistine Chapel and Vatican Palace into a temporary polling place and hotel, and for food and drink for the electors, the officials, and the technicians who are locked up inside the conclave. For such splendid theatre, worldwide publicity, and dramatic suspense, four or five million dollars does not seem too high a price to pay, not for an organization which reports a membership of 700 million people. Whence, then, the financial crunch?

The Vatican's annual budget, according to the estimates you get around here, runs anywhere from 75 to 100 million dollars; less than that of a good-sized American liberal arts college and about one-third of that raised annually by such evangelists as Garner Ted Armstrong. With the Vatican's annual expenditures, you could buy a few jet fighter planes, or a supersonic transport (assuming $6,000 a year average annual salary to Vatican employees, $18 million of the budget would go into salaries alone). It is generally conceded that for several years the Vatican has been operating at a deficit of between 25 to 40 million dollars a year.

How come?

The answer is that the Vatican is poor, that's how come. Estimates of the "fabled Vatican wealth," which is alleged to run from 25 to 50 billion dollars, are absurd appeals to anti-Catholic bigotry or to lovers of a conspiracy theory or to the mindless enthusiasts on the Catholic left who want the church to "give away all its wealth."

There's not much to give away.

Estimates of the Vatican's "wealth" must distinguish, if they are to be of any use at all, between book value and income-producing property. How much, for example, is St. Peter's worth? Twenty-five million, fifty million, one hundred million, a billion dollars? You name it—St. Peter's is, of course, irreplaceable and, indeed, priceless. It is also, alas, worthless.[3]

Friday, August 25

This is the day they go in, and tomorrow morning they begin to vote. They had the mass this morning for the election of the pope; 110 cardinals standing, the Samoan cardinal, with his sore foot, sitting. Cardinal Villot preached the sermon. I avoid recording the various sermons, because they're generally pretty dreary affairs.

Between the mass and the procession into the Sistine Chapel this afternoon, I sit down to prepare dispatches describing the outcome of the conclave. Each one is a kind of scenario of how a particular man got elected. The Vatican Communications Office has thirty-four biographies. I'll have less than half that: the three Italian favorites, Bertoli, Baggio, and Pignedoli; the old, non-Italian compromise candidates, Villot, Koenig; the Italian liberal dark-horse candidate, Pellegrino; long-shot Hume, to keep the English happy; then one on Pironio, who seems to me the only serious foreign candidate; also, on two real non-curial Italians, Pappalardo and Ursi. I don't think I'll do Benelli—I just can't imagine a fifty-seven-year-old who has made as many enemies as he has winning. As I look them all over, I'm trying to figure out where I'd place my money if I were a betting man, especially because Grace Ann and Judy are having a party tonight and I have to predict the winner at that. Well, I'll say Koenig as an elderly interim candidate, but that's what I said on the *Today Show* almost three weeks ago. I just don't see how any of these folks can possibly win.

I'm going to take a walk.

I am now watching the cardinals processing in full robes from the Pauline to the Sistine Chapel, singing the hymn to the Holy Spirit.

The procession into the Sistine Chapel has a certain drama. The cardinals look solemn, serious, and responsible, some of them quite vigorous, some of them very haggard and infirm. There is a long, long wait while people scurry around fulfilling their various requirements. Now finally the papal master of ceremonies, Monsignor Noè, says "Extra omnes" in a reasonably firm voice, and with Villot standing by, the door is slowly and dramatically swung shut.

Despite the reports that there was great tension and nervousness among the cardinals, it was quite peaceful, if already very stuffy, inside the conclave the first night. The cardinals seemed relaxed now that the long period of waiting was over and at last they were getting on with their task. Conversation at the evening meal was subdued but friendly. Most of the electors retired to their rooms were hot, and the full cardinalatial robes already were corridors as they searched for the right room. If there was any consultation in the nighttime hours, it was done very quietly. The rooms were hot, and the full cardinalatical robes already were beginning to show the telltale effects of human perspiration.

Scene III

The concelebrated mass over and a light breakfast eaten in the refectory (at other times part of the modern art gallery of the Vatican Museum) the cardinals, with mounting tension, proceed to their chairs in the Sistine Chapel. First of all, voting cards are distributed by the master of ceremonies to the cardinals, two or three to each elector. Then by lot are chosen the names of three infirmarii (who collect the votes of any sick cardinals, though there was no need for such this first day) and of three revisors (in effect, recounters).

The cardinals grow somewhat impatient now. The long, tedious ceremonies have begun to wear on their nerves, and they wish to get down to business. The upper half of the card contains the printed words "Eligo in summam pontificem" (I choose as supreme pontiff) and the lower half has a space for writing the name of the person chosen. The card is designed so that it may be folded in two and be about one inch in size (Paul VI was not one to leave a single detail to chance). After the cards have been distributed and before the writing may begin, the various functionaries—the secretary of the conclave, the master of ceremonies, the assistant masters of ceremonies—must leave the chapel. The doors are shut and finally the cardinals are able to vote. Paul VI was careful to remind each of them that he had to write the name of his candidate down secretly even to the extent of disguising his handwriting. He also wanted them to write no more than one name, as this would make the vote invalid. With some awkwardness and embarrassment because they are seated so closely together, the cardinals write a name and fold a ballot, nervously trying to reassure one another by gazing rigidly straight ahead that they are not trying to peek at each other's ballots.

Then, one by one, in order of precedence (oldest in terms of service first—cardinal bishops before cardinal priests, cardinal priests before cardinal deacons), they walk down the aisle, holding up their cards so that the others may see them, to the altar where the scrutineers are standing, upon which is placed a chalice cov-

150

ered with a plate. When each reaches the altar, he kneels, prays for a short time, and then rises and pronounces aloud yet another oath, "I call to witness Christ, the Lord, who will be my judge that my vote is given to the one who, before God, I consider should be elected."

He places the card on the plate—nothing so hasty as putting it into the chalice—and then drops it from the plate into the chalice. He bows to the altar and then returns to his place. The tension grows perceptibly as this tedious process continues. Benelli wonders if the Luciani strategy will really work. The first ballot should give at least some hint.

Finally, the 111th card is in the chalice. The scrutineer shakes it several times in order to mix the cards (Paul VI was quite careful to make sure that they wouldn't forget to shake the receptacle), and the last scrutineer counts the ballots, picking them out of the chalice in full view and depositing them in another chalice. Fortunately, the number of cards is 111, and there is no need to burn the cards and start over. The cardinals are relieved, and at last they are about to get a count.

The three scrutineers sit at a table and begin the count itself. The first opens a card, unfolds it, notes the name on a piece of paper, passes the card to the second who does the same, then in turn, passes it to the third, who finally announces the name on the card and also writes down on his tally sheet the name of the candidate. The process continues, with the last scrutineer piercing each card with a thread and needle through the word "eligo" (again nothing left to the imagination). As the names are read, there is visible relaxation among the Luciani supporters. Nothing unexpected is happening. Siri and Luciani are getting about the same number of votes. The others are spread out: Pignedoli, Baggio, Koenig, Bertoli, Pironio, a couple for Lorscheider and Felici.

After the names have been read out from each ballot, the ends of the thread are tied in a knot and the scrutineers count up the votes on their tally sheets. Siri has the most votes, twenty-five.[1] Luciani is behind him, but only by a few votes; Pignedoli has less than twenty votes; the others are widely distributed, with Baggio, Koenig, Bertoli, Pironio, Lorscheider, and Felici all having less than ten votes. The coalition leaders relax. No surprises, everything according to plan. Pignedoli and Baggio hide their emotions. Luciani frowns. How could it be possible that he got so many votes?

He shakes his head, mutters something under his voice which a cardinal near him thinks sounds like the word "Absurd."

They look at their watches. The whole process only took an hour. It seemed longer. The revisors hastily recount the ballots, check the tallies. The count is accurate. They proceed to a second ballot. Again, the tension increases slightly. The first ballot was exploratory: compliments were being paid, feelings were being protected—though the feelings of Pignedoli and Baggio are beyond protection. But the second ballot is the serious one. Will it be Siri or Luciani who gains the votes? They are now going to drift away from the other candidates. Halfway through the count, it becomes clear what is going to happen and Luciani is visibly upset. It is truly absurd. There is absolutely no reason why he should be pope. He should have stopped Benelli when there was time. Now it is too late. Cardinal Ribeiro, the handsome young patriarch of Lisbon, leans over and whispers to him, "Courage, the Lord gives the burden. He will also give the strength to carry it." And on the other side, tall, thin, bespectacled Johannes Willebrands, one of Luciani's many close friends, whispers to him, "Don't worry. All over the world everyone is praying for the new pope." The ballots are counted, the tally sheets are added up, totals are announced, and a sense of relief passes through the Sistine Chapel. The job is virtually over, the task has been done. It turned out to be easy after all. The conclave will be over before the sun goes down. Tonight will be the last night.

Tomorrow they will be out of the purgatory of the Vatican Palace and the Sistine Chapel. Luciani has gained thirty votes and now has fifty-five. Siri supporters remain unmoved with their solid block of approximately twenty-five votes. Pignedoli has slipped back now to fifteen votes, and Lorscheider has risen to twelve. In the afternoon, surely, enough of the Lorscheider and Pignedoli votes will switch to Luciani to guarantee his election. The ballots and the tally sheets are placed in the stove at the back of the chapel and black smoke goes up. The cardinals again look at their watches and smile. It is earlier than most people believe would be possible for them to have finished two ballots. Many are going to be caught unawares over in the piazza. Someone whispers in Luciani's ear, "The next time it will be white." He smiles hollowly. Lunch is now affable and relaxed. Pignedoli is cheerful; Baggio smiles and chuckles; Luciani tries awkwardly to ignore what is happening; Benelli,

Suenens, Arns, Lorscheider exchange pleased smiles. Felici decides that he and his less than completely intransigent curial allies have stayed with the Siri ship long enough. Luciani is a happy solution to the problem.

The patriarch of Venice goes back to his room, room 60, and tries to take the brief siesta which is his daily custom, but he does not sleep.

Back in the chapel in the late afternoon, the cardinals are in an almost frolicsome mood. The Holy Spirit is working among them. Particularly happy are the electors from the disorganized middle, who really had no idea of the candidate for whom they ought to vote. Cardinal Carberry will speak later of a feeling of revelation. It was clear on the first ballot that Luciani was most likely going to be the winner, and so many of the uncertain cardinals in the middle promptly jumped on his bandwagon. The coalition leaders expected to pick up fifteen more votes. They got double that number. Perhaps the third ballot will do it, certainly the fourth. It is easier than anyone had expected. The coalition of the left and the moderate right against the far right and the disorganized center had now won over much of the center too, and was about to elect Albino Luciani as pope.

But not quite. Some of Pignedoli's supporters and some of the Siri supporters (including Felici) turned to Luciani on the third ballot, but not quite enough. He still fell five or six votes short. The cardinals are smiling, happy and carefree. The next ballot is a formality. Luciani will certainly win and the conclave will be over. A sense of peace and joy flows through the Sistine Chapel. The Holy Spirit had done his work well. "Now," says Luciani to a colleague smiling warmly, "it begins to get dangerous for me."

The cardinals have now dispensed with taking the oath each time they vote (thus frustrating Paul VI's cautious safeguards against the possibility that a cardinal would on a later ballot not vote for the man he thought was best suited for the job). As the third scrutineer reads off the votes, only Luciani's name is heard. At 6:05, the seventy-fifth Luciani vote is recorded and the cardinals applaud enthusiastically. The Swiss Guard posted outside is startled. A pope so soon? There were some ninety votes for Luciani, one dogged ballot for Aloisio Lorscheider (the new pope himself, of course), and twenty blank votes cast by the stubborn Siri supporters, who are sending a message in this election just as they had in

153

the last, so that the new pope would not have a unanimous mandate—but they are dissenting more gently than their predecessors had against Montini. (Later they would try to claim they had voted for him much earlier in the day and that it was the Pignedoli supporters who stuck it out until the bitter end.)

The doors of the chapel are opened and the various masters of ceremonies come in to accompany the smiling camerlengo, Villot, to the speechless, flustered Luciani. His face beaming with joy, Villot says the words required by Paul VI's constitution. "Do you accept your canonical election as Supreme Pontiff?" Luciani replies, "May God forgive you for what you have done in my regard."[2] Having reached into his memory for a quotation out of the past for which he would later apologize, he then added "Accepto" —"I accept." "By what name do you wish to be called?" asked Villot. "John Paul," replies the now smiling Luciani. The cardinals are delighted; the name is marvelously appropriate.

Luciani is led out to don the temporary white papal robes, grinning happily now—never in his life could he repress the grin—he takes the chair in front of the altar, and the joyful cardinals approach one by one to embrace him and kiss the papal ring. He has a kind and friendly word to say to every one of them.

"Holy Father, thank you for saying yes," said Leo Suenens, who had perhaps more to do with electing him than anyone else.

The new pope, who knew that he had Suenens to blame for his plight, responded with his broadest grin, "Perhaps it would have been better if I had said no."

I got to St. Peter's too late for the first smoke this morning. They certainly got through the early ballots in a hurry. By 12:00, the black smoke had appeared and was gone. A lot of people did see it, though. There were tourist buses on both sides of the street, and a crowd of tourists in the piazza. I was off in a little hotel in the Borgo Pio being interviewed by Irish Radio and got there a few minutes too late. At lunch time, the English press secretary told me that Peter Hebblethwaite had assured him that Hume would get fifteen votes on the first ballot. I gather that Peter was quite emotional at the party last night about what the meaning of a Hume election would be for him. I still think the English are kidding themselves, but if there were an American candidate, I suspect we would be doing the same thing. I'm going back to the Visconti

Palace Hotel to try to work out some more scenarios.

Saturday Evening—Piazza San Pietro

Just two minutes ago, I was sitting in the press office talking to a reporter from an Irish magazine when the television screen showed smoke going up. I dashed out into the piazza. There were horns honking and people shouting "è bianco, è bianco"—"it's white, it's white." But now the smoke that's pouring out looks black and everybody is confused.

6:30—Vatican Radio has now said that the smoke appeared at first to be white, but now it appears to be black. It looks like a false alarm. I'm standing here with Alain Woodrow, Molly McGee, Judy Fisher, Grace Ann Barry, and Jordan Bonfante of *Time*. Jordan is clutching my Sony radio desperately, because if the smoke was white, he has about eight hours to get in a cover story on what could be the most important event he will report in his whole life. Why can't they do this right? he keeps mumbling. The horns have stopped honking, the babies have stopped crying, the people are drifting out of the piazza.

6:45—Vatican radio has been telling us what might be going on inside if the pope had been elected, but black smoke is still pouring out, or, more precisely, gray smoke, "Grigio," people are saying, laughing. The air of expectancy and excitement has diminished. People are streaming away. The cops are relaxing. The sun has set behind the Sistine Chapel. The evening is turning cool. Everybody has enjoyed the excitement even though it was a false alarm. A car from RAI (the Italian TV network) just went by, and the man said there was no pope. Well, that settles that.

7:15—Smoke puffed away merrily for about forty-five minutes and was certainly gray, which I suppose means black—still, why so much smoke?[3]

Sometimes some of the smoke that puffs out doesn't look gray, it looks white, but it has all stopped now, and I guess it's over. Jordan has relaxed, and he and I are going out for supper.

7:19—Just as we are beginning to walk away, a voice booms out of the massive public address system they have in the piazza: "Attenzione." We turn around immediately, and the big door over the balcony of St. Peter's swings open. A cross-bearer comes out. Talk about drama. There's someone in red on the balcony now. It's

Felici, grinning broadly. Well, that means he hasn't been elected, thank heaven. "Annuntio vobis gaudium magnum, habemus Papam!" We have a pope . . . "Eminentissimum ac Reverendissimum Dominum . . . Dominum . . ." More cheers . . . "Albinum . . ." Albinum, who in the hell is that? "Cardinalem Sanctae Romanae Ecclesiae LUCIANI!" The crowd is going wild. The piazza is only one-third full, but they are cheering wildly. Albino Luciani, the patriarch of Venice, is the new pope. Felici is continuing, "Qui sibi imposuit nomen Joannis . . . ". So, John XXIV. That's a good sign . . . "Pauli . . . " Another huge cheer, John Paul! Give him credit for knowing how to use symbols . . . "Primi !" Bedlam in St. Peter's. I've got to go back and write another dispatch. Serves me right. Thirteen scenarios—now I must come up with the fourteenth.

7:45—Back in the Visconti, pounding away at the typewriter, watching his blessing on television. Lord, the man has a magnificent smile. Everything I know about him says that he is a conservative, at least of a sort, not perhaps as conservative as the curial people, but after all, they were pushing him last week, weren't they? What did Adolpho say about him last year? Something like a nice, intelligent man, but frightened by Venice. Still, that smile is irresistible. Maybe I have my smiling holy man. I feel completely flat—trying to understand what happened and to write a dispatch that makes some sense out of the whole thing. Emotion will come later, I guess.

Dom and Grace Ann just dashed in. Both under considerable emotional stress. Dom says his childhood faith has returned to him. Grace Ann fell to her knees and made the sign of the cross when the pope was giving the blessing. They had picked up some interesting information about Luciani. Perhaps he's not as conservative as he had been originally typed. And he certainly can smile. All right, you wanted a smiling holy man, you crazy so-and-so, you got one. But now to try and put some sense into my own confused emotions.

As was clear from his behavior on the balcony of St. Peter's, he is an amiable and friendly man of considerable intelligence and broad cultural sophistication. After the mass yesterday, as he was entering the conclave, Luciani was seen signing autographs and kissing babies as he walked past the crowd. No one here dislikes Papa Luciani; he is the kind of man it is impossible to dislike.

But his experience has been in Italy. He was a strong supporter of the reforms of the Second Vatican Council and is unlikely to try to undo any of those changes. Politically and socially, he seems to be somewhat conservative. However, he is certainly a friendly, openhearted, and attractive man. There is no reason to think that he has any detailed sense of the problems of the church outside Italy. But he may have the capacity to learn.

His personal charm may carry him a long way, but for many Catholics and non-Catholics personal charm is not going to be enough to cause the papacy to be taken seriously as the world's most important evangelistic pulpit.

Like Pope John XXIII, Papa Luciani is known for his long walks through the streets of Venice talking with the people. A man with pastoral experience, he seems to have the common-man style of Pope John. One Italian newspaper quoted him as once having said that he would have preferred to be a journalist rather than a bishop. A man with an apparent passion for journalism, he told *Il Tempo* that his favorite authors are Mark Twain, Petrarch, Dickens, Sir Walter Scott, and G. K. Chesterton.

The full story is not yet out. Luciani has more pastoral experience than any other of the leading candidates. He may have persuaded the non-Italian cardinals that he will make major changes in the way the papacy is run. He may have indicated that he will retire at seventy-five. They may have preferred him to any of the curial diplomats who were touted as favorites—simply because he seemed to be a nicer man. He may have made some commitments about upgrading the Synod of Bishops and decentralizing authority to the national churches. He will probably not be an impressive pope; he does not seem to be the kind who will restore the impact of papal leadership in religion and morality around the world.[4]

Tonight I called one of my friends in the American hierarchy who knows Luciani well. His reaction was interesting: "He was a marvelous bishop in a small diocese. In Venice, he was uneasy and nervous, pressured by the problems of the city and by the decisions imposed on the Italian hierarchy by the Curia and the pope. Now that he's pope himself? It may sound crazy, but I've got a hunch that he may go back to being Don Albino, the country bishop."

I hope he's right.

Sunday, August 27

Vatican Press Office, 12:30—I'm sitting here telling myself that Luciani was elected by impulse voting. They had to have a candidate. Some people came up with this candidate. They elected the pope in a day and got out (this morning). I'm angry at men like Koenig and Suenens and Tarancón, who should have been down here participating in the preparations.[5]

Yet, there are good things too. Benelli was the floor leader of the Luciani victory, according to just about everybody. Benelli's speech on Friday about the need for greater collegiality doubtless was a reflection of John Paul's feelings. Luciani himself once said he would never overrule a decision made by his priest senate. He did his dissertation on Rosmini. He seems to be part of the northern Italian tradition of intellectual openness mixed with intense charity, a tradition reinforced, if not created, by Rosmini. During the Second Vatican Council, he was on John Courtney Murray's side in the religious liberty debate. His statement on the birth of the test-tube baby a couple of weeks ago was a masterpiece of charm, sensitivity, and intelligence. Some people say that the move from the pious place of Vittorio Veneto to the empty churches and open paganism of Venice has had a profoundly depressing effect on him. Lefebvre supporters around Rome are rejoicing. The cardinals wanted a smiling Italian pastor. They got one. But can such a pastoral man with conservative tendencies actually stabilize the church? Maybe the key will be whether he changes the rigid and indeed impossible election system which made him pope.

But having said all of those things, I am beginning to wonder if maybe I've missed the point. A half-hour ago, he came out with his first Angelus address to a crowd that was almost three times as large as the one that saw the white smoke last night. The talk was dazzling. It was delivered with simplicity, humility, and that incredibly contagious smile:

"Yesterday morning I went to the Sistine to vote peacefully. I never would have imagined what was about to take place. As soon as it began to be a danger for me, two of my colleagues who were sitting near me whispered words of encouragement. One said to me 'Courage, if the Lord gives a burden, he also gives the strength to carry it,' and another said, 'Don't be afraid. The whole world prays for the new pope.' When the moment came then, I accepted.

"As regards the choice of names, because then they asked me and I had to stop and think a while. My thoughts were like this: Pope John had wanted to consecrate me with his own hands here in the Basilica of St. Peter. Then, though unworthy, I succeeded him in the Cathedral of St. Mark, in that Venice which is still filled with the spirit of Pope John. The gondoliers remember him, the sisters, everyone. On the other hand, Pope Paul not only made me a cardinal, but some months before that, on the footbridge of St. Mark's Square, he made me turn red in front of twenty thousand persons, because he took off his stole and placed it on my shoulders. I was never so red-faced. Furthermore, in the fifteen years of his pontificate, this pope showed not only me but the whole world how he loved the church, how he served it, worked for it, and suffered for this church of Christ. And so I took the name John Paul.

"Realize this, I do not have the wisdom of heart of Pope John. Nor do I have the preparation and culture of Pope Paul. However, I stand now in their place. I will seek to serve the church and I hope that you will help me with your prayers."

Then at the end of the talk, which was interrupted by frequent cheers from the throng in the piazza, he began to say the Angelus in Latin. Now I believe in prayer, but I haven't said the Angelus in twenty-five years. Still, I stood up here in the Vatican Press Office, surrounded by apostates, pagans, agnostics, and other varieties of non-Catholics, and said the Angelus with him with tears pouring down my face. How he came to be elected and what he is going to mean for the church, I just don't know right now, but what looked last night like either bad news or not really encouraging news now could turn out to be incredibly good news. I'm too confused to know what to make of any of it.

Earlier today as the cardinals poured out into the courtyard of St. Damascus, leaving behind, doubtless for a good many years, the cramped, uncomfortable conclave area, they seemed happy men. "It was the greatest day of my life," said Cardinal Thiandoum. "It was a grace, a gift of God," said his African colleague, Gantin. "The Holy Spirit helped us," said Austria's Koenig, who just a few weeks ago was calling for a young, non-Italian pope. Benelli was ecstatic in his enthusiasm, "A striking manifestation of the unity of the church supported by the presence of the Holy Spirit. . . . The electors came from every part of the world, from every culture, and with very different mentalities and, in a single day, reached complete agreement."

Well, maybe there were creative energies at work, picking unity out of diversity. But if the Holy Spirit was to be, in Basil Hume's words, "paying someone the compliment of collaboration," it seems reasonable to believe that the principal collaborator was the energetic, wheeling-dealing, enormously forceful Giovanni Benelli. In the terms of city hall, he was the man who cut the deal. Come to think of it, Adolpho was right. Benelli was the kingmaker, except he didn't wait for the deadlock to happen. He must have won over an awful lot of people. As I try to figure out how he did it, I remember that Suenens is a close friend of Benelli and Arns is a close friend of Suenens. I'll bet that was the link. Well, at least, it's a clue to trace down.[6]

The American bishops had a press conference. They repeated pretty much the same sort of thing that the cardinals said emerging from the conclave area. It was an experience of peace and joy, a happy, joyous day. John Dearden insisted that it was wrong to try and describe the pope as a conservative, and Cardinal Cody, in one of his more sublime moments, when asked by a reporter how one could explain to the American people that the pope's father had been a socialist, said, "What's so difficult about that? My father was a fireman, and I'm a cardinal."

Entr'acte

John Paul's September was a revolution. He swept away the throne, the crowning, the majestic "we," the word "pontificate," the formal and aloof monarchical style of the papacy—even the "sedia gestatoria" (chair on which the pope is carried). The last was brought back later as a functional necessity so that the people could see him when he came to his audiences. (He never used it in solemn ceremonies.) He shook hands with the Communist mayor of Rome and promised cooperation. He walked unannounced in the Vatican gardens with Cardinal Villot (throwing the Vatican security forces into confusion and disorder). He wandered around the offices of the Secretariat of State to see who was doing what. He spent long hours preparing his seemingly spontaneous homilies and Sunday remarks. He grinned, he smiled, he laughed. He quoted nineteenth-century Roman romantic poetry as well as Jules Verne, Mark Twain, Napoleon, and St. Bernard. He asked children questions at his audiences, he charmed the simple and ordinary people of the world. He never did quite manage to make it with the more sophisticated of the world press. Le Monde commented: "The audiences attracted the immediate sympathy of the public but disappointed and sometimes worried church officials. The pope expressed a philosophy of existence that recalled on occasion the Reader's Digest *common sense, a little simple at that, which broke with the grand theological flights of oratory of Paul VI. Visibly, he did not have the cultural and intellectual training of his predecessor."*

Le Monde *was simply wrong. In fact, John Paul had a far richer cultivation and far more sophisticated training than Paul VI. He was so cultivated and so sophisticated, in fact, that he was able to be simple. An Argentinian archbishop would remark, "The other day on the street in Rome, a little boy was asked if he loved the pope and he said yes. He was asked why. 'Because I understand everything he says.' "* Newsweek *thought that when he condemned the equation of political, economic, and social freedom with salvation in Jesus Christ (in his rejection of the dictum "ubi Lenin ibi Jerusalem"—where Lenin is there is Jerusalem), he was attacking the theology of liberation. In a classic non sequitur,* Newsweek *added, "Since Luciani had been elected pope with the considerable support of the progressive cardinals in Latin America, his remarks were widely seen as a rejection of the Third World efforts to liberate the poor through church-based social action." In other words, if you refuse to equate religion with politics, you are not only rejecting Marxist liberation theology, you are also rejecting the progressive Latin Americans who elected you. Of course, none of the Latin American cardinals are Marxists, none of them could be considered radical liberation theologians, and certainly none of them would remotely disagree with the pope's rejection of "ubi Lenin ibi Jerusalem."* Commonweal, *with its usual marvelous ability to miss the point, said, "We followed first with eagerness, then with a growing sense of the ridiculous, his generous efforts to discover who he was. He smiled, his father was a socialist, he rejected the tiara for a simple stole, he spoke informally at his audiences."*

He was, according to the all-wise editors of Commonweal, *the "unknown pope." It was as though the wise and the learned of the world (and is not one wise and learned if one writes for* Newsweek *or* Commonweal *or* Le Monde*) bitterly resented the pope's ability to instantly capture the imaginations of ordinary folks. He was a peasant, a conservative, a simple man. Given more time, his true conservative orientations would have shaped a papacy perhaps not even as broad as that of Paul VI (none of them seemed to notice his personal correspondence with Hans Küng congratulating that controversial theologian on the publication of his best-selling book,* On Being a Christian—*scarcely "conservative" behavior). The world, you see, was wrong and the wise folks of the press were right.*

The Curia was bitter and tried to censor his speeches, reinserting the majestic "we" where he had used the simple familiar "I." It ignored him, harassed him, tried to freeze him out, and complained that he wasn't doing his administrative work. Papers were going unsigned and major problems of the church were being ignored while he prepared his Sunday homilies and his catechetical instructions for his audiences. He himself admitted that he had to get out the Annuario Pontificio *to find out who did what in the Vatican administration, and he confessed to one of his friends that about the operation of the Curia, "I know nothing." A nice, simple, pastoral man, yes, but scarcely qualified for the administrative tasks of the Curia. The crowd applauded and the Curia murmured.*

The Curia also dissembled, as it frequently does. For a newcomer, in his first month on the job, John Paul made remarkable progress in understanding and beginning to control the recalci-

trant bureaucracy. He began an investigation of Vatican finances, a subject on which he already had strong feelings; he did not need the exposé in the respectable Italian financial paper Il Mondo *(kind of an Italian* Business Week*) on September 6, which was accompanied by an open letter urging him to straighten out the financial mess. When Archbishop Casaroli came to him with seven questions about the church's relationship with countries in Eastern Europe, he gave prompt answers on five and asked time to think about the other two. Casaroli left dazed. Paul VI had never been that decisive.*

So some of the world press tried to present him as a conservative (which he was not, save in some very limited sense of the term), a political reactionary (based on the premise that you are either a Marxist or a reactionary), and as unsophisticated (which he most assuredly was not); and the Curia tried to portray him as irresponsible and incompetent, when, in fact, he was all too competent for their liking.

Such is the punishment that mediocre men and women impose on someone who captures the popular imagination. When at his first talk on faith he quoted Pinocchio and compared the soul in the modern world to an automobile that breaks down because it runs on champagne and jam instead of gasoline and oil, the learned folk shook their heads in dismay. When he casually remarked that God is even more our mother than our father, the Italian papers produced learned articles asking if this was a change in the church's theology and whether a fourth person was to be introduced into the Blessed Trinity (only to have the pope come back at a later talk and dismiss the whole controversy with a laugh by saying he was only quoting the prophet Isaiah). When he quoted Jules Verne in his audiences, the solemn Vatican protocol-types shook their heads; his incorrigible habit of calling little kids up to interview at his audiences dismayed those who were responsible for keeping the papacy presentable.

A few people noticed that when the pope was interviewing children at these audiences, he always very carefully pushed the child's head towards the microphone so his response could be heard. His public presence was that of the carefully prepared professional.

The papers played up his talk to American bishops in which he warned of the dangers of divorce. But they ignored the question period afterwards during which the pope admitted that there were many questions to which he did not know the answers and added, with the usual winning grin, "After all, I am only a bambino pope."

His little-noted Angelus talk on Sunday, September 17, was a masterpiece, directed at young people who were going back to school. Again, there was a reference to the ever-present Pinocchio and a lament that when young people came out of school there were not enough jobs for them. But the principal point was that young people should work hard in school, because only after graduation would they appreciate how important the knowledge can be. "If anyone had ever said to me," he concluded, " 'you will be pope,' I would have studied harder so I would be better prepared. Alas, now I am an old man and there is no time."

Some of us read his books. Some studied his remarkable catechetical style. Others were awed by the professionalism of his TV presence. A few knew the decisiveness with which he was working inside the Curia, but most people were totally unaware of any of these things. What, then, was the secret of his powerful appeal to the ordinary people of the world, an appeal which seems to have escaped the Curia, Newsweek, Commonweal, and Le Monde? The secret of John Paul's success with the ordinary folk of the world is that the ordinary folk of the world are not concerned about ideology, liberation theology, or collegiality. Differences of the right and left don't mean very much to them. But personal holiness of the kind which says that hope and even joy are still possibilities in human life remains extraordinarily attractive. Christianity has not been tried and found wanting, G. K. Chesterton once remarked, but found hard. Similarly, a religious papacy hasn't had much of a try either, not for a long time, and a religious papacy with instant access to the world has never been tried before. I indeed did have my hopeful holy man who smiles—a man who fit the job description far better than I could have hoped or expected. And the world response was more striking than I would have dreamed possible. Religious leadership which radiates joy and hopefulness will be successful 100 percent of the time, and when that leadership operates in the world's oldest pulpit with the world's largest church, there is almost no limit to the amount of influence it can have.

But, the elitist argues, Pius X smiled and he was repressive. Yes, Pius X was a holy man and he was repressive. I strongly suspect that Pius X on TV, for all his holiness, would have turned people off. It is only a special kind of holiness that makes for effective world religious leadership—a leadership which emphasizes hope and joy. There wasn't much hope and joy in the man who signed the condemnation of modernism and permitted the white terror that followed it. No matter how virtuous he may have been personally in other respects, would Luciani have turned repressive? I find it very difficult to see how a man who talked about Mark Twain, who quoted romantic poetry, who cited jokes about marriage from Montaigne could have ever turned repressive. His changing positions on religious liberty and birth control, his correspondence with Hans Küng, and his collegial governing of Venice with his priest-senate seem to me to preclude the possibility that beneath the warmth and the wit and the smile there lurked an authoritarian inquisitor. If the emblem of liberalism is the acceptance of liberation theology, I suppose he was not a liberal. The people of the world who saw him on the television screen couldn't have cared less.

The curial ideologues of the right objected to him because he spent more time on sermons than signing papers. And the liberals on the left objected to him because his style was not that of a radical theologian. But the kids in the streets knew what he meant and so did the people of the world—and they loved him and he revolutionized the papacy.

Not merely because he discarded many of the medieval and Renaissance customs; not merely because he demolished the monarchical papacy; not merely because he laughed and smiled— though all those things helped: in September of 1978, Pope John Paul reintroduced the specifically religious dimension of papal leadership in such a dramatic and exciting way that it could never again be excluded. The idea of a hopeful holy man who smiles could be dismissed by Roman journalists in August as American "packaging," but by October (in the second conclave) it had become clear that henceforth that was the only kind of pope the cardinals dared to elect. The pope had definitively and irrevocably become a world religious leader in the era of mass communications, and the implications for Catholicism are so many and so complex we have not even begun to sort them out.

As I look over what I wrote at the end of August, I confess that I am disappointed in myself. I had my hopeful, smiling holy man, and one part of my personality was completely captivated by him. But caught up in the frantic, exhausting, ideologically charged atmosphere of the final week in August, I wasn't able to appreciate the full force of what I had written earlier—that it does not matter whether he is a liberal or a conservative, a pastor or a diplomat, an Italian or a non-Italian, as long as he incarnates the Christian vision of hope. The first hint was in his smile at the blessing after his election. The second was the little Angelus talk the next day. I began to understand what kind of man he was when I read the marvelous statements on the birth of the test-tube baby, and I was captured completely by the installation mass on the Sunday of Labor Day weekend.

Sitting once again on the shores of Lake Michigan at Grand Beach, with the spinnakers of the Chicago Yacht Squadron dashing recklessly across the blue lake, I watched on TV his greeting of each of the cardinals after the pallium had been put on his shoulders. It was an astonishing manifestation of graceful charm. Several people who dropped into my house also stared, transfixed, at the drama on the television screen. The choreography of the liturgy in the piazza was perfect again, the slowly moving shades of night transforming San Pietro into a glowing marble dome against the black sky. The man himself was the best part of the drama, skullcap awry, broad grin, warm embrace, expressive gesture— one knew that Catholic Christianity was now being seen by the world as something very special. Later than some but before a lot of others, I climbed on the Luciani bandwagon, realizing that the papacy and the church would never be the same again.

At the beginning of the last week of September, I returned to Rome with some friends on a previously planned vacation to finish my reconstruction of the conclave events and to try to get a feel for what conclusions one might draw in the first month of Papa Luciani's pastorate.

Tuesday, September 26

The first reaction came from my friend Ernie Primeau. "Well, personally, I think we have a hell of a good pope, though he doesn't know anything about how this place works, because he stayed away from the city, and you can't blame a man for doing that."

Tonight, I was to have supper with Father Carter. I did,

indeed, go over to his apartment and show him my manuscript just to get his reaction. However, that was the end of it, because I got my annual midday migraine headache—except that it came midday Chicago time, which was 7:00 P.M. here—and that thoroughly wiped me out for a while. So I had to depart just at suppertime, leaving him in charge of my traveling companions, who spent a delightful evening with him while I was home in the hotel being sick. I also got caught in the rush-hour traffic, and it took me forty-five minutes of pounding headache and violent nausea to get back here so I could be sick in decent peace.

Later, Father Carter and I talked on the phone. Carter said that we all ought not to have been surprised, though we all were (he himself included), because the cardinals had made it clear enough that what they wanted was a pastor, somebody who had never been contaminated by the Curia. And that's what they got. Now whether or not they got somebody who will be able to deal with the Curia is another matter.

He continues to be high on Benelli. He said he's a tough man. Benelli shouted at him on the phone once, "I disagree with you totally and completely, but if you say that's the way it should be done, we'll do it that way." He says he knows of no situation, no case, where Benelli has ever turned away from talent.

Carter told me about John Paul's meeting with the American bishops. The bishops were there at the general audience, and after the audience was over, John Paul chased everybody out, including the translator, read a talk to them in English, and then had an American bishop translate in a question period afterwards. He said, "Now it's your turn to ask questions," and engaged in give and take for a fair period of time with the bishops. They asked him whether his first encyclical would be on the priesthood, and he said he would like it to be but thought he was pretty much committed to doing the first one on catechetics, because that was the last thing the synod had treated—which shows his emphasis on collegiality.

Collegiality means different things to different people. It is one thing to the Synod of Bishops, for whom it means bringing people together in Rome to thrash something out; it is quite another thing to someone like Felici, who figures you get together a small staff of your own folks, draft a document, and send it around to the bishops of the world, most of whom don't react at all, while a few react one way and a few another, so that they cancel each other out. If there is a fairly strong consensus against what you are saying, you modify it somewhat. That's consultation and collegiality for those folks, and this is the way the new canon law reform has been put together—it will be a disaster if promulgated (and John Paul is apparently committed to promulgating it).

Wednesday, September 27

This morning we went to the papal audience. It was something else. Ernie had gotten us tickets up front in Section A. We got there about 10:15, and the place was already two-thirds filled. It was completely filled by 10:30—there were perhaps sixteen thousand people in there. Paul VI filled the audience hall, too, but not the way this man does. Most of the seats in the back were taken out so there would be more room for people. The pope had seen a large number of German people in St. Peter's before he showed up to see us. There was a band playing—Swiss Guards all around the place, Vatican police, bishops and Capuchin religious superiors, nuns, priests, men, women, young, old, rich, poor, black, white (by the way, every time a black bishop appeared in the hall, he was cheered wildly—but then all sorts of people were cheered wildly). The audience hall is big and ugly. The Resurrection scene behind the podium is bigger and uglier than anything; but still the hall is reasonably functional and allows lots of people a chance to see the pope up close.

He came in about twenty minutes late. His talk was about love—simple, declarative sentences—delivered in a rather low, somewhat timid voice, but with a great deal of conviction, charm, and, of course, the famous smile, which just dazzles people. You get the impression that he likes his job and—my traveling companions thought this too—that he's a little bit uncertain about what to do, somewhat overwhelmed by it all, but pleased, particularly when he's able to talk to people. One had the impression that he was fairly hemmed in by the monsignors who accompanied him and that at times he would have liked to break away from them and go over to shake hands with people—really work the crowd—but was almost afraid to do so. He read a summary of his talk in English, the first time he's done that, and his English pronunciation is excellent—some people said better than Paul VI. His rapport with crowds, no matter what the language, is also better than Paul VI's because of the simplicity and the timid charm of his manner. His voice leaves something to be desired, but it's made up for by his smile. He really turned the crowd on—I mean, they just cheered wildly, including my fairly sophisticated traveling companions, who aren't easily taken in by piety. Indeed, Andy Burd said it was the only time in the trip he was really excited. Mary said to me, "You were smiling like a delighted little kid through the whole audience!" I'm sure I was.

So you have this simple, kindly man, smiling and giving a simple catechetical talk to smiling and cheering people. It almost seems utterly spontaneous, until you realize that Don Diego, his tall, bespectacled secretary is up there flipping the pages of the text as he talks. The pope is speaking from memory, but his secretary has the exact text, and according to those who have listened to him on tape and seen the text afterwards, he doesn't deviate from the final text (which he has revised himself by hand before he uses it). So, on that stage one had a sort of symbol of everything, a man hemmed in, a man uncertain, but also a smart man with a tremendous memory, one who has not been stopped from doing what he wants to do by the people around him now. All in all, it was a virtuoso performance. The distaff side of my traveling entourage decided that he was "cute," which from that type of Irish female must be a compliment of considerable power, since the same word was used of a very handsome Swiss Guard. Incidentally, the papal audiences tear the hell out of Roman noonday traffic. The thing was over about 11:30; at 12:20 the tourist buses were still lumbering around the Piazza San Pietro and the Via della Conciliazione, and traffic was all messed up. I had to walk to the Piazza Cavour to get my cab to get to the Piazza San Calisto to meet with a source.

Thursday, September 28

It is an absolutely gorgeous Roman day. There was some kind of brief front that passed through here last night and cooled things off. It is a cool, clear, crisp day—just marvelous.

Adolpho is delighted with the new pope. Things are going much better than he would have dreamed possible. He is convinced that the meeting of the permanent council of the Synod of Bishops is absolutely critical because the Synod is likely to be the one effective counterpoise to the Curia, which the pope needs for his independence. The first session will be tremendously important. Vigorous leadership from these people is absolutely essential. The council needs to be represented in Rome by a powerful cardinal, not someone like Ladislaw Rubin, the poor Polish fellow who is saddled with the job now and who doesn't have enough power to do it effectively. It needs a very powerful secretariat with not only cardinal rank but lots of prestige. Someone like Lorscheider, in other words, has to be in Rome permanently to represent it.

What are the character and personality of John Paul? After the recommendation of the birth control commission had been rejected and it looked as though there would be an encyclical, Luciani sent the report of his own small commission to the pope, arguing that now was not the proper time for a decision and that any action should be delayed until more study had been undertaken—which was very wise advice. He received no response. *Humanae Vitae* appeared about a month later, and, as Adolpho put it, he threw the documents in his drawer and locked them up and never mentioned it again. Similarly, on the Italian divorce referendum, while he dissolved the student union and silenced the priests who were arguing, not in favor of divorce, but that Catholics should be able to vote in favor of the referendum, Luciani, in fact, in the Italian bishops' conference opposed the divorce referendum, realizing that the church would lose, but went along with the decision of the church. So at least some of his more conservative behavior, according to Adolpho, can be attributed to his conviction that when the church has made a decision, one goes along with it. In both the above cases, his own personal opinions represented a change from the church's previous positions—certainly in birth control and probably in divorce. Mind you, he still would be personally opposed to divorce but would support freedom of divorce for people in Italy who believed in it. At the least he would not have gone to the wall to fight such freedom.

Thursday Night

We had supper tonight with Bob Tucci, the director of Vatican Radio and an old friend of mine. He was delighted with my traveling companions and they with him, and the charm was flowing all over Trastevere. My friends are completely taken with the pope, and so, for that matter, is Tucci.

Just as we were leaving Tucci, he told us about the new pope's first phone call after the election. He called the bishop in Belluno, where he had been bishop, and his first line was, "Well, the fox may have lost his hair, but he still is a fox," implying that "even though I may be pope, I'm still bothering you on the telephone."

The pope had a hard day. He spoke about justice and liberation to a group of Filipino bishops in the morning and talked with Milan's Cardinal Colombo in the afternoon. Apparently he tried to persuade someone to accept the diocese of Venice as his replacement and was rudely rejected. The Curia was still freezing him out. He huddled with Cardinal Baggio about some critical appointments and replacements in the world hierarchy. (In the interview with Cardinal Baggio John Paul had given orders for the replacement of Cardinal Cody. The papers of the Cody case were in his hands when he died.) He saw Cardinal Villot, the secretary of state, and may have received reports from him about troubles in a certain Catholic country. After night prayer in the chapel, the staff told him about the ambush of a Communist by right-wing extremists: "They kill each other—even the young people." He shook his head and with a sheet of paper in his hands, some German notes and some appointment material left by Baggio, went into his bedroom. Later, in the early morning, taxis could see that the lights were still on in the papal apartment.

At 4:30, Sister Vincenza, his housekeeper, brought the usual cup of coffee and left it on the table outside the door of his bedroom. She came back later to take away the coffee cup and discovered it had been untouched. There was a light on in the papal bedroom. She summoned Father Magee . . .

Act Two

Scene I

The pope is dead.

Last night at eleven o'clock, just when Tucci and my friends and I were breaking up the meal at Sabatini's, he died in his bed while reading a book. A man who had spent much of his life reading died with a book in his hand.

At 5:30 this morning, Monsignor Magee, the Irish priest who was one of his two secretaries, went to his room—the pope was usually in his chapel before that—and found his body. At 7:15 A.M., Tucci was called with the information, at 7:27, he announced the death to the world on Vatican Radio before he began the morning mass on the radio. He then said the Mass for the Dead.

Ernie Primeau called me at 7:45; about 8:30 I woke up my friends and told them. We all sat here feeling dazed, confused, shocked. Jack Saletta said that it is clear that if the church is to give the people strong, vigorous leadership, it has to turn to younger people. It is hard to think about a successor. All the cardinals are going to have to come back to Rome again, this time not to mourn a pope whose death had been anticipated for some time, but to mourn a pope for whom they had expected at least ten more good years. They have indeed worked out a job description, but how will they find a man to fit it? In particular, how will they get a man who can follow the example set by John Paul in his vigorous, month-long pastorate? The task is going to be harder this time. Right now all is confusion.

Noontime

The Piazza of St. Peter's at noontime—bells tolling. There are people in the square—tourists, as always, somewhat more subdued than for Paul VI, perhaps, but hard to tell. People with cameras and flight bags moving through. There is supposed to be a viewing of the body by journalists, which is why I'm down here. I don't know whether anything will come of that or not. It sounds pretty gruesome to me. Black headlines in the paper. The jour-

nalists are here, all right. I needed to get a pass to come in through
the bronze door, so I ran to the press office and am breathless now
with pass in hand. There is a crowd here, most of them people I
don't know; mostly Italians, I would imagine. A fairly big crowd of
people out under the Bernini columns, just kind of watching.
Photographers are shooting away like mad taking pictures. There
was a simple announcement of the pope's death in the Vatican
Press Office. It's only 5:30 A.M. in the United States. Americans
are just waking up to find out about what happened during the
night. *L'Osservatore Romano* is already out with a black band
around it. A number of Italian papers have got out special editions.

We've been waiting about fifteen minutes here. Others have
been waiting longer than I have. No sign of movement. As always,
everything in Rome is inefficient.

We're back in the Vatican Palace, the Apostolic Palace, as it is
also called, climbing the stairways on the way up to the room where
the preliminary exhibition is to be. Marble, baroque staircase put
in by Pius IX. Through the Belvedere Courtyard, up another set of
steps, to the door of the Sala Clementina. Another wake.

The pope's body is in a Renaissance hall built in the 1500s,
walls covered with paintings and frescoes. It is hot and stuffy;
people are pushing in typical Italian fashion. The television folks
are up in front now blazing away with their cameras at the corpse.
It's all very grim and macabre.

I'm walking down the steps away from the room by myself. I
was in the first rank of the third group they let in. I walked by the
casket, said a couple of quick prayers, and got out. They had taken
off his glasses; it doesn't look like him at all. Which is, of course, a
stupid Irish thing to say, isn't it? It's all very ghoulish. Reporters
and photographers, chattering away, plying their professional
trades, in the presence of what, less than fifteen hours ago, was an
extraordinary human being. *The frailty of all things human.*

It's a whole new ball game, and while the players are virtually
the same, give or take one or two, they are the same men who are
now experienced conclavists, men who have lived through a month
of John Paul. And that changes the whole thing. It is not enough
just to pull out the notes of the previous game. They are not
freshmen anymore, not rookies; and there has been a month of
world experience of what the papacy can be with the right kind of
man.

There is a heaviness, a lethargy, in everyone here, a going through all the motions again, a sense of *déjà vu*, of replaying an old movie. And from Cardinal Villot, who once again is camerlengo, on down, there is a weariness and a heavy heart, a special sting of sorrow for what might have been, as people prepare for the making of another pope.

The AP stopped my friend Mary Burd in the piazza. Her quote went out all over the world. Said Mary Catherine Whelan Burd that was, explaining why she would not go into the wake, "I saw him in the audience Wednesday and prefer to see him smiling. I loved Rome when I came a week ago; now I want to go home."

Saturday, September 30

The papers this morning are filled with explanations—from the traditionalists, who suggest that God punished John Paul because he hadn't wanted to be pope, to the liberals, who contend that a papabile should have a physical examination (What was his blood pressure?). Cardinal Marty is supposed to have said sometime yesterday (I heard about it from Jordan Bonfante last night), "What is God trying to tell us?" There is no lack of answers in Rome just now to that question.

It was not the shortest papacy in history; Urban VII ruled for only twelve days. But the thirty-three days of John Paul I were surely the most dramatic and decisive of the short pastorates of Catholic history. They were brief, glorious days; in my notes the day before he died I wrote, "We don't deserve a man like this." I guess we didn't.

He threw away without a backward glance much of the old monarchical trappings of the papacy—the throne, the crown, the majestic "we." He spoke easily of the maternal love of God. September, 1978, shook the papacy to its core. It will never be the same again.

Even the members of the world press reassembling here, normally hardened to human tragedy, are dazed and saddened. "I am not a Catholic or even very religious," said an American TV reporter to me, "but that man made me feel peaceful and happy whenever I saw him."

Then, of course, there is the cynicism of the Romans over in the Trastevere section of the city who darkly hint at poison—an absurd charge which cannot be refuted because papal law prohibits autopsies.

Caricatures, perhaps, but we humans are meaning-creating animals—"suspended in the webs of meaning that we ourselves have spun." Faced with senseless and ironic tragedy, we search for meaning, with far more confidence in our ability to divine the will of the ultimate powers than we should have. You must, however, whistle in the dark as you pass by the cemetery.

It might be argued that it was the important, if brief, role of John Paul to present a model of what the papacy might be: the most influential religious leadership position in the world, capable of exercising enormous power, but only on the condition that it shed its outmoded monarchistic trappings. The creation of such a brilliant model, it could be said, was a sufficient accomplishment for one "pastorate"—John Paul's term for his pontificate. The pre–John Paul Renaissance papacy, with all of its royal anachronisms, can never return, according to this interpretation. Now it is up to the new pope—whoever he may be—to move the church forward in the substantive directions toward which John Paul's style pointed.

But that interpretation can easily be confounded if the cardinal electors, not perceiving the impact of the Luciani revolution on the ordinary people of the world, elect a man who may indeed be an "Italian pastoral type," but who will nevertheless bring back the old trappings of papal power.

With its usual skill in such matters, the Vatican is doing just the opposite this time of what it did last time in beginning the conclave. Last time they waited the full three weeks that they are permitted; this time they are starting at the earliest possible date, the fourteenth, just fifteen days after the pope's death. The funeral mass will be Wednesday, and then a week from Saturday the cardinals will go into conclave. The big question now is whether they will simply pull out the notes from the last time and do the same thing all over—that is, pick the next one down on the list rather automatically—in which case it will be a short conclave, or whether they will realize the change worked in the church by Luciani and declare it a whole new game, in which case it could be a somewhat longer but better conclave. The decision, by the way, to make the discussion period as brief as possible was made by the curial cardinals, twenty-nine of whom met today—all of them are in Rome this time—and, of course, gives the *stranieri* less time to act, and perhaps Benelli less time to concoct a plot. However, as we know from the last time, the *stranieri* waited till the last week anyhow, so it may not make much difference. Indeed, it could be that while the Curia's decision to have a quick conclave is certainly in its own interest, that decision reflects the attitudes of the other folks too. Nothing much is going to happen this week, I think—that is to say, the week beginning tomorrow. The following week should be fascinating, though.

Saturday Night

They are transferring the body of Pope John Paul from the Vatican Palace to St. Peter's. The piazza is filled, the sun is setting, there are red and pink skies behind the dome of St. Peter's. The crowds are absolutely silent, reverent.

Apparently, Don Diego, the pope's secretary, blames the pope's death on a great sorrow; he had been deeply moved by the outburst of terrorist assassinations, the news of which he had heard just before he retired. The newspapers are saying that the Curia was not cooperating with him in the last several days and had left him isolated. That added to his burdens, and the terrorist thing must have added to them even more. Apparently, he had complained to a number of people about how difficult his task was. It was obviously a massive stroke he had—and you can't tell, because you can't do autopsies on popes, but there had to have been a precondition. Jack Saletta (a doctor friend traveling with me) wondered what his blood pressure was before and after the election and when he last had a physical checkup. There are also hints in the papers, doubtless from the Curia, that the burden of moving into Rome is too much for a man without curial experience (those folks never give up). One could easily have argued that lack of cooperation from the curialists was as much the cause of his death as his inability to understand how the Curia worked. To top things off, the newspapers today carry a detailed description of Cardinal Siri's blood pressure and heartbeat, suggesting that despite his seventy-two years, he has the vigor of a much younger man.

Many Italians believe that Pope John Paul I was murdered. The conspiracy theory is not news, and there is not a shred of evidence to support it at this time. But the fact that people are

179

willing to believe it is news and must be recorded as such.

There may be a stronger strain of paranoia in Italian culture than in American—not without reason, given the tragic past and the tragic present of this battered nation. Just now there is some reason to believe that Aldo Moro's life could have been spared; there is some evidence—not much—that enemies in his own political party were not eager to save him (the Moro family has publicly resigned from the party). There is also some hint that he may have been held for a time in a foreign embassy. None of this is likely, but none of it is impossible either, especially in Italy.

So both Italian culture and the current crisis in Italian political life incline people here to take conspiratorial scenarios even more seriously than do Americans, and heavens knows we take them seriously enough.

The Vatican's refusal to perform an autopsy on the grounds that it is at least implicitly excluded by the regulations Pope Paul established concerning the death of a pope has fed the hunger for sinister plots. Italians do not believe the Vatican; some reporters openly laughed at the announcement that the pope died reading *The Imitation of Christ*. Sure enough, his secretary has said that he was reading personal papers. I was taken in by the *Imitation of Christ* report, maybe because I'm a naive American.

But an autopsy wouldn't be accepted either, unless it was performed by some objective outside agency; and even then those who need conspiratorial explanations would still not believe the evidence. The Vatican, in other words, has handled the suspicions badly, but even if it had handled them skillfully, the plot theories would still flourish. The Warren Commission did a bad job investigating President Kennedy's death, but even a superb and thorough inquiry would not have satisfied the unbelievers. For all the bungling done by the Warren Commission, the publicity-hunting House committee has stretched credibility to the breaking point in order to muster a faint challenge of the commission's basic explanations.

Monday Night, 11:15, October 2

Still raining, indeed, it's pouring again. It has been raining for forty-eight hours straight. The poor church. Crowds at one papal wake wiped out by the *ferragosto* and crowds at another wiped out by the autumn rains. I suppose the cardinals will say it's the work of the Holy Spirit.

The Curia is keeping up through its contacts in the press a campaign of criticism of John Paul—very tasteless—for his supposed inability to deal with the problems of the church. It is stupid, considering that he only had a month to demonstrate whether he could or could not do the job. It is self-defeating, too, because every cardinal who gets off the plane talks about the need to have somebody like Pope John Paul. Still, maybe the curialists will have an impact of some sort, since what they say does get into the press here. Some of the Hispanics, particularly the archbishop of Barcelona, Narciso Jubany Arnau, are talking about the possibility of a non-Italian. He mentioned Aloisio Lorscheider. Unfortunately, and perhaps disastrously, the newspapers today say that Lorscheider has apparently had some kind of heart attack and won't be here until the conclave itself. It's a tremendous blow to everyone. However, it does appear that Cardinal John Wright is out of the hospital and will be here.

Tuesday, October 3

The poison theory continues to gain credence here in Rome. Jordan Bonfante tells me that there are people by the bier complaining that their pope was killed by the Curia. They pass by the body and scream out, "Who did this to you, who did this to you?" *Corriere della Sera*, the most responsible of the Italian newspapers, has called for an autopsy. The Vatican has dug in its heels and says there will be no autopsy, that there is no need for one. Given the suspicions here, the paranoia that is part of Italian society, and the state of Vatican finances, there may be grounds for suspicion. Obviously, there is only one chance in ten billion that the pope was murdered, but if his health was perfect a week ago, which one doubts (you can't believe anything these people say), then how come he died so quickly? The question is legitimate.

Wednesday, October 4

Yet more rain. Four straight days. They are forging ahead with their plans for having a funeral mass outdoors regardless of the rain. That might be trust in God, or it might be tempting God; but in any case that's what they propose to do. More power to them. The real problem seems to be that if they have it inside St. Peter's, people simply won't be able to see what's going on.

There was apparently some sort of medical examination of Pope John Paul's body. Last night the Italian newspapers were all headlining it. However, according to Jim Roache, it was merely a kind of embalming examination and nothing else. The Vatican continues to insist there is no need for an autopsy. The suspicion continues to be widespread, not only here, but, I gather from Jim Andrews in the States, all over the world, that the pope was murdered. The problem is that you can't believe the so-and-so's. I mean, they were telling us the pope died reading *The Imitation of Christ*. I figured they wouldn't lie about that. Now it turns out from Don Diego Lorenzi, the pope's secretary, that he was reading some papers of his own, preparing a Sunday homily. So instead of dying reading a book, he died preparing a catechetical talk. If they'll lie about little things, they'll lie about big things; there's no reason to trust anything they say.

The word today is that Cardinal Lorscheider will not be at the conclave. That will be an enormous loss. I have a hunch that the church is tumbling into a new era, that what Roache calls "the image factor" created by John Paul's short pastorate may dissolve questions of age, nationality, and previous experience. It will be a total victory for those of us who talked about the image of the papacy before the last conclave—though we're not likely to get much credit for it.

The Italian satirical magazine *Male* has an horrendously tasteless but very telling edition suggesting that Benelli poisoned the pope. It's absurd and funny in a black humor sort of way, but it shows what's going on here.

St. Peter's has a peculiar, grim festivity about it in the early afternoon. People in dark suits and ties are now streaming in for the mass. The security precautions are enormous. There will be more people here at this funeral than at the last one. It is gray and drizzly with occasional downpours—multicolored umbrellas going up now from the crowd, the sky darkening throughout the mass. Somehow, it is much grimmer, much more melancholy, but also much more real than the August funeral. The grief here today is being forced by no one, except possibly some of the curial cardinals.

To tell you the truth I couldn't stay for the whole funeral. But I sorrow in my own way, and I'm afraid that the splendidly choreo-graphed liturgy, even with intermittent rain showers adding to the grimness, just doesn't even begin to get at the depths of emotional frustration and loss that I feel.

Pope John Paul began his administration with the support of much of the Third World, the more progressive Northern Euro-peans, and some of the moderate Italians, as well as the belated, if enthusiastic, endorsement of those who were too out of it to know for whom to vote. But he was also given a tough warning from the traditionalists, especially from those members of the Roman Curia who had been more or less on the shelf during the time of Paul VI.

What are the chances of such a scenario happening again? The best predictions here are that such chances are very slim indeed. The coalition leaders will have to find a cardinal whose life experience has been pastoral, who is committed to power-sharing in the church (to please the progressives), who is cautious on doctrine (to reassure the moderate traditionalists), and who dem-onstrates the sort of transparent goodness that will reassure the uncertain and leaderless center. They will also have to satisfy a world which had fallen in love with John Paul and which will judge his successor by the brief but brilliant performance of the man with the big grin and the unruly skullcap. There was something in the Luciani victory for absolutely everyone—except the most intransi-gent.

The leadership of the coalition—Cardinal Giovanni Benelli, Cardinal Leo Suenens, Cardinal Paulo Evaristo Arns, Cardinal Johannes Willebrands, Cardinal Aloisio Lorscheider, Cardinal Francois Marty—will be hard put to duplicate such a victory. Their coalition could easily splinter and come apart—and then anything could happen. This time it may not be a religious experience for anyone.

Insiders here are beginning to speculate that the only man who can hold together the "Luciani coalition" is the man who created it, Florence's energetic, forceful Giovanni Benelli. They do not necessarily predict that Benelli will be pope; rather, they point out that there were three constituencies in the original Luciani coalition: Northern Europeans, including Benelli's good friend Leo Suenens of Belgium; moderate Italians, who look on Benelli as their leader; and the "Brazilian connection"—a Third World faction led by Brazilian Cardinals Arns and Lorscheider, whose link with Benelli is through Suenens. With sufficient guarantees, it is suggested, both the Brazilian and the Low Countries connections (the latter represented by Suenens and Holland's Willebrands) might find Benelli preferable to any other available Italian.

Benelli would have to give "assurances" that he would support a vastly expanded role for the Synod of Bishops and would accept a limited term as pope (perhaps ten years); while he might find such restrictions galling, Benelli, who can be imperious when pragmatism requires it and charming when pragmatism demands it, might go along, especially if there is no other candidate around whom his tenuous coalition might rally. He is already acting like a candidate. "We must find a young, vigorous, and heroic pope," he said yesterday. In an obvious appeal to progressives, he went on to say that the church must move ahead with the reform of the Vatican Council, "not only in the liturgical field, but in every aspect of the church's relationship with the world," adding that the church must prepare itself to face the "problems of the third millennium" and must, in particular, address itself to the opportunities of ecumenism.

A small, bald man of great personal intensity, Benelli is in many ways the exact opposite of his friend, the late pope. Most of his life he has been a diplomat (in such places as Ireland, France, Brazil, Spain, and Senegal). Luciani had the style of a simple parish priest; Benelli is very much the tough administrator and adroit political operator. Luciani was a man of transparent personal holiness; Benelli seems to many observers to use his considerable personal charm as a political tool. Luciani was widely read and theologically cultivated; while unquestionably intelligent and perceptive, Benelli is short on intellectual sophistication. Everyone trusted Luciani, while Benelli is a man with many enemies, including most of the curial cardinals (even though he is a product of the Curia).

But though he has many enemies, Benelli is also a man with many friends. Others respect him, even if they are not personally close to him. "He is a man you can fight with, shout at, make him change his mind," one American prelate told me. "That's more than you can say for a lot of them."

He has been accused of being a power-hungry tyrant during Paul VI's years, so offending other curial officials that he ultimately had to be shipped off with a red hat to Florence. An English newspaper carried an article blaming him for most of the "conservative" decisions of Pope Paul's years. He was accused of setting up a super-Curia under his own office that was far more dangerous than the other Curia because it was efficient and worked an eight- or ten- or even twelve-hour day (no siestas for Benelli's staff was the Vatican joke). If one favored a conspiracy theory of the Pauline years and looked for an evil genius, Benelli was the perfect target. An H. R. Haldeman in the Vatican.

There are a number of progressives in Rome and elsewhere who take a different view. Benelli did not seek his power but was forced into a vacuum created by the easygoing Cardinal Villot (his nominal superior when Benelli was in Rome and a man who will certainly not vote for him). It was his job to get done the things Pope Paul wanted done. Without the vigor and, indeed, the ruthlessness of Benelli's office, Pope Paul, they say, would have been a virtual prisoner of curial inertia. Men who work in the ecumenical and social justice areas insist that he protected them from repression by curial Neanderthals. His shock at the confusion in American Catholicism eight years ago brought an end to the curial conspiracy to appoint mediocre men to American bishoprics in order to punish the United States for the vigorous part the Americans played at the Second Vatican Council. Even if his support for ecumenism and collegiality is pragmatic, they say, who cares about motives so long as the support is there. Benelli knows how to read the signs of the times better than most. He knows the days of the monarchical papacy are over. Consultation, power-sharing, openness to new ideas, a pastoral style, simplicity of manner, and support for talent are now pragmatic necessities. If you can't have a smiling saint, they conclude, you find the next best thing in an open-minded pragmatist who can smile as well as anyone if need be.

The Benelli critics respond that a flexible, collegial, humble Papa Benelli would be not merely a leopard changing its spots, but a leopard without spots; and, make no mistake about it, they say, Benelli is a dangerous leopard.

However, he would certainly shake up the central structure of the church, which almost everyone agrees needs a good shaking. In any case, he is now a serious candidate in his own right, not merely the "advance man" for an old friend. If he cannot be the "young,

vigorous, dynamic pope" of his own job description, he will probably have even more to say about who the new pope is than he did
the last time.

No one today denies the wisdom of that choice. It took a man
of no little ability to engineer the election of an unknown on the
first day. Few question Giovanni Benelli's ability; but a simple
pastor of the countryside he is not. Paradoxically, by presiding over
the emergence of the magic Luciani image, he may have damaged,
even destroyed, his own chances of becoming the next pope.

Friday, October 6

The tragic death of the "pope of smiles," as everyone here
called him, has raised again the question of medical care of a pope.
Why not physical exams for candidates? Why burden with major
responsibility a man who is at an age when he would be retired by
most corporations? Both China and Russia may be gerontocracies,
but where is the rule that Catholicism must also be?

The only answers you can give to the health-care questions are
"tradition" and "papal dignity." These infuriate the medical profes-
sion. Maybe there was a time when a pope was safer in his own
apartment than in a disease-ridden hospital, but if dignity means
anything it means the best health care. The dignity and the importance of the office should make accurate information about the state
of a candidate's health absolutely essential.

When Cardinal Gregory Agagianian, a Russian-born Armenian who spent most of his life in Rome, was a serious candidate for
the papacy in 1958, he requested an immediate physical checkup
and informed an American reporter that he would be a bad choice
for the papacy because of the findings of his doctor. He was a
leading candidate in several early ballots and might well have been
elected instead of Roncalli (Pope John XXIII) if it had not been for
his resolute integrity about his own health status. As it was, he
outlived Pope John by several years.

Some of the cardinals will doubtless say that questions of
health must be left to the Holy Spirit, dismissing the importance of
modern medical science. No detailed data on the health of the
papabili will be available to the cardinals when they begin their
work in this conclave. Instead of dealing with the health-and-age
issue directly, they will be forced to rely, as they do in so many

other things, on rumor and hearsay. The whispering campaigns against many candidates last time hinted of dark things about their health.

About the only concrete result of the sudden death of Pope John Paul will be more vicious and more detailed whispering campaigns. "Cardinal So-and-so looks tired, don't you think? . . . No, it is merely jet fatigue . . . So pale, poor man . . . So much like poor Luciani . . . Did you know that he had to go to the mountains for six weeks last year?"

Health and age will be on the cardinals' minds, of course, but they won't know quite what to do about the problems. "Anyone who wants the job," said a cynical American curialist, "had better buy himself a sunlamp."

Even though he thought his chances of being pope were minimal and he had absolutely no desire to be elected pope, Karol Wojtyla still had an electrocardiogram before he returned for the October funeral and conclave.

Saturday, October 7

The cardinals are taking the weekend off, many of them going up to Turin to look at the sacred shroud there; others are retiring into the hillsides around the city to various shrines and villas and hideaways where there may be some politicking going on, though I suspect much of it in this conclave is being done on the telephone. It is a good opportunity to talk about the National Opinion Research Center (NORC) computer models which we have used to simulate the conclave. These models were commissioned by Universal Press Syndicate for my Rome coverage. The models weren't ready last summer when Pope Paul VI died, but Christian Jacobsen, the research assistant in charge, forged full steam ahead with the model construction and produced a list of highly rated candidates just as the election of John Paul was announced. Interestingly enough, among those who were considered to be likely candidates for the papacy at that time, Albino Luciani was ranked third, after Cardinal Antonio Poma, who was presumably excluded on grounds of health, and Cardinal Sergio Pignedoli, whose curial background was counted against him by the non-Italian voters. Thus, the computer simulation in August was remarkably successful in that few, if any, human Vaticanologists were willing to rank Albino Luciani so high.

All of those of us who were involved in it as social scientists would insist that our simulation is an approximation, a tool for understanding rather than a flat prediction. It is based on an estimation of the electors' positions on fourteen issues facing the church and of their relative influence on one another. It does not take into account the personality factor, age, importance of nationality in an elector, health, or possible anger at the Curia. In all our attempts to model the conclave, we predicted not a single winner, but a range of possible winners.

First of all, data were collected on each of the cardinal electors from people in a position to know their attitudes and behaviors on a questionnaire.[1]

In addition, a number of experts on the College of Cardinals rated each of the cardinals on a scale of relative influence from one to five, five indicating a highly influential cardinal and one a cardinal with relatively little influence on others. The cardinals who were rated five were: Giovanni Benelli, Pericle Felici, and Aloisio Lorscheider. Those who scored four were: Evaristo Arns, Vicente Enrique y Tarancón, Giuseppe Siri, and Sebastiano Baggio. The rating of three was assigned to Joseph Cordeiro, Bernardin Gantin, Franz Koenig, Sergio Pignedoli, Jaime Sin, Leo Suenens, Hyacinthe Thiandoum, and Johannes Willebrands.

Using a complex decision-making model developed by NORC's James Coleman, a weighted profile which calculated the attitudes and behaviors which would be most typical of the college was constructed from the data. Each of the cardinals was then assigned a score based on his deviation from that profile, a score on a scale running from zero to two hundred.

Like all computer simulations, the NORC model is an over-simplified version of reality. It does not have nearly the amount of input information Professor Coleman uses in his application of the model to the decisions of political groups such as legislatures or national assemblies. Nevertheless, its success in the August conclave seemed to indicate that we should take another look for the October conclave. Of the men listed as candidates in the October conclave, the following was the rank order of "profile deviation" among the top candidates: Corrado Ursi, Salvatore Pappalardo, Johannes Willebrands, Sebastiano Baggio, George Basil Hume,

Michele Pellegrino, Eduardo Pironio, Franz Koenig, Ugo Poletti, Pericle Felici, Paolo Bertoli, Giovanni Benelli.

The first six candidates are all closely bunched, and none of them could be described, strictly speaking, as "favored."

The closest profile of all to Luciani's, differing from his only on two points in a score of two hundred, was a cardinal who was not considered a candidate at the time of the computer simulation, Karol Wojtyla of Cracow. Once again, the computer Vaticanologists were smarter than the human ones. "Are you looking for that cardinal who is most similar to Luciani?" the computer said to us. "Well, it's Wojtyla of Cracow." And our human response was, "Sure, but he's not a candidate."

In order to more accurately simulate the process of a conclave, a method called "cluster analysis" was used to permit coalitions of cardinals with similar values to emerge. The critical stage in the clustering process produced five distinct groups, the largest being a curial group made up of such electors, for example, as Giuseppe Siri, Giuseppe Sensi, Francesco Carpino, Pericle Felici, Ermenegildo Florit, Silvio Oddi, Pietro Palazzini, and Mario Ciappi. The other four groups included: two moderate groups, one made up of men like Cardinals John Dearden, Paul Léger, Timothy Manning, and Narciso Jubany Arnau, and the other made up of such men as James Freeman, Maurice Roy, Pio Taofinu'u, and Thomas Cooray; and two progressive groups, one counting in its number the Northern Europeans, such as Basil Hume, Franz Koenig, Bernard Alfrink, and François Marty, and the other more Latin and Third World members, Aloisio Lorscheider, Maurice Otunga, Vicente Enrique y Tarancón, and Jaime Sin.

As the simulated conclave continues, the four non-curial groups cluster with one another and the curial group acquires no more allies; when finally the arranging of the cardinals is finished (and it must be stressed that this is entirely an empirical, machine-executed process, based on no a priori assumptions about how the college ought to divide up), it appears there are two coalitions, a curial one-third and a non-curial two-thirds. Thus, the cluster analysis produces a division of the college of cardinals not unlike the one which informed sources say was working in the August conclave and confirms that there is a strong tendency among the cardinals who are outsiders to organize themselves in a coalition sharply distinct from the curial insiders.

There are two observations that are important to make about the cluster analysis. First of all, the majority coalition falls a couple of votes short of the necessary two-thirds-plus-one majority. Given some measurement error, some unpredictability, and some personal loyalties and rivalries, it seems safe to say the majority coalition doesn't quite have what it takes to force its will on the rest of the cardinals. However, the curial block and its allies have little chance to elect a pope of their own, though they are in a position to have a disproportionate say as to who the compromise candidate will be.

Second, when one looks at the cardinals appointed in the last two consistories, one sees that they accurately reflect the existing division of the sacred college. Two-thirds of them fall into the majority coalition, one-third into the curial minority; thus, Pope Paul really did not change the balance of power in the college when he named his last two groups of cardinals, as so many people here contend that he did. Rather, he merely preserved the existing balance of power despite tremendous pressure from the curial group to shift the weight of power back in their direction. Whether Pope Paul realized how precise and finely drawn was the division between the minority and the majority in the group that would elect his successor no one knows. Nonetheless, he left the impress of his own personality very firmly on the College of Cardinals. It is split in such a way that decisive action remains very difficult.

The computer model also enables us to understand the curial weakness in the August conclave. Many of us thought that because it more or less controlled the central structure of the church, the curial faction would be able to win over disorganized and perhaps uninformed foreign cardinals. However, the foreign cardinals "clustered" with one another in reality as well as in the computer model. It would appear, then, that they did perceive quite clearly the differences between themselves and the more conservative wing of the college. The predictions by my Roman sources that they would be co-opted by the Curia assumed that their behavior would not be rational. The prediction made by the NORC model assumed that their behavior would be rational. The outcome of the August conclave confirmed the latter prediction.

The big question now for the October conclave is whether the

Luciani coalition will be able to hold together, and whether it will be able to find a candidate sufficiently acceptable to some of the more moderate members of the conservative minority to win five or ten votes from them.

On the one hand, it might be argued that the leaders of the majority coalition have now had experience at their work and ought to find it somewhat easier to keep their amorphous alliance functioning in a second conclave despite the high-pressure tactics of the now-aroused Curia. On the other hand, leaders are likely to be hard-pressed to find so easily a candidate around whom their own coalition can coalesce and to whom enough members of the other coalition might be attracted to assure victory.

I must confess that I flew back to NORC after John Paul's funeral to work on the computer models. I didn't accept the computer's analysis of Wojtyla's chances. I returned to Rome after a few days and acted like a journalist instead of a sociologist.

Scene II

Today, Benelli's secretary had lunch at the Church of St. Stanislaus, on the "Street of the Covered Shops" where it crosses a romantic curving alley called the Via dei Polacchi just off the Piazza Venezia, with Cardinal Wojtyla, Bishop Andre Deskur, Wojtyla's close personal friend, and Bishop Rubin, the Polish bishop who is the secretary general for the Synod of Bishops.[1] It is not known what transpired at this meeting, though there is some speculation that the message from Benelli to Wojtyla was that the former would be prepared to throw his support to the latter as a "compromise" non-Italian. Wojtyla did not at this time consider himself a serious candidate, and if such a discreet commitment was made, he probably responded by saying that he was grateful for the compliment but hardly expected it to be necessary for Cardinal Benelli to honor such a commitment. Wojtyla, for his part, however, promised that he would support Benelli.

Tuesday, October 10

The Giuseppe Siri forces are still pushing their man very strongly. It seems to me to be utterly senseless and futile behavior because all the foreign cardinals giving interviews at the airport have absolutely insisted on the need for a man who will appeal to the world the way John Paul did. It would appear that the Curia is saying, "Well, look, isn't our man a pastor? He's always been, ever since he was made a cardinal, twenty-four years ago." There's also a lot of talk about Archbishop Ballestrero of Turin, whom a number of people had the chance to meet when they went up to the Holy Shroud Festival over the weekend. The Italians are really running scared this time, and that's why Ballestrero is being trotted out as a last-ditch Italian compromise, for apparently they don't want Pappalardo or Ursi. Having destroyed Pignedoli and Baggio the last time, the curialists are in a real bind, which may be why they are standing by Siri. They also may feel that they gave up on him too soon the last time around. Frantisek Tomasek, the Czech archbishop, has seriously raised the possibility of a non-Italian. So has Arns. It looks to me that just as the Curia people may be making a bigger play for Siri this time, so the non-curialists are digging in, at least for negotiating purposes, for a non-Italian.

Even in retrospect, it is difficult to understand the extraordinary phenomenon of the Siri candidacy in the week before the October conclave. John Paul II's "inauguration" talk to the cardinals (see Appendix), like that of his predecessor, was prepared for him by staff members of the Secretariat of State, based on conversations of the cardinals during the "congregations" which led up to the second conclave, and, therefore, can be taken to be an objective summary of the morning public deliberations of the cardinals. The emphasis on the Second Vatican Council seems to have been even stronger in the October congregations than in the August congregations. Therefore, it seems inconceivable, on the basis of their public pronouncements at the congregations, that the cardinals could have been thought to be preparing to elect the man who resisted the reforms of the Council during the years it was in session and who would say that he did not know what the collegiality of bishops meant. Nonetheless, Siri dominated public discussion in the week before the October conclave. There was undoubtedly a concerted and well-orchestrated offensive on his behalf in the Italian press, probably engineered by those who knew who the curial sources were that the Italian Vatican reporters would call for gossip. It was a brilliantly executed plan aimed principally at the uncertain "center," which had jumped so quickly on the Luciani bandwagon in the August conclave. Yet the uninformed and unaligned cardinals (such as many of the Americans) were interested only in voting for the winner, and if they carefully read the Italian press to find out what was going on (and most of them did), then the psychological warfare on Siri's behalf might have tipped things in his direction. It is difficult to believe, however, that the most sophisticated members of the Siri bloc really believed that they could win with the seventy-two-year-old archbishop of Genoa. Perhaps they were only seeking a dramatic and powerful showing on the first ballot to hide the numerical weakness of their own position, but to some Siri supporters, perhaps more than half of them, the kamikaze strategy was not a ploy. They stuck to the archbishop of Genoa to the bitter end, as they had done in

*the August conclave, and as their predecessors had done in the
1963 conclave.*

*The coalition leaders chose not to respond in public, a wise
decision, since they did not have access to the media through
carefully controlled "sources" as did the conservative minority.
Ultimately, press manipulation would backfire on the Siri supporters. We will never know whether if Siri had not given his interview
to* Gazzetta del Popolo *he would have come any closer either to
victory or to dictating the name of the compromise candidate.*

Thursday, October 12

The French cardinals are indicating that they are aware of the
world image problem, that they know they have to come up with
somebody who'll have the popular appeal of John Paul, and that
they are taking their responsibilities very seriously indeed. I was
impressed. I was not impressed with the comment of John
Dearden, quoted in one of the American papers, that he knew of no
caucusing that had taken place the last time around, and that the
only thing that had happened was that the cardinals had all gone in
to the conclave and very quickly worked toward consensus.

I bumped into an American archbishop and quoted Dearden.
He said, "What the hell's the matter with John? He knows better
than that. What does he think happens when they go out to dinner
or talk to each other on the telephone?"

I haven't seen Adolpho yet, but I was talking to Tony Blake a
few minutes ago; he said Adolpho had been on the phone to him
and that Adolpho was concerned about the Siri bandwagon. It
would appear that Cardinal Confalonieri, who because of his age
has got all kinds of influence (people don't imagine that he might be
senile, but just think he's wise), has been pushing for a good
administrator and a strong anti-Communist—for Siri.

Thursday Afternoon

At the end of the day, I managed to get a detailed description
of the strategy of the Northern European cardinals, at least as that
strategy is perceived by Cardinal Leo Suenens. I must note here
that Suenens is *not* my direct source.

First of all, they do not take seriously the Siri boom; they think it's a smokescreen the Curia is using to scare people, and they expect the curial people to come back with a compromise candidate, someone like Felici—the old curial game. The coalition leaders say they won't play that game; that they will block Felici every bit as much as they blocked Siri. They will try on the first day to find a compromise Italian candidate on whom the Italians can agree and whom the foreigners can accept (another Luciani). If, in the first day and a half, there are no Italians to fill the bill, then they will turn to foreigners: George Basil Hume or Johannes Willebrands, or possibly Bernardin Gantin, will become the candidates. Suenens is quoted as saying that he thinks they will be out by the end of the second day, or, if there is some delay in finding an acceptable foreigner, perhaps by the morning of the third day. One has the impression that these people really do not expect to find a compromise Italian and, hence, do indeed expect to elect a foreigner. I may be reading that into them and my contact is indirect, but still, I would be willing to bet that close to half of the cardinals right this minute are ready to vote for a non-Italian.

There had been a meeting a day or two before of the coalition leaders. Suenens, Jubany Arnau, Alfrink, Koenig, Arns, Lorscheider (he made it to Rome), and perhaps Tarancón, Marty, and Willebrands, as well as some others, were present at the meeting. The strategy of the "Italian day" followed by the "day of the foreigner" emerged at this meeting. Some of the leaders of the coalition felt strongly that on the first day Benelli ought to be supported, then, if he did not receive enough votes (even his supporters feared that he would not do so), an attempt should be made to find a Luciani-like Italian compromise, perhaps Poletti, the cardinal vicar of Rome. There was stronger commitment to the Italian compromise among some leaders of the coalition than among others.

Everyone agreed that it was strategically correct, but some, particularly the Brazilians, saw no reason why the long-delayed shattering of the Italian hold on the papacy should not occur in this conclave. These men, in fact, were fully prepared to give the Italians the choice of Benelli or a foreigner. The names of various foreigners were discussed. No specific commitment was made to back any one of them, though some of the coalition leaders argued in favor of Johannes Willebrands as a man who knew the Curia

195

well, had pastoral experience, and had more practice in ecumenism than any other cardinal. But a number of other names were discussed as "acceptable" candidates. The name of Karol Wojtyla was discussed, perhaps at Koenig's suggestion. There was no strong objection to him and a good deal of positive comment. It was noted that John Krol of Philadelphia, an American Pole, might be expected to bring virtually all of the American votes, some of them out of the Siri camp, to the support of Wojtyla; the Germans were already solidly behind him, giving him a nucleus of ten to fifteen "free" votes. Furthermore, no one could deny either the strength of Wojtyla's personality or his realism on Marxism, the characteristics that would make him attractive to some of the Italian curialists and their allies. Other candidates were also mentioned: Pironio, Hume, Gantin, Cordeiro. But no definite decisions were made on any of them.

The coalition leaders, in other words, were sufficiently confident of their position and their communication network to develop a loose and flexible strategy. Indeed, one so flexible that if those of us watching from the outside realized what it was, we would have been terrified. In retrospect, the confidence of the coalition leaders was barely justified.

A few of them left the meeting convinced that Wojtyla would be pope. Hume did not speak Italian well enough, Gantin lacked intellectual depth, Pironio didn't have the administrative skills, Cordeiro, the experience. Koenig, Jubany Arnau, Tarancón and Suenens were moderately certain that Wojtyla would be elected. (Tarancón and Jubany Arnau had arrived in Rome with Wojtyla's books in their luggage.)

The role of the German cardinals in supporting Wojtyla was critical, not because, as the Italian press hinted before the conclave, the Germans were able to swing Third World votes from the countries supported by their money, but because they were a solid base of five or six votes that were always in the archbishop of Cracow's camp. Such votes would be of decisive importance when it came to gaining support for the tradition-shattering election of a non-Italian. Those who favored ending the tradition knew that at the critical time they would need every last vote—until the trend was securely established, when there would be a bandwagon effect.

The German strength was based on the fact that others knew that Wojtyla and Wojtyla alone was the non-Italian they would accept. In effect the Germans had the power to designate which of the non-Italian possibilities became a probability.

That the Germans, who were less numerous than the North Americans, were able to exercise such influence while the Americans just went along with the rolling bandwagon is not evidence of German conspiracy but of American ineptitude.

The reasons for the support of the Germans were mixed. All of them were profoundly impressed with the prince archbishop's powers of reconciliation, brilliantly displayed when he asked the German church to forgive the Polish church for whatever offenses it had committed at a meeting of the two hierarchies earlier in the year. The ruthless and reactionary Hoeffner of Cologne admired Karol Wojtyla's toughness; Ratzinger, made even more neurotic than usual by his encounter with "Marxist liberation theologians" just before the conclave, was impressed by his sophisticated tenacity in face of the Communist government in Poland; Koenig, Austrian but German-speaking, had enormous respect for Wojtyla's intelligence and charm as well as his political pragmatism. Obviously some of the Germans supported the archbishop of Cracow for reasons different from those which motivated men like Lorscheider and Pironio. As in every coalition some participants were more likely than others to be disappointed by their favorite in the months and years after his election.

Friday Morning, October 13

Friday the thirteenth may turn out to be a very unlucky day for Giuseppe Siri.

The morning Italian papers are down on the Siri candidacy, hinting that it might finally have been nipped in the bud. A priest for the diocese of Rome warned that it would tear the church apart and that Catholicism as an institution would appear to the whole world as unreformable. One of the things that Siri is supposed to have said is that he does not believe that women should wear trousers because that makes them forget their natural function. How a man like that could possibly be seriously considered, particularly after John Paul, simply staggers the imagination. Well, we shall see what happens.

The Italian papers are also saying that the secretaries to the cardinals are remarking that Benelli has it in the bag. At the present time, compared to Siri, Benelli looks good. He may be playing a waiting game, encouraging somewhat the Siri candidacy so that he can move in and save the day.

An extraordinary mood of pessimism seems to have come upon the cardinals, perhaps induced by jet fatigue, perhaps caused by the tragedy of John Paul's death, perhaps exacerbated by the charges that John Paul was murdered, and certainly fed by the poisoning environment of the Roman Curia. They see atheism, agnosticism, Communism on all sides; they see the church threatened with dire calamities.

The English journalists are going wild over the candidacy of Hume. Some of the stories seem to suggest that he is as good as elected. I'm afraid that this is self-deception, though doubtless we would be guilty of it too if there were a strong American candidate.

There is a serious attempt going on at the last minute to find a candidate like Luciani who is acceptable to all. There's a good reason for this. No matter how you look at it, neither one of the two main wings has the two-thirds votes. Basically, you can count on thirty-six or thirty-seven people, curialists or curialist creatures, to vote against any foreigner, and you can also count on, minimally, forty-six votes to block any curialist; there are about twenty-five votes that you really couldn't put in either camp and that would probably split, say, down the middle, when push came to shove.

So, the maximum one could see for the non-curialists would be sixty-two to sixty-five votes and the maximum for the curialists between about forty-five and fifty votes, enough to block each other but not enough for either to elect its own candidate. The anti-curialists are bigger but less well-organized, though they may be, despite the absence of newspaper publicity, more organized than they appear. Under those circumstances, then, it would seem that the seventy-six-year-old bishop of Milan, Cardinal Giovanni Colombo, is the likely winner.

If that happens, the world reaction is going to be outrage. Angered at the loss of John Paul, who was a symbol of hope, the world would get a man eleven years older and with no more experience than John Paul had. If something like that happens, it will be clear that the electors could not agree and that they settled for a temporary pope who might broaden the base of the papal election or increase the number of cardinals or something of that sort (and give Benelli seven more years to develop pastoral experience). Presumably, if Benelli and his crowd count up the votes and see they haven't got enough, then they'll go the Colombo route. But that would be an insult to the world, however charming an old man Colombo is.

In May, 1938, the prince-archbishop of Cracow, Cardinal Adam Sapieha, came to the small city of Wadowice, thirty miles from Cracow.[2] An eighteen-year-old boy, the brightest in the school, Karol Wojtyla, was chosen to greet the bishop. After the greeting, the archbishop asked what the boy planned to do. The reply was that he was going to the Jagiellonian University in Cracow to study Polish literature. A pity, the archbishop said to the head of the school, we could do with someone like that in the church.

His mother (Emilia Kaczorowski) and father had moved to Wadowice from their original home, a small village in the Carpathian mountains on the border of Czechoslovakia, after World War I. His father was a petty officer in the army of the Austrian Empire and served briefly in the army of the newly independent Poland. In the 1920s and 1930s, however, there was little employment for professional soldiers, and the Wojtyla family eked out a living from his father's pension as a reservist.

Karol was born in 1920. By 1930, his mother and older brother were dead (the latter, a physician, died of scarlet fever he caught from a patient). Alone with his tough-minded, pious, and intelligent father, Karol already knew loneliness and privation. The dimensions of his personality that most of his childhood friends remember were his wit, his athletic ability (goalie on the school soccer team), his popularity with other students, boys and girls, and his commitment to literature and the theater. While still in secondary school, he was the producer and chief actor in a school troupe that toured the region doing Shakespeare and modern Polish plays.

There was another side of his personality. He went to church every morning, did not drink or smoke, was head of the religious society at his school, and occasionally gave hints of a thoughtful, reflective side to his personality. Still, no one remembered him as especially pious, and only a few of his friends were not astonished to discover after the war that he was a priest. In 1938 he entered the Jagiellonian in Cracow, intending to study philology.

Author James Michener interviewed Wojtyla in July in the cardinal's garden in Cracow for the PBS series James Michener's World. *As Michener was leaving after one of the conversations, the prince-archbishop of Cracow said, "Now, if this goes well, I will expect a call from Hollywood . . ."; and taking Michener by the arm, he added, "You know, Mr. Michener, I trained for the stage as a young man. I was going to be an actor."*

The archbishop of Cracow has traditionally been called the prince-archbishop because in former times he was not only the religious but also the civil ruler of the city. Sapieha was a royal prince in his own right; hence, doubly a prince.

Wojtyla's adolescence is shrouded in obscurity by the dark, deadly clouds of World War II. His years at the university had only begun when the Polish republic was snuffed out again after but two decades of independent existence. It was invaded from the west by the Nazis, stabbed in the back from the east by the Russians. The university was closed and the Rhapsody Theater was abolished. Wojtyla's father and then his other brother died. The young man went to work, first of all in a mine in Zakozowek and then in the Solvey chemical factory near Cracow to escape deportation to a slave labor camp. He became active in the cultural and political underground, performing in the suppressed Rhapsody Theater, smuggling Jewish families out of the ghettos, finding them new identities and hiding places. He was a very busy young man, working in the factory by day, performing in the theater, participating in the underground, and from 1942 on, also studying for the priesthood by night in the palace of the prince-archbishop, Cardinal Sapieha (Andre Deskur's uncle; Bishop Deskur is a close friend of Wojtyla).

The details of those years are little known. They were troubled, dangerous times about which few people even today are willing to speak. But Wojtyla was on the Nazis' wanted list, had several narrow escapes from the Gestapo, and finally ended up hiding in the prince-archbishop's palace in 1944, when the archbishop became convinced that the peril to the young man's life was too great to permit him to remain on the streets of Cracow. He began to study for the priesthood after reading the sixteenth-century Carmelite mystic, St. John of the Cross and, according to one story, applied for the Carmelites but was rejected because of his interest in the theater, which was thought to indicate a lack of "seriousness." The origins of his priestly vocation amid the dangers, sufferings, and privations of Poland's long twilight between 1939 and 1945 are not on the public record and are perhaps known only to Karol Wojtyla himself. In any event, the year after the final liberation (1946), he was ordained and sent to Rome for doctoral studies in philosophy at the two Dominican orders' Angelicum University (his doctoral dissertation at the Angelicum was on St. John of the Cross).

It was during those twilight years, according to some rumors, that he was married and lost his wife to Nazi killers shortly afterwards. The story is false. If it has any basis in fact at all, it may be in that it's not at all unusual for young people in their teens or early twenties to have brief, if intense, friendships, and such friendships are even more likely to occur when death is a danger every day. Many of the young people the young Wojtyla knew died in the horrible turmoil that swept back and forth across southern Poland. It is not impossible that there could have been one special friend whom he might have married but who was killed in the war. But quite properly, no one in Cracow speaks of such things, because they are a part of a person's private, instead of his public, biography. The facts of the matter are that he did not marry and that, by 1942, he was already in the underground seminary in Cardinal Sapieha's house.

Friday Afternoon

My interview with Adolpho was grim. He admits he's under the heavy weight of fear and that this may cause him to exaggerate the chances of the people he doesn't want. But he thinks Siri may very well win it, and that, if he does, the last twenty years of our lives as Catholics will be canceled out. He says that it's astonishing how utterly and completely the atmosphere has been changed; the emphasis is now on strong discipline and firm doctrine, and not much on pastorality. A lot of people are saying that Luciani was not a good pope, that he wasn't able to run the church.

Adolpho was very glad to hear my report about Suenens because he believes Suenens is a smart politician and that if he has a strategy it might work. "Leo Suenens may have become a charismatic," said Adolpho, "but he can still count."[3]

The coalition absolutely needs thirty-six votes to block Siri. Adolpho's fear is the huge amorphous middle that you can't count on; if it looks like somebody is going to win, those of the middle will sweep along after him. One cannot imagine people like Arns, Alfrink, Willebrands, and Suenens being reduced to such a state that they can't command thirty-five or thirty-six votes, but they may finally end up that way.

It dawned on me some time after I left Adolpho and while I was being interviewed by CBS television that I was an empirical social scientist; instead of worrying about the Siri candidacy, I ought to count votes. So, not having our computer printout, I sat down at the Sala Stampa (the press office) with just a sheet of paper and a pencil. It takes thirty-six votes to defeat a candidate and I came up with forty votes against Siri. Those were forty certain votes, of people who just wouldn't vote for him. I got back to the hotel a few minutes ago—it's now about 3:30 in the afternoon—got out *The Inner Elite* and our computer printout and easily came up with forty-three certain votes against him and another ten probable. It is a remote possibility that Siri could come up with fifty-five votes, counting the curialists and the center that might drift in that direction, but fifty-five votes is only half of the electorate and it falls twenty short of the total needed for election. Maybe with luck he could push it to sixty-five, but I would think there are between forty and forty-five hard, firm, solid votes against him.

Saturday, October 14

Everybody is still talking about Siri's interview in *Gazzetta del Popolo*. He seems to have lost his temper several times; said he was one of the most maligned men in the whole world; said he was neither a liberal nor a conservative but a supporter of the Gospel; ridiculed John Paul's inauguration speech; took several sharp digs at the Secretariat of State; and dismissed the idea of the collegiality of the bishops. As far as one can tell from the accounts in the Italian papers, he was thoroughly irascible throughout the interview. That should be enough to frighten even more people away from him.

Siri gave the interview with the condition that it be embargoed—not published—until the cardinals were in the conclave. A Gazzetta reporter realized that the Siri interview was

dynamite and informed his friend, Benelli, who was rumored to have urged him to break the embargo. (At least one top journalist questioned this involvement of Benelli.) The embargo was indeed broken, on the grounds that Siri had given the same interview to Italian radio stations. However, the radio interview was much less ill-tempered than the one in Gazzetta del Popolo. Many Italian cardinals were furious at Benelli—for embarrassing Siri—and one of them said, going into the conclave, he was so angry he would vote for Siri to the bitter end. That the backlash over the broken embargo injured Benelli's candidacy is problematic. The electors who were offended by the "injustice" done to Siri would not have voted for Benelli in any event. One also has to wonder about the ethics of imposing such an embargo in the first place. If the Siri interview had been released to the world while the cardinals were in conclave, so that the electors were the only ones who didn't know about it, the shock and scandal would have been enormous. I disapprove of journalists breaking embargoes, but I disapprove even more of cardinals agreeing to go on the record only when their fellow electors can't read the record. It is the sort of slippery behavior that one does not normally expect of Siri, who may be a reactionary, but who is an honest reactionary. Perhaps he didn't realize the full implications of the embargo or the great impact the interview would have had on Sunday morning. One suspects that Siri and many of his supporters had begun to believe their own propaganda and saw victory snatched out of their hands by the premature release of the Gazzetta interview. In fact, probably the only effect of the broken embargo was to reassure those who were worried about the Siri blitz that it would not be effective. Final analysis: the ineffectiveness of the Siri candidacy could not be attributed to the Gazzetta interview. Siri and his supporters lost for a classic political reason stated by the late Mayor Richard Daley in his discussion of the 1968 presidential election: "Mr. Humphrey lost because he didn't have the votes."

It is altogether unlikely that the Benelli election will come very quickly; still, if he is able to buy off some old curial adversaries with certain commitments to them, most of the other people in the Luciani coalition would vote for him if he makes a run for it.

Great weather these days: warm in the day, cool in the evening; lovely clear air. The Via della Conciliazione is filled with bustling people. All very lively. I met Mary McGrory, Bishop O'Donnell, and Jim Roache and we sat and talked. Mary is obsessed with the thought that Benelli is a raw political operator interested in power, a curial power-broker, and not a religious leader of the quality of John Paul. I made the case that he would reform the Curia, straighten out the mess here, put the church's ministry in order, and she said, "Who cares? How many people does that appeal to?"—which is a fair comment.

Men who work here, like Adolpho and Carter, may rejoice at Benelli's election, but it doesn't make a damn bit of difference to most of the world that he's going to straighten out the curial mess. He's already typed as a political operator, and it's very hard for political operators to have any deep religious impact on the world. Anyhow, I'm sure Mary McGrory reveals the attitude of the American press.

Father Carter, with whom I had lunch at Roberto's, had a much broader view of the thing. He says that Benelli is concerned about the church; he has a very weak papal theology but is open to learning even there; he would practice collegiality, at least with people whose intelligence he respected—hence in a small group like the Council of the Synod he would not be nearly as imperious as he might be with a large group. You take a calculated risk, I guess, with a man like Benelli. He'd straighten out the financial and administrative mess in the Curia; he'd push ecumenism and social justice; he'd probably not harass the theologians too much but he would find it very hard to practice democracy.

While the Siri-Benelli conflict was holding the attention of the outsiders, some of the more sophisticated leaders of the coalition realized that neither could possibly win. Leo Suenens, despite his sympathy with Benelli, was asking friends and acquaintances what they would think of Colombo as pope. Most of the reactions were unfavorable. Colombo, he was told, was simply too old, especially too old to replace a man who had died at sixty-five. You must not be disappointed, Suenens responded to several of them; after all, remember what Pope John did and he was seventy-seven when he was elected.

Those who knew Suenens well guessed that Lorscheider was his own personal choice but unelectable because of his health and that Hume and Wojtyla were his other favorites, but that he

*realistically assumed that there would have to be an attempt at a
compromise Italian, that neither Poletti nor Ursi nor Pappalardo
would be acceptable (the first because of his curial affiliation, the
second because of his mercurial disposition, and the third because
the Italians would not accept a Sicilian). Colombo was then the
only obvious compromise choice. Toward the end of the first day,
Suenens seemed to think, there would be an attempt, quite possibly
successful, to put forward the seventy-six-year-old archbishop of
Milan as a last desperate effort at an Italian compromise. None of
the coalition leaders were enthusiastic about such a prospect, but
with the large "drifting center" and the conviction of at least half of
the electors that there ought to be "one more" Italian pope, a
Colombo compromise seemed to insiders a very distinct possibility.*

It is interesting to watch the switch in the American cardinals.
They came in talking about John Paul's impact on the world and
they ended up talking about the need for a strong administrator.
Absolute pushovers for curial propaganda. They came with the
right instincts, but these people just lied to them about John Paul's
administrative abilities and they bought it. John Carberry is bringing his ten chocolate bars into the conclave and told people at the
press conference the other day that it was like an illumination from
the Holy Spirit to vote for Luciani. Carberry is also saying that the
time is not right for a non-Italian because none of the non-Italian
candidates know Rome intimately. "There is no doubt that the
church moves out of Rome," he said. He also missed the point
about John Paul when he said that the next pope could not have the
same charm as John Paul. "God made him, then threw away the
mold." Nobody's insisting on someone from exactly the same mold,
but the good cardinal of St. Louis does not seem to comprehend
that people are not expecting a Xerox copy. What they are expecting is another man of hope; presumably, God did not throw away
that mold.

They are now in the conclave. It's all over but the waiting.

It's 8:30 Saturday night and I'm having supper alone at the
restaurant right across from the Visconti Hotel. Didn't set anything
up for tonight. I'm tired of big, elaborate meals. I'll walk over to St.
Peter's and soak up the atmosphere over there.

"What percentage of Italian cardinals ski?" Wojtyla asked at a

meeting in Milan. He was told that none of the Italian cardinals skied. "A pity," he said, "forty percent of the Polish cardinals ski."

"But," said one of his confreres, "how can that be? There are only two cardinals in Poland."

"Wyszynski counts for sixty percent," he replied, smiling ruefully.

At the same meeting, Wojtyla dashed out early one afternoon to watch Poland play Brazil in a World Cup soccer match.

As bishop and cardinal, Wojtyla has lived a life of complete disregard for physical comfort. He was made archbishop of Cracow in 1964. He wanted to remain in a two-room flat he had as auxiliary bishop. He moved into the episcopal palace only when the vicar-general forcibly removed his belongings—after four weeks of persuasion had failed. His staff members despair of his physical appearance; his shirts, shoes, and clothes all look battered and worn. He has only one set of cardinalatial robes, and that's second-hand (this part of the unofficial biography makes one wonder: Where do you buy secondhand cardinalatial robes?). But there is one prized luxury in his possession, a pair of top-quality skis. Both an opera and a soccer fan, Wojtyla has maintained the athletic enthusiasms of his youth, with skiing, canoeing, hiking, and mountain climbing his favorite sports. The Tatra mountains in southern Poland and the Masurian lake district in northern Poland (nearly three thousand lakes) are his favorite outdoor haunts. Not only does he write poetry (which is published in the magazine Znak *under the pseudonym Andrzej Jawien), but he plays the guitar and sings folk songs.*[4] *He was on a canoe trip in the Masurian lakes when he was named a bishop. After accepting the appointment, he went right back to his boat. He delights in walking through the mountains, guitar in hand, singing old folk songs and making up new ones. A woman from New Hampshire, according to* Time *magazine, remembers being serenaded by a group of fellow skiers after she broke her leg in an accident. She only learned later that the bishop was playing the guitar for the serenade. He once said to a reporter, as he gazed out of his residence in the direction of the mountains, "I wish I could be out there now somewhere in the mountains, racing down into a valley; it's an extraordinary sensation." On canoeing or kayak trips, he says mass with a portable altar, a cross for which is made by lashing two canoe paddles together. And on retreats with the priests of his diocese, he stays up late at night, playing his guitar and singing with them.*

Later Saturday Night

I'm especially depressed by the gloom that seems to be gripping Rome this lovely October. The death of John Paul was a terrible tragedy, but scarcely enough to account for the pessimism. Cardinal Ursi said earlier in the week that the next pope would have to suffer much. *Osservatore della Domenica* has an article predicting a nuclear war during the reign of the next pope, a prediction based in part on the prophecy of St. Malachy (which responsible scholars consider a sixteenth-century forgery) and partly on a very dubious text linked with the shrine at Fatima. (The Fatima "secret" at one time was supposed to be that the world was going to end in 1960. Indeed, I remember one affluent and pious Catholic matron at a New Year's Eve party on December 31, 1959, suggesting that we enjoy the party because it would be the last one. The world would end before the beginning of 1961. It didn't.)

Osservatore della Domenica doesn't normally fall back on pseudoprophecies and private revelations to fill its pages. Maybe the pessimism is a curial manipulation, too. Still, I will confess that right now, although maybe it's just fatigue, I feel very pessimistic indeed.

The big difficulty with this election is that the ordinary Catholic folks got a glimpse in September of what the pope could be. They saw the pope, ever so briefly, as playing the role for which the papacy was designed. As Nancy McCready said to me, "It made me proud to be a Catholic again."

All right, we lost John Paul; *why* is God's problem. If John Paul is replaced by business as usual, the people will be profoundly disillusioned. That's where lots of Catholics are today. They went through an interlude of being proud of Catholicism and had it snatched away from them; they want it back, yet many of these clowns who are doing the voting don't perceive that.

As Wojtyla said to James Michener in his interview for PBS, "We are a Polish church, the church in Poland is a thousand years old; in the United States, only two hundred years old; there are different political and economic systems. . . . The church in Poland is living its own life. This is very important. And I suppose it is important for the church everywhere, living its own life, to be different, to realize its own mission."[5]

His training at the Angelicum under Reginald Garrigou-Lagrange *was in the most rigid, traditional, and mystic categories. After returning to Poland in 1948, he earned a doctorate at the University of Cracow, balancing his theological training in Rome with phenomenological philosophical research in Poland. (His doctorate in Rome was on John of the Cross, and in Cracow he studied the ethical system of a twentieth-century sometime-Catholic philosopher, Max Scheler.) He taught for a time at the Catholic University of Lublin and served as chaplain to the students in Cracow. In 1958, he became auxiliary bishop of Cracow. In 1962, de facto archbishop. In 1964, he was officially appointed prince-archbishop, and he received the red hat from Pope Paul three years later.*

He spoke up repeatedly at the Second Vatican Council. "The church should so speak that the world may see that it is not only teaching but also seeking a just solution to human problems . . . helping the world find the solutions by itself and excluding an ecclesiastical mentality; lamentations over the wretched state of the world . . . moralizing and exhorting are to be avoided. Atheists think that we believers are alienated from this life because we subject ourselves to a God who is an unreal projection of our minds. In beginning our dialogue with atheists, we must then demonstrate that we are not alienated from the world but precisely because of our faith, we feel deeply committed to it; . . . and again, the human person must be shown to be not a mere economic instrument of the state but as enjoying the dignity of a rational nature which has its apex in religion and which transcends all secular power."

Like many other physically strong men who have known great suffering, Wojtyla is a person sensitive to the feelings of others, soft and gentle in his manner. But he is tough-minded about getting things done. He rarely raises his voice, argues his position modestly, and spends far more time listening than he does talking. In his relationship with the priests of his diocese and with the priests and laity who are part of the seminary's small-group discussions at the diocesan center in Cracow, he earned a reputation for being a patient listener and a brilliant summarizer. At the Synod of the Bishops, he played the same role with such effectiveness that he has been elected to the permanent council since the beginning of the synod (and chaired the meeting of the Council of the Synod last spring). He eats a big breakfast (bacon and eggs or ham and eggs, instead of the uncivilized Italian colazione of coffee and rolls). He pays little attention to food, but is pleased if people serve him tripe and potato pancakes. For lunch he has a glass of wine or light beer, avoiding all stronger liquor.

His walk is slow and deliberate. His eyes miss nothing. His lips are habitually pursed, as though ready to break into a smile. While his eyes take in every detail, they light up frequently with interest or humor. He gives the impression of being a strong, shrewd, cheerful, gentle person with deep resources of experience, faith, and intelligence.

His profound concern for and sensitivity to others is reflected in his philosophical scholarship. Wojtyla is a personalist, a man whose fundamental philosophical assumption is the irreducible value of the human person. As a philosopher, he is good enough to earn the praise of Harvard summer school director Thomas Crooks, who said after Wojtyla's lecture at Harvard in 1976 that Wojtyla was "one of the most impressive men I've met in my life . . . an absolutely radiant personality."

I'm now here at the obelisk in the Piazza San Pietro looking up at the Apostolic Palace. There are a lot of lights on up there; some of them individual bedroom lights, other lights in the corridor; there are a fair number of them off, too. I watched a couple of lights flick off as I stood here. There are people in the piazza, maybe a hundred or two hundred, mostly tourists with cameras. Police are scattered about, a couple of dozen of them, not very much on the alert. The dome of St. Peter's looms in the background, the night sky is clear; there's a moon behind my left shoulder shining down. The outline of the Sistine Chapel stands vaguely in the background. What's going on up there?

Scene III

Inside the Apostolic Palace there were many different moods. Cardinal John Carberry patiently awaited the revelation of the Holy Spirit. Giovanni Benelli fretted and worried; he did not want to run for pope, but his friends and allies insisted that he was the only Italian left who was acceptable to many of the foreign cardinals. He knew that there would be many votes for him the next morning. He was also reasonably certain that there would not be enough.

In room 96, Karol Wojtyla tossed a Marxist philosophical journal on his desk, something to read during the monotonous hours of ceremonial voting in the Sistine Chapel. Wojtyla planned to vote for Benelli and told his friends before he came that he had booked an open return flight to Cracow for the day after the conclave.

Leo Suenens and Franz Koenig met briefly in the corridor; one of them went to see Vicente Enrique y Tarancón. The curial Italians were grim and tight-lipped. The coalition leaders figured that this would mean a bitter battle. Despite his weariness, Aloisio Lorscheider roamed the corridors, cheering up his uneasy Latin American colleagues. Joseph Malula, archbishop of Kinshasa, remembered the words he had spoken to Jordan Bonfante earlier in the day: "All the imperial paraphernalia, all that isolation of the pope, all that medieval remoteness and inheritance that make Europeans think that the church is only Western—all the rightness makes them fail to understand that young countries like mine want something different. We want simplicity. We want Jesus Christ. All that, all that must change."

Malula was exhausted and uncertain and could not even be sure that some of the African cardinals were not going to vote for Siri on the first ballot.

Sunday Morning, the Piazza of St. Peter's

The piazza is swarming with people. It's Sunday; Romans are coming home from church and are out walking. They've all come around to see the first smoke. It will almost certainly be black

Pope John Paul II — Karol Wojtyla
— poses with a candle in his hand
after receiving First Communion in
Cracow, Poland (date not known).

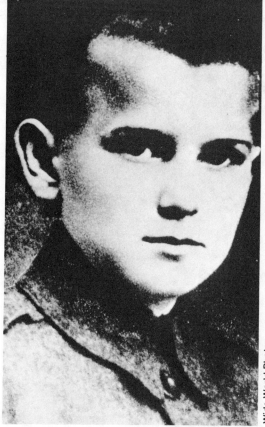

Wojtyla at the age of twelve as a
schoolboy in Wadowice, Poland. He
was an actor and an athlete — serious
but not pious.

As Poland's junior cardinal, Wojtyla was known as a pragmatist, reconciler, coalition builder.

Pope John Paul II waves to dignitaries and cardinals in St. Peter's Square during the open-air Mass which consecrated the beginning of his pontificate.

Pope John Paul II accepting the mantle of the supreme pontiff on the night of his election, October 16, 1978. Many said he had not wanted the job.

John Paul II, the fifty-eight-year-old pope, embraces the primate of Poland, seventy-seven-year-old Cardinal Stefan Wyszynski, at a reception after the investiture ceremonies for the first Polish pope in history.

Pope John Paul II touches a small baby in the crowd that welcomed him to the papal residence at Castel Gandolfo, the hilltop resort south of Rome.

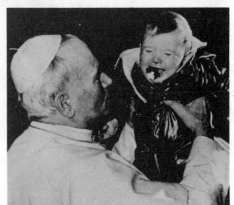

Whether he was praising the poetry reading of a ten-year-old boy in a small parish in Rome . . .

. . . or trying to calm a crying two-year-old during a formal Vatican audience . . .

. . . the new pontiff regarded the children of the world as the symbol of his faith in the changing church.

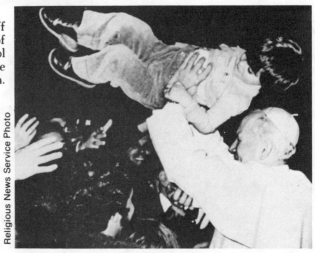

An enthusiastic skier, John Paul II received a pair of skis from members of a Sulmona, Italy, ski school.

Now known as the pope who can't keep out of a crowd, John Paul II chats with Cardinal Ugo Poletti, vicar of Rome, after an audience.

After less than five months in office, the pontiff leaves on a "pilgrimage of faith" to Latin America.

His Holiness John Paul II kisses the ground on his arrival in Santo Domingo, the first pontiff to visit Latin America.

From Santo Domingo, it was on to a six-day tour of Mexico. Wearing a native straw sombrero, Pope John Paul II hugs an Indian girl.

Throngs of well-wishers greet John Paul II in Mexico.

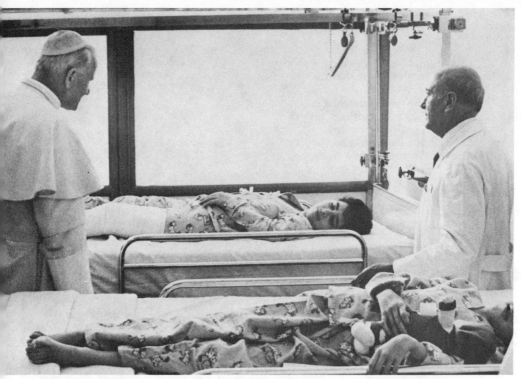

The pope of children. Pope John Paul II visits Mexico City Children's Hospital.

The pontiff is surrounded by Indians in various feathered costumes during his visit to Cuilapam, Mexico — the headdress is worn during "dance of the feathers".

Cardinal Sebastiano Baggio introduces Pope John Paul II at the opening session of the Latin American Bishops Conference in Puebla, Mexico. In his address, he spoke of social justice, human rights and church involvement but no identification with systems . . . right or left.

United Press International Photo

United Press International Photo

Then, like a good pluralist, Pope John Paul II went home so that the bishops could work out their own programs.

smoke. Nonetheless, the tendency now is to think of it as a brief conclave, ending probably with Giovanni Benelli, though if one is to judge anything by the Italian papers, there's a little less confidence about Benelli than there was yesterday.

The piazza is absolutely jammed. Nine minutes to noon. The Via della Conciliazione is crowded halfway back, too. Tom Drape and Dom Mariani (both part of the UPS team) and I are under one of the colonnades looking up to the Sistine Chapel. There's an air of excited expectancy among the people; I think mostly they've come because it's Sunday at noon, and a lovely day, and if there is white smoke, they don't want to miss it.

The crowd is getting thicker; everybody really kind of seems to think it's going to be white this time. They enjoy the suspense and the show, which may mean that the absence of people in August truly was the fault of *ferragosto*.

Well, there was a puff of white smoke, then it's turned black again. They're playing games with us.

It is now black again. You'd think they'd never invented the telephone. The crowd is so big, it's hard to get out of the piazza. Now the smoke has turned white and clearly white. White. More white. Now there is clear white smoke coming out, there can be no doubt about it. Now it's gray. Vatican Radio is signing off, saying that the white smoke was a false alarm and that it was actually black.

Walking back to the hotel, a little before one o'clock, there's a massive traffic jam around St. Peter's as the tourist buses and the cars try to pull away. It was warm enough in August, but now it's so hot here that I seek the shady side of the street to walk on. One can only guess what's going on inside there. Maybe the Siri people showed all the strength they could this morning and didn't quite make it. A fellow in the press office was saying that Siri had fifty votes. I'm guessing, myself, no more than thirty-five, which is forty votes away from what he needs. I also suspect that if the first stage of the strategy is to beat back Siri, then we're not going to be safe until we get black smoke this afternoon. If there is black smoke this afternoon, that means there isn't going to be any election by acclamation and the conclave will be a somewhat strongly contested one, which is what it ought to be. If it goes on to Tuesday, it's all up in the air. A foreigner has a shot, and if they don't do it Tuesday and they take some time off Wednesday—which they may, to prepare and reflect—then I think the chance of an outsider, either Archbishop Anastasio Ballestrero of Turin or a foreigner, will go up tremendously.

The tension as the electors walked down the aisle to cast their ballots was stronger than during the first conclave, and the nervous anxiety more apparent. The curial Italians cast their votes with a flair and a gusto that bordered on arrogance. Some of them were confident this would be Giuseppe Siri's day; others made a brave show of certainty despite their fear that the papacy might finally slip out of the Italian grip that had held it for four and a half centuries. Pericle Felici was depressed. The acrimony of the previous week had deprived him of much of his leverage within the conservative bloc.

At the end of the first ballot, Siri was ahead, as he had been at the end of the first ballot in August, but he had fallen substantially short of the fifty votes that his supporters had confidently expected. Benelli trailed Siri but was not far behind. Other Italian candidates–Ursi, Poletti, and Colombo—had substantial blocks of votes. Siri supporters knew that they were not likely to capture many of these electors.

Their faces were glum as the second balloting began. The coalition leaders, Tarancón, Koenig, Suenens, Lorscheider, Arns, Alfrink, and Marty, were worried. Siri had fifteen more votes on the first ballot than he had at the August conclave. Could this be enough to start a stampede in his direction? They didn't think so, but they could not be sure. The second ballot would be critical. If Siri lost votes, he was finished. If Benelli picked up votes, it might be another one-day conclave as in August.

Karol Wojtyla, reading his Marxist journal, frowned when it was announced that he had five votes. The men who were voting for him were casting their ballots away. It would be impossible for seventy more electors to vote for him, he reassured himself. Still, they were going to be looking for a compromise candidate before the day was over, though they would hardly look for a Polish compromise candidate.

The advantage tilted in Benelli's direction as the ballots from the second scrutiny were strung on the thread. Siri fell behind, losing a half-dozen votes from those cardinals who had thought they were backing a winner and had been disappointed by the first ballot evidence that Siri would not be the winner. Benelli forged into the lead as the members of the majority coalition abandoned the other Italian candidates and cast their votes for the Italian who now seemed most likely to be able to defeat Siri. There was an air of cautious optimism at lunch, but none of the non-Italian cardinals were persuaded that Benelli was in striking distance of victory or that the one-day August conclave would be duplicated. The Italian curialists and their allies were glum and silent. They had a stormy gathering in a tiny courtyard after lunch and before their siesta. Benelli must be stopped; he was a creature of the stranieri (foreigners), he would betray the Italian papacy, he was arrogant and ruthless, he was responsible for the Luciani nonsense in August. Even if they were not going to elect their man, they would not tolerate the election of Benelli.

Even before they got wind of the courtyard meeting, Benelli and his allies in the coalition were uncertain. There were perhaps a dozen cardinals (including such anti-Siri electors as Baggio, Pignedoli, and Villot) who had experienced and still resented Benelli's ruthlessness when he was undersecretary of state. Others had personal scores to settle with him, and still others were uneasy about his qualifications for the papacy. Added to the Siri faction, these dozen or so doubters meant that Benelli would fall between ten and fifteen votes short of winning no matter what happened. The Siri faction was quite implacable. Many of the doubters would not be easily moved, Suenens sighed as he opened his Bible. If Benelli had not so vigorously and effectively engineered the election of Luciani, he might not have had such strong opposition.

On my way back to St. Peter's to watch for the evening smoke, I got worried. If we can get through this one with black smoke, then we can start relaxing again. The Siri business will have been stopped; it will mean the non-curialists are sufficiently well-organized to dig in their heels and not be swept away. The illusion of curial power which was developed so well this week by the Italian press can be pretty well smashed even in the cardinals' minds. Then they can get down to the serious business of working out a selection which will reflect the sentiments of everybody in the college in a somewhat more mature fashion.

Looking through my old notes this afternoon, I was struck by the question of the influence of the foreigners: whether they would be stampeded by the Curia or not; whether leaders would emerge;

whether they would be sufficiently well-organized to resist the curial blitzes. The fear somebody raised last night, and that I'd forgotten about, is that the sheer size of the group makes it a diffuse body, difficult to organize intelligently, but easy to manipulate and panic, which is the game the Curia people are so good at playing.

In the Luciani election, a number of the unaffiliated, unintelligent cardinals—the Americans among them—did indeed panic when they saw that Luciani had a lot of votes and jumped on the bandwagon on the third ballot to be with the winner.

In that election, the panic wasn't used by anybody and was something of a surprise, even to the people who had organized the Luciani campaign. But this time around, there has been a very clear effort to orchestrate events so as to produce panic, and then to use it for the Siri candidacy. The effort, I suspect, was doomed to failure to begin with; but Siri certainly did his best, unwittingly, in the *Gazzetta del Popolo* interview, to torpedo it yesterday.

Jim Roache reported that Ernie Primeau's prediction is Siri by noontime, so as I came into the press office today, Jim walked up to me and said, "Computer one; Primeau zero."

I'm sticking with our computer, which sees forty votes at the most in the Siri camp. Where's the smoke? Make it black!

The third ballot dashed all hopes of a one-day conclave. Siri continued to lose votes, but they drifted to Giovanni Colombo. Benelli had peaked short of the magic seventy-five. His candidacy was finished. His enemies relaxed as the tallies were announced. They had not elected Siri, but at least they had blocked Benelli.

On the fourth voting there was a sudden and dramatic surge of votes towards Cardinal Giovanni Colombo, the seventy-six-year-old archbishop of Milan. Many of Siri's supporters and a considerable number of the drifting "centrists" jumped on the Colombo bandwagon. He was a compromise candidate acceptable to all Italians. As Felici would say later, this was Italy's moment of glory at the conclave. What would world leaders say about a seventy-six-year-old Italian "compromise"? But Colombo seemed to have the momentum. Karol Wojtyla relaxed. The chance of a Polish compromise pope, never in his judgment very serious despite the ten votes that he had amassed at the end of the afternoon, was now almost nonexistent. Lorscheider wondered to himself whether this had been the secret design of the Siri backers all along: a genial, well-liked elderly Italian whom they could dominate.

It became evident, however, that Genoa had not been a stalking-horse for Milano. To the astonishment of the non-Italians and chagrin of many of the Italians Giovanni Colombo bluntly stated that even if he were elected he would not accept. The conclave was now plunged into chaos.

Immediately after supper two of the leaders of the coalition met by prearrangement in a darkened corner in the fringes of the conclave area. The conclave, one of them remarked, was like a wild horse, untamable, unpredictable, reckless. They might have beat us, the other responded. Can you imagine the letdown back home if they had?

But, the first one replied, now they're disorganized and un-certain. We must have a candidate before tomorrow morning. His companion agreed. Now was the time for the discreet meeting of a handful of leaders which had been tentatively agreed upon before the conclave began. A word was said here, a word was said there—late in the evening, quietly, so that the antagonism stirred up by the noisy noontime caucus of the Siri supporters would not be roused again.

(The dramatic shift to Colombo illustrates how dangerously impulsive a modern conclave can be with its large numbers of uncertain drifting electors. Giovanni Colombo had far more sense than did those who voted for him.)

Later in the evening one older European cardinal remarked to another as they sipped a glass of wretched cognac together that the conclave was a terrible method for electing a pope. "The Holy Spirit saved us today," replied his friend ruefully.

The other shook his head, "There has to be a change."

"Ah, my friend," replied his companion, "we will not live to go through this again."

The other cardinal made a face atop the cognac glass and shrugged his shoulders expressively. "We thought that before."

The sun is going down behind the Bernini columns; it's five minutes to five. The waiting is driving me nuts. The piazza itself is about nine-tenths full; only one little corner, from which you can't see the Sistine smokestack, is empty. It's part of a day's Sunday outing to discover whether you can be there to see the white smoke.

It's 5:25. Obviously they didn't do it on the third ballot. The sun is now completely set; it's twilight, turning to dusk, in St.

Peter's; the television floodlights are on. Half an hour more and we'll know.

Somebody was playing with a searchlight a few minutes ago; just testing it, I guess. It looks to me like it will still be fairly difficult to see what color the smoke is; it's getting darker and darker here. Apparently there is some line to the Vatican Press Office, even though that's not officially admitted; we suspect the line because Monsignor Romeo Panciroli confirmed at noontime today that it was indeed black smoke almost immediately after it came out. To add to the drama of the situation, a magnificent full moon is rising just over the Tiber. Jordan Bonfante is praying it's black smoke for tonight, because the best *Time* can do is two sheets in the center of the magazine if there's an election tonight, whereas *Newsweek* can do a cover—which is an interesting way of looking at it. The crowd is hushed now, and it's getting dark, though there's still enough light up there to see the color of the smoke. We have about fifteen minutes . . . You gotta say one thing: the church is good at squeezing the drama out of things, whatever else it may or may not be good at.

The bells are ringing—I don't know if that means anything in particular or not—it's twelve minutes to six and counting, and the lights just went on in the Conciliazione. It's stirring up some interest in the crowd. The moon has now turned to brilliant orange in the sky, almost smack in the middle of the Conciliazione. A perfect setting.

Six o'clock and nothing yet. It's quite dark now—it's going to be awfully hard to tell.

The searchlight is on the smokestack now; that doesn't mean they know anything any more than we do.

It's after six o'clock. The tension is so thick you can cut it.

6:05—nothing yet.

Now the smoke is going up, and it sure looks white! It's 6:34 and it's white smoke this time. Vatican Radio is saying black, but people are cheering. Hard to tell. Vatican Radio is still saying black.

They've got an observer way up on the roof who is closer to it. Another puff that looked white and then turned black. I'm so damned confused—nobody knows what's going on.

6:53—in the press office. Jim Roache just came in and confirmed that Monsignor Panciroli said it was black; so it took them a little longer to confirm it this time. I told him, "Computer two, Primeau zero."

Scene IV

The coalition leadership avoided the Curia's mistake of staging a noisy public rally. A word was said discreetly here and there; a hurried phrase was exchanged in the corridor; brief visits were made to various rooms—all so quietly that many of the electors hardly knew that decisions were being made. The light-touch strategy was continuing. It was not necessary for the "foreign" candidate to leap into a dramatic lead at once. But, if on the next morning ballot there was a major shift from Benelli to the designated foreigner, it would be clear to all in the coalition what had happened.

The electors hesitated briefly between Willebrands and Wojtyla, leaning toward the latter. It was argued that he already had a dozen votes, presumably American and German, and that he was younger by more than a decade than Willebrands and had greater physical strength. Not only was Franz Koenig supporting Wojtyla, as he had all along, but also the Spaniard Narciso Jubany Arnau, who had come to Rome determined to support Wojtyla and was one of the few cardinals who had read his books. He strongly insisted during that evening of confusion that Wojtyla was not only a happy compromise but just what the papacy needed. Sebastiano Baggio and Eduardo Pironio also rallied to Wojtyla's support in the course of the evening. The chaos of suppertime was dissolving and a new plan was emerging. Like all conclave strategies, however, it was casual, informal, delicate, and indirect. Many of the cardinals would not get the signal until the next morning. Whatever the case, when the tense leaders of the coalition went to sleep that night, the choice had been made. Tomorrow would be the day of the foreigner.

Monday, October 16

11:15 A.M. Something strange just happened. Black smoke, followed by white smoke, followed by black smoke, followed, thank heavens, by an announcement on the public address system from Vatican Radio. The smoke was indeed black. But the strange thing is not that it finally occurred to someone that whoever is making phone calls up to the conclave to find out the color of the smoke could make an announcement on the public address system (it only took us two conclaves to arrive at that happy solution, but better late than never); the strange thing is the timing. The smoke was fifty minutes early. Why was the smoke so early? Did they begin earlier or was there only one scrutiny? And if there was only one vote, by what authority do they cancel the second one? The rules of the conclave seem clearly require two scrutinies at each voting session. Maybe they are convinced that it is within their authority to suspend the second scrutiny. Maybe they simply began earlier. White smoke an hour early would make sense. Black smoke an hour early? There's something strange going on.

I just walked into the Vatican Press Office. Jim Roache was there trying to fend off reporters who wanted to know the basis for the confirmation that it was black smoke. Technically, he was not able to tell them that his boss, Monsignor Panciroli, had called an official who was lurking outside the door of the conclave and who confirmed the color of the smoke. He saw me come in, shrugged his shoulders, and said "Primeau zero, computer three."

The basic outline of what happened on the day of the foreigner is clear. There was an overwhelming shift of votes to Karol Wojtyla, with Willebrands and Sebastiano Baggio vigorously endorsing the archbishop of Cracow. There was also a vigorous and totally negative reaction from Karol Wojtyla. His reluctance was overcome, it would seem, through the persuasiveness of Cardinal Stefan Wyszynski. There was a stubborn, last-ditch resistance from the Siri forces and then victory for the coalition. But something is missing in this account.

On the first morning scrutiny there was almost a doubling of Wojtyla's votes, from about ten to about twenty, as well as a surge in favor of Willebrands. Siri and Benelli were both losing votes. Colombo's gains were modest. There was no time between the first and second scrutiny for the spent curialist forces to devise a new strategy, and, indeed, by now they were psychologically incapable of a new initiative. The smarter among them realized that they had won the Benelli battle only to lose the Italian papacy war. Many of those who had voted in the first scrutiny for Benelli and

Willebrands now perceived that Wojtyla was their best candidate. The light-touch strategy of the coalition leaders was successful again. When the cardinals adjourned for lunch after sending up their early, befuddling black smoke, the archbishop of Cracow had approximately forty votes. The number of ballots bearing his name had doubled twice during the morning session.

Karol Wojtyla was no longer reading the Marxist philosophical journal. He had spent a troubled and uneasy night knowing that the number of votes for him had inched up on each ballot that day and perhaps perceiving for the first time that he might, after all, be an acceptable compromise candidate. He did not want the job. The mountains and lakes of Poland, the streets of his beloved Cracow, his philosophy books and poetry, his tough but stimulating fight with the Communist party—all of these would be lost in a job that his friend Bishop Andre Deskur, now dangerously ill in a Roman clinic, had often described as impossible. His neighbors in the Sistine Chapel smiled encouragingly at him as the ballots were tallied, but Karol Wojtyla grew increasingly somber. Later he would tell the crowd in St. Peter's that he was afraid to accept the nomination.

Some of the coalition leaders noticed the mask of concern on Wojtyla's face and his indifference to the congratulations that he was already receiving as they filed into the dining room. Wyszynski was urged to encourage him. Theirs had been a long relationship of affection, respect, cooperation, and, on Wojtyla's part, extraordinary patience with his tough-minded and sometimes insensitive senior colleague. Wojtyla had learned long before that it was fruitless to argue with Wyszynski.

Between lunch and the first afternoon ballot, Willebrands indicated to his friends and supporters that he thought Wojtyla would be an excellent choice and that while he himself was grateful for further support, he felt now was the time to unite behind Wojtyla. Most of the Luciani coalition was now solidly in place in support of the archbishop of Cracow. There are reports that Benelli also threw his votes to Wojtyla, though this is not true. In fact, Benelli was bitter because Wojtyla was a year younger than Benelli and age had been used against him in his candidacy.

"The Holy Spirit spoke to us through mathematics," said one cardinal. They saw the sudden surge of Wojtyla's support in the morning. The signals were clear. He would be elected before the

day was over. On the first ballot in the afternoon it was all over. Wojtyla was so close that it was evident that the papacy could not be denied him even though he cheerfully would have denied it himself. There was still a scattering of votes for other cardinals, with the bitterly stubborn Siri faction resisting to the end. On the final vote, some of the Siri supporters finally defected (probably including such voters as Pericle Felici and Silvio Oddi, who admired Wojtyla personally and realized that in any case their cause was finished). Wojtyla had more than ninety votes, well over the seventy-five that were required, yet no one would speak of election by acclamation.

Just as they had in August, some of the curial electors stubbornly voted for Siri, even on the last ballot. Karol Wojtyla wept openly, his face in his hands, despite the applause around him. There was a long pause before he accepted. In response to Villot's question he finally raised his head from his hands, answering in solemn Latin: "Knowing the seriousness of these times, realizing the responsibility of this election, placing my faith in God, I accept."

When asked by Villot by what name he wanted to be known, he paused again and then said thoughtfully and in careful, precise Latin: "Because of my reverence, love, and devotion to John Paul and also to Paul VI, who has been my inspiration, my strength, I will take the name of John Paul."

There was more applause and even John Krol—not known for the sensitivity of his feelings—was moved by the pathos of the broad-shouldered, strong-visaged man slumped wearily, head in hands, near the fresco of the **Last Judgment.**

6:10 Monday evening. Back in the Piazza San Pietro, the setting much like last night, the moon showing down by the Tiber, the sky turning black, the floodlights and the searchlights on, the large crowd—not nearly as large as last night but still good-sized—filling much of the piazza but leaving plenty of room to move about. Dom Mariani, Tom Drape, and I are standing near the obelisk, eyes glued to the smokestack coming from the Sistine Chapel, waiting, waiting, waiting. There is an air of expectancy, even more than last night, as though we sense that it is going to happen tonight. No reason especially to think so. But then the tension and the expectancy are so great at a moment like this that reason seems to stop working . . . There it goes! White Smoke! No doubt about it this time! The smoke is white! It's 6:13 and we have white smoke!!

Now comes the waiting, the terrible anxious waiting. In a half-hour we will know and the whole drama will come to an end. Who will it be? I can't even think very clearly anymore.

There is a beautiful vintage moon, orange, coming up now. By the time the pope comes out, it's going to be shining brightly. The Swiss Guards just marched in; all the floodlights are on and the Sistine Chapel is glittering; kids are standing on the obelisk; the searchlights are now focused on the door on the balcony in front of St. Peter's. A light just went on inside the second floor of St. Peter's, so they are on their way.

They seem to be almost ready to open the door now. The Swiss Guards are marching around. I can barely see their red and white plumes. No, it's the Italian army band that's marching. He's going to come out and see the full moon looking right down upon him. An auspicious beginning, I guess.

6:43—The floodlights are on behind the balcony, so we're going to get an announcement almost at once. The curtains are pulling back—lots of clapping—the door swings open, the door has opened—no one's come out yet. They are setting up the mikes.

"None of us gave much thought to the political implications,"
one cardinal said. "Oh, perhaps Koenig and a few of the Germans
did, but not the others. We had the man for the job and he was
Polish and that was fine. It was only afterwards, in retrospect, that
we thought of political strategies. The most nervous moment of all,
though, was when we waited behind the windows wondering what
the reaction of the Roman crowds would be to a non-Italian pope."

Another delay. Finally, the door opens . . . out they come. Applause, applause. Cardinal Felici (so, again, it's not him) begins to speak (everyone hushed now). "Annuntio vobis gaudium magnum . . ."

Big cheers.

"Habemus Papam . . ."

Loud cheers from the audience! "Carolum Sanctae Romanae Ecclesiae Cardinalem." Another long pause. Charles who?

"Wojtyla!"

Wow! A Polish pope!

He chooses the name John Paul.

The first non-Italian pope since 1522, and he's Polish. I can't help it; I'm laughing; they crossed us up again, good for them.

I'm still laughing. Neither Tom nor Dom recognizes the name. Most people in the piazza don't seem to know who he is. They're silent, dead silent, angry, disappointed. Someone just asked me if the pope was black. No, I said. "Asiatico?" No, I said: "Un Polacco." "Un *Polacco*?" The man pounded his head in astonishment. An angry, confused, sullen crowd. There were virtually no cheers, even some boos, I think, but mostly dead silence.

I went into the press office for a few minutes. A very harassed Jimmy Roache just came in distributing English-language biographies of Karol Wojtyla. He saw me, moved his left hand sharply parallel to the floor (clutching the stack of biographies with his right hand), and said, "Computer zero, Primeau zero."

7:21. Outside again. The doors are opening again. Here he comes—he's a really big man, a broad and strong-looking man with a strong Polish face. He looks like a pro football linebacker. He simply has got to say something to these people tonight. He has to heal their wounds. He has to let them know he is their bishop. God, I hope he's smart enough and brave enough to break the precedent and speak to them.

He did it. He began by saying to them in Italian, "Praise be Jesus Christ." A lot of people in the crowd responded, "Now and forever." He has a deep, powerful voice and a strong presence up there. He's talking to them now. I'm no expert in Italian, but it sounds flawless to me.

"May Jesus Christ be praised. Dearest brothers and sisters, we are still all grieved after the death of the most beloved Pope John Paul I.

"And now the most reverend cardinals have called a new bishop of Rome. They have called him from a distant country, distant but always so close for the communion in the Christian faith and tradition.

"I was afraid to receive this nomination, but I did it in the spirit of obedience to Our Lord and in the total confidence in his mother, the most holy Madonna.

"Even if I cannot explain myself well in your—our—Italian language, if I make a mistake you will correct me.

"And so I present myself to you all to confess our common

faith, our hope, our confidence in the mother of Christ and of the church, and also—and also to start anew on that road, the road of history and of the church—to start with the help of God and with the help of men."

An absolutely perfect beginning. There was a moment there when he said that he was afraid to receive the nomination but did it in the spirit of obedience. He was very close to tears and he had to grip the railing of the balcony to control himself. When he made his slip about "your" Italian language, he had the crowd laughing. Even Cardinal Jean Villot was laughing, the first time I've ever seen him laugh. The reference to the Madonna was cheered by the Italians; a marvelous way to link the religious traditions of the two countries. They gave him a huge ovation at the end. It looked to me like one of the functionaries up there tried to cut him off, but that didn't stop him. He kept right on talking.[1] A brilliant, brilliant move, speaking to them in their own language. He's gone a long way toward overcoming Italian hostility, and on national television, too. Wyszynski was up there with him, just as he was at the first blessing of Pope John XXIII. A lot of history tonight, old history and new history. I've got to get back to my writing and then off to NBC and CBS to explain how this happened.

Tuesday, October 17

The first day of the new era. Yesterday, incidentally, was the feast of St. Hedwig, one of the patron saints of Poland; make of that what you will! I was up until 2:30 in the morning being interviewed by television people. Harry Reasoner asked me what I thought it would be like in Chicago, and I said I imagined they were dancing in the streets on Milwaukee Avenue. "Would you like to be there dancing with them?" he asked. I responded, much to his delight, that I sure would, though I wasn't sure that they would let an Irishman in.

I said to hell with it and slept late this morning and am now sitting once more in the press office. Everybody is trying to analyze the text of the talk he gave this morning to the cardinals. As far as I can tell from reading through the Italian it seems to be a solid enough document—more emphasis on collegiality and the Vatican Council than in the August inaugural address of the first John Paul.

My own initial reaction is that the cardinals took a big

gamble—but not on whether he is conservative or liberal, not on whether he is pro–Vatican Council or anti–Vatican Council. He is about as liberal as anyone could be and still be a cardinal in Poland. He is on the record time after time in favor of the Vatican Council, and he has served on the permanent council of the Synod of Bishops for the last two times (as a matter of fact, he was the first European to be selected to the Council of the Synod, which, had I taken Adolpho seriously a year ago, should have been a tip-off).

The big risk, it seems to me, is whether a man can make the leap from Cracow to Rome, from being the brilliant leader of a garrison church to being the one who presides in charity over a worldwide pluralistic church.

Before the final mass in the Sistine Chapel, one of the cardinals bumped into Wyszynski at the breakfast table. "There is sure to be great jubilation in your country today, don't you think?"

"Yes," was the somber reply, "but there will be none in Wojtyla."

After Pope John Paul's first discourse and the concelebrated mass in the Sistine Chapel, the cardinals streamed out into the courtyard in various stages of formal dress: from Benelli, merely in a scarlet sash and skullcap, to Siri, in full robes, including a red Roman hat. The Italian reporters and TV people closed in with a barrage of questions. The cardinals looked tired and distracted. No one was claiming that it was spiritual experience this time. Agnelo Rossi shrugged his shoulders; it was impossible to find an Italian. He didn't seem all that happy about it. Salvatore Pappalardo shrugged his shoulders; you have seen and heard what we have done, what do you think, he responded to the reporters. Giuseppe Siri was sullen: "Did you think it would be such a brief conclave?"

"I know nothing."

"Was the outcome a surprise for you and the others?"

"I'm not able to say. Perhaps it was a surprise."

"What did you think of the discourse of the new pope?"

"I do not remember anything."

Agnelo Rossi: "I'm not able to reveal anything besides that the conclave was longer than last time."

Antonio Poma was asked whether he was satisfied. He refused to respond.

Giovanni Benelli was willing to say more, but he seemed nervous and agitated: "The right man at the right time."

"A revolution?"

"There aren't revolutions in the church, always continuity," Benelli snapped back. "The Holy Spirit guides the church."

"Did you expect a foreign pope?"

The feisty little man lost his patience and exploded, "In the church there are no foreigners, no boundaries, no divisions. There are no foreigners in the church." Then the famous Benelli smiled as he headed for his car.

Aloisio Lorscheider was beaming with happiness. So was Michele Pellegrino, who was absolutely radiant, in fact. His warm, handsome face was alive with joy. (Later in the day, Pericle Felici would snarl at a journalist who made a mild comment about the outcome of the election.) It is pretty clear which side is happy and which side isn't.

Not much more at the press conference of the American bishops, either. John Cody promptly claimed that the pope was a good friend of his, that he'd spent ten days as his guest in Poland, and that he had had lunch with him just before the conclave. John Krol, asked how he felt about the election of a Polish pope, responded with characteristic graciousness, "What do you think?"

Tuesday Evening

The pope went to the Gemelli Clinic late this afternoon to see his good friend Bishop Andre Deskur, the head of Vatican communications (he had a stroke last week). Deskur is fifty-four and is a close friend and seminary classmate of the new pope. John Paul II rode in an open car and the crowds cheered him in the streets for the third time in twenty-four hours. He wept at Bishop Deskur's bedside. As he was leaving, someone reminded him that he hadn't given the papal blessing. "I must learn how to be a pope," he laughed. And then, shaping his hands like a megaphone, he bellowed the apostolic benediction.

Bishop Deskur was not expected to recover. He was told after regaining consciousness that his friend had been elected pope. He said, "Who will protect him from them? Now I must recover!"

No one needed to ask who "they" were.

The pope would visit Deskur again in the hospital, this time wearing only unofficial black (much to the annoyance of Roman and Vatican security forces). Deskur is still partially paralyzed and is in Switzerland, completing his recovery.

Wednesday, October 18

John Paul II has not yet confirmed the existing papal "cabinet." The rumor now is that he is not going to, but is going to decide each appointment on its own merits. I bet that has all kinds of folks scared stiff.

I was appalled with the junk in much of the world press about the new pope. Coverage of the two elections has been terrible. This is partly the fault of the newspapers, which generally do not maintain competent correspondents in Rome to cover the Vatican. Whenever something happens in the papacy, they send off well-meaning but uninformed amateurs to cover it. It is also partly the fault of the Vatican, which does its best to keep everything secret from journalists. When push comes to shove, the Vatican is not above lying to them.

Hence the newspaper and TV and radio newscasts are filled with idiocies. But the worst idiocy of all came from Henry Tanner, the *New York Times* bureau chief in Rome. Writing about the alleged conservatism of Pope John Paul II in the *International Herald Tribune* (the *New York Times* was silenced by a strike), Tanner observed, "The new pontiff is known as a conservative theologian. Specialists said that this conservatism was evident today in the fact that twice in his address he referred to the Virgin Mary. Liberal theologians have lately avoided references to the cult of the mother of Jesus to spare Protestant feelings."

One would dearly love to know who the specialists were with whom Mr. Tanner spoke, because just about everybody I have talked to was well aware that it was not the pope's intention to speak about theology at all when he mentioned the Madonna. Rather he was attempting to establish a link between Poland and Italy (in both nations the ordinary people have historically had intense devotions to the mother of Jesus). Indeed, when the pope mentioned the Madonna, the largely Italian and still-skeptical crowd in the Piazza of St. Peter's broke into enthusiastic cheers. They knew what he was up to, even if Mr. Tanner's so-called "specialists" did not.

Nor, apparently, did the "specialists" know of the great historical link between the famous shrine of Our Lady of Czestochowa and the Polish nation's fight for freedom. Some specialists!

Why didn't they tell Mr. Tanner that virtually every one of the great Catholic theologians—Karl Rahner, Yves Congar, Edward Schillebeeckx, Henri de Lubac—has a book about Mary, and that the Protestant superior at the ecumenical Abbey of Taizé has also written such a book? Nor did the "specialists" point out that such liberal Protestant theologians as Harvard University's Harvey Cox have spoken warmly of the devotion to the Virgin. Maybe some Catholics shut up about Mary because they are afraid to offend some Protestants, but the decline of Marian devotion in the United States has nothing to do with the Protestant-Catholic dialogue and a lot to do with (a) the sad shape of American Catholic self-identity and (b) the sugar-sweet concept of Marian piety on which so many of us were force-fed when we were children.

Apparently the "specialists" did not inform Mr. Tanner that Mary is one of the most powerful religious symbols in the history of the Western world, and that devotion to her has generated great cathedrals, lovely paintings, and magnificent music. Catholics should forget about that symbol just because it is offensive to Protestants? And a pope shouldn't mention it lest he be considered conservative?

Nor has Mr. Tanner been told by his nameless "specialists" that the function of Mary in the Catholic Christian heritage is to reflect the feminine aspect of God. God is a blend of both the masculine and the feminine, a blend which Papa Luciani had in mind when in one of his addresses he said that God's love for us is more like the love of a mother than of a father. Mary is the only religious symbol in the modern world that can embody meaning for authentic feminism (however badly that symbol may have been abused at times in the past by male chauvinists). The Mary symbol links Christianity directly to the ancient religions of mother goddesses and also stands for the tender, loving, life-giving affection of the ultimate powers of the universe.

So much for Henry Tanner and his "specialists."[2]

The search to find a label to paste on the pope has become absurd. Cardinal Wojtyla, we are told by the press, has been a strong opponent of Communism in Poland, so he is a conservative; but since his opposition has been more adroit and less rigid than that of Warsaw's Cardinal Stefan Wyszynski, he is at least not as conservative as the latter. Thus he can be safely labeled as a "moderate conservative."

This is baloney. As a Polish-born colleague said to me, "Wojtyla supports freedom of the press, freedom of expression, freedom of worship, freedom for striking workers, better pay and working conditions in the factories, civil and human rights for Poland. Anyplace else in the world, a man who stood for those things would be considered a liberal or even a radical. Why is it that when you stand for them in Poland, you are written off as a conservative?"

A fair question. What my Polish friend didn't understand is that if you support freedom of the press, expression, and religion and the rights of workers in countries like Chile and South Korea, you are a liberal; but if you support them in Marxist countries, you automatically become a conservative—at least in the eyes of this country's literary and journalistic elites.

It is also amusing to watch reporters try to figure out what the cardinals were up to politically when they elected a Polish pope. What was the message they were sending to Russia's Leonid Brezhnev and Poland's Edward Gierek (the Communist party boss)? What new strategy for dealing with Marxism had the cardinal electors chosen? What complex, secret, and obscure conspiracy to fend off the Communists had emerged from the conclave?

The answer to all of these questions is that most of the cardinals weren't thinking in political terms at all. Their vigorous denial of that when they came out of the conclave was honest.

But the worst thing going on here is a kind of snide, anti-Polish reaction. Thus one woman columnist is complaining that Wojtyla will kick off a third world war and that he is anti-Semitic. When asked how she knows he is anti-Semitic, she responds by saying that all Poles are. I guess that settles that.

In fact, as a young man during the Second World War, Wojtyla was active in an underground movement which assisted Jews. He helped them to find shelter, to acquire false identification papers, and to escape from the country. He was blacklisted by the Nazis for helping Jews, and one of the reasons for his remaining hidden was to avoid arrest by the Nazis.

After the war, he defended the Jews who remained in Cracow from Communist anti-Semitism. He helped to organize the permanent care of the Cracow Jewish cemetery after that cemetery had been desecrated by secret police–inspired thugs. The cardinal called upon the students of the University of Cracow to clean and restore the defiled tombstones. In 1964, on the Feast of Corpus Christi (the most popular Polish national religious festival), he condemned the Communist government for its anti-Semitism. In 1971 he spoke at the Cracow synagogue during a Friday night Sabbath service. As a young man, his closest friend was a Jewish schoolmate named Georgy Gerzy Kluger. His diocesan Catholic paper in Cracow, Common Weekly, *repeatedly publishes articles about Judaism and the Holocaust. A Roman official of the Jewish Anti-Defamation League, commenting on this paper, said, "There are in my judgment very few Catholic newspapers outside the free world which would devote more space to the Holocaust, Jewish martyrdom, Catholic-Jewish relations. . . . Cardinal Wojtyla played the guiding role in the operations of this very important publication."*

Saturday, October 21

The pope is going to be installed, or invested, or inaugurated, whatever you want to call it, tomorrow. It was his decision that the inaugural mass be in the morning so that people would be able to watch the soccer games on European television in the afternoon. That's a little rough on the American TV networks, who wanted to do it live and who are now going to have to broadcast taped versions Sunday morning in the States. On the other hand, it is good for all the pro football fans in the States. Sunday games won't be interrupted by the Vatican ceremony. I guess all the sports fans in the North Atlantic world benefit from the pope's choice. He's probably going to go back into the papal apartments and turn on TV to watch the soccer game himself!

Yesterday, he met the diplomats of the world and gave a very low-key speech that will drive the reporters here who are trying to figure out his political strategy wild—they'll be digging through each paragraph, each sentence, each word, searching for clues. In fact, everything we know about the Wojtyla personality by now suggests that such parsing of his texts is a waste of time. He is a flexible, pragmatic, adroit man, who is absolutely unshakeable at the core of his convictions. He is not very interested in politics. He will play the secular politics game for itself. The appeal yesterday was for religious freedom and for human rights. My guess is that he will meddle in politics both here in Italy and in the rest of the world much less than did Pope Paul VI.

If he dazzled the diplomats yesterday, he wowed the world press today. Listen to some of the things he said:

"Merely on the professional level, you have lived through days as tearing as they were moving. The sudden, unforeseen character of the events which occurred has obliged you to draw upon a great fund of knowledge in regard to matters of religious information which were perhaps somewhat unfamiliar to you, and then to face conditions which were sometimes nerve-racking and an imperative which is known as the disease of the age: speed. For you, waiting for the white smoke was not a restful time.

"Thank you for having made so large an effort to call to mind, with unanimous respect, the great and truly historic work of Pope Paul VI. Thank you also for having made so familiar the smiling face and evangelical attitude of my immediate predecessor, Pope John Paul I. Thank you, too, for your favorable reporting of the recent conclave, my election, and the first steps I have taken in discharging the heavy duties of the papacy. In all of these cases, this was an occasion for you to speak not only of persons—who pass—but of the See of Rome, of the church, of its traditions and rites, of its faith, of its problems and hopes, of St. Peter and of the role of the pope, of the great spiritual goals of the present day; in brief, of the mystery of the church."

After he finished his talk (in French), he did something totally unexpected. He descended from his chair in the Apostolic Palace's Hall of Blessings and began to move among reporters to answer their questions.

Monsignor del Gallo, one of the "busy" monsignors whose job it is to keep the pope in line, reached out to grab his arm to prevent him from joining the press. Decisively, the pope shook him off. A radio journalist pushed a microphone towards his mouth. Del Gallo pushed it away. The pope reached out, pulled the microphone back, and spoke into it. The functionaries managed to get him away from the crowd of reporters for a few moments, but then he went back to them a second time. "Would you like to visit your

native Poland?" someone asked him. "If *they'll* let me," he replied.
"Would he continue to ski?" "If *they'll* let me," he said, nodding
towards the furious monsignors. "Will you visit Russia?" someone
else asked. He made an expressive face and said, "If *they'll* let me."

Then there was no stopping him. He walked through the hall,
speaking Polish, English, German, French, Italian, and Lithua-
nian, as if they were all one language. To two young Lithuanians he
said, "Half my heart is in Lithuania." Would he hold regular press
conferences? "As soon as I'm allowed to." Another nod toward his
now-resigned aides. "We'll see how you treat me!" he laughed.
Will you return to Poland? "I'm too young not to go back home."
Will you visit Ireland, Canada, Brazil, the United States, and New
Bedford, Massachusetts? To each one, he responded, "I'd love to."
Will you come to Colorado to continue your skiing? Again, rich
laughter. Was he prisoner of the Vatican? "I've only been here four
or five days."

He told an American reporter, "I hope the American press is
good to me and the church." Then, finally, at the end, at the back of
the hall, after a forty-minute impromptu press conference, somebody reminded him that he had forgotten the apostolic blessing.
He apologized to the reporters, cupped his hands like a
megaphone once again, and shouted the blessing above the noise of
the milling crowd.

One reporter asked him just before he left whether he thought
that, like his predecessor, he would be a pope of hope. "I hope so,"
he said. It was a show-and-a-half. Even cynical Mary McGrory
seems to have liked it.

Sunday, October 22

John Paul II received the pallium (the small white band worn
around the neck and shoulders) as bishop of Rome before 200,000
people in the Piazza San Pietro. Upon receiving it, he said: "To the
See of Peter there succeeds today a bishop who is not Roman, a
bishop who is a son of Poland. But from this moment he too
becomes a Roman. Yes, a Roman. He is a Roman also because he is
a son of a nation whose history, in its thousand-year traditions, is
marked by a living, strong, unbroken, and deeply felt link with the
See of Peter—a nation which has ever remained faithful to the See
of Rome."

It was a simple talk made dazzling by the fact that he spoke to the crowd and to the world watching on television in Latin and in eleven other languages and by the strong, poignant plea to the whole of humankind at the end, "Pray for me! Help me to be able to serve you!"

The sky was leaden and overcast with the sun breaking through intermittently. Thank God, it didn't rain again. The Polish contingent went wild, waving their red and white banners furiously. The most dramatic moment of all was when Cardinal Stefan Wyszynski came up to make his pledge of loyalty. The pope stood up, embraced him, and kissed Wyszynski's ring to the tumultuous applause of the whole crowd, with the Poles again leading the way in enthusiasm. At the end the pope walked down toward the crowd carrying his crosier as though it were an Alpine walking stick. Then, holding it in both hands as if it were a battle-ax or a giant sword of faith, the pope shook the crosier at the cheering crowd. When a little boy rushed up with flowers, a fussy monsignor tried to chase him away. But the pope grabbed the little bambino and hugged him.

After the mass was over and he had returned to his apartment, the crowds kept cheering and the pope repeatedly appeared at his window. Finally he said, "It's time for everybody to eat lunch, even the pope!" and ended the momentous events of the day with a laugh.

You can tell, somebody said to me, that he studied for the stage. He doesn't miss a trick.

He sure doesn't. We lucked out twice. Whatever else is going to come in the months ahead, we have for a second time a hopeful holy man who smiles, who hugs little children and climbs mountains and waves a crosier like an Alpine stick or a shillelagh.

Epilogue

The Making of the Popes 1978

ROME

Thanksgiving Day, November 23, 1978

It was just three years ago this week that I began my first reconnaissance of Rome to study the making of the pope. Now the story comes to an end. I feel some relief at having the enormous burden of the book and the repeated transatlantic flights off my back. Maybe nostalgia is setting in, too, but the excitement of the story in retrospect is appealing. I'm going to miss Rome and I'm going to miss the various people I've come to know here.

The weather is as much unlike the first time I was here as I can possibly imagine. It is clear, crisp, cool but not cold; one can survive the day nicely in a suit coat and the evening in a light topcoat. It's interesting—almost December and one rides through the streets of Rome and sees flowers blooming in the balcony gardens. The city has its usual fascination for me. I'm delighted to see it again, and I'm sure I'll be delighted to leave it. St. Peter's Square, the Via della Conciliazione, the Sala Stampa all seem curiously deserted without the crowds of people, the reporters with their typewriters, the TV people with their cameras, the radio men with their cassette recorders, the guards at the door, people swarming in and out; even the tourist trade is down. If you could guarantee this kind of weather in late November, it would be a wonderful time to come to Rome. One doesn't even have to wait for taxis, which is a marvel.

Karol Wojtyla, Papa Jan Pawel, owns this city backwards and forwards, up and down, every which way. Right now it is his. His moves, his presence, his smile, his friendliness, his gestures have thus far pleased everyone. He has handled the first six weeks of his job with the accomplished skills of a professional actor and a professional politician. One cannot help but marvel at the flawlessness of his performance. I suppose the best symbol of it is the poster one sees on the pillars and walls of the Via della Conciliazione put up by the Communist mayor of Rome welcoming the Polish pope as a hero of the resistance against the Nazis during the war and welcoming him in the name of the Polish soldiers who died in the liberation of Rome.

He received Archbishop Marcel Lefebvre the other day at Lefebvre's request. Such old quasi-Lefebvrists as Silvio Oddi and

Giuseppe Siri paved the way. Oddi is one of the "Piacenza mafia." (Piacenza is a city in northern Italy which is a stronghold of traditionalism and of Lefebvre's supporters. There are three cardinals there, each more reactionary than the other: Opilio Rossi, Silvio Oddi, and Antonio Samore. All are substantially to the right of the last Etruscan ruler of this district.) Lefebvre apparently wanted to make peace. It is not clear that he will be able to yet, but apparently John Paul has charmed him. He embraced him when he came into the office and he embraced him again when he left. He embraces everybody—Communist mayors and right-wing bishops. Similarly, he received Bishop Méndez Arceo of Cuernavaca, Mexico, who, while still a bishop in good standing, represents the left wing of the church. The right-wingers are happy he saw Lefebvre, the left-wingers are happy he saw Méndez Arceo of Mexico; if he had omitted one or the other, half the crowd would have been unhappy. Now he has pleased everyone.

He has won the Romans. Indeed, wherever he goes there are tens of thousands of them. Visits to Assisi and to the Church of Santa Maria sopra Minerva to venerate the remains of St. Catherine were the gestures that finally won over the Italians completely. He is great with crowds—shaking hands, smiling, talking, kissing babies. The Italians have almost claimed him as one of their own. Adolpho told me yesterday that many of the Italians he knows opened bottles of champagne to celebrate his election simply because they wanted a cleansing of the Italian clericalism that has dominated the Vatican. They are opening second bottles of champagne now that they have discovered how thoroughly Italian, in the good sense of the word, his style is.

The protocol types are still trying to close in on him, but without success. He just dismisses them. The more serious problem is with the security types, who are worried silly about what's going to happen—as is the Italian government, which has to worry about traffic jams whenever he moves out of the Vatican. There's a story in one of the papers that sometime relatively early in his papacy he wanted to go over to see Wyszynski, so he said to his Polish secretary, "Let's go see the primate. How can we go?" The Polish secretary suggested a taxi, but John Paul replied, "No, the taxi drivers would recognize us." So they simply put on black cassocks, walked out of the gate of the Vatican, walked over to Wyszynski's house, saw him, and walked back. The Italian security people went bananas when they heard that. They say that the Swiss Guards who saw the pope walk back into the Vatican still haven't got over the shock.

He is working like crazy—they say eighteen hours a day; he has read all the documentation of Paul VI's administration; he's seeing everybody; he has a tremendous output of writing. He writes most of the talks he gives, and when he doesn't write them, he asks for materials and suggestions and puts them together himself. In the morning he receives visitors; in the afternoon he deals with the Curia, which means they don't get much chance to sleep; in the evening he reads. This makes for a very, very tough day. It's not clear how much exercise he's getting; he half-walks, half-jogs in the Vatican garden a couple of days a week. He told one man that to avoid nervousness he needs three hundred hours of exercise a year, which comes down to about an hour a day. Thus far he doesn't seem to be getting it.

Friday, November 24

I bumped into John Long from the Secretariat for Christian Unity today and heard some interesting stories and ideas. John said that when the pope talked to the ecumenical people, he was speaking in French and used the plural *nous* for "we"; then he smiled, because he had banned the use of the majestic "we," and said, "I mean, all of us here," gesturing to his ecumenical staff to make sure they understood that when he was using the plural he meant the plural and not the majestic form of the first person.

John said that we have a *kairos* going now. *Kairos* is a Greek word meaning a time of opportunity, an appropriate time, a time of grace. The pope is an absolute genius, a man of extraordinary skills and powers and abilities; he is forcing us to rethink our theology of papal influence. It may not be all that important what the papal powers are or how they are defined. What counts is the person who is pope and the way he radiates goodness.

Saturday, November 25

I have come into possession of a curious document. It's a memo, a series of notes from the Italian government's spy in the Secretariat of State. The Italian government apparently has on

retainer a staff member of the secretariat who keeps Giulio Andreotti personally informed about what happens there. It's a memo
put together the day after the election of John Paul II. My impression after having read over the document is that Andreotti is
wasting his money. There's very little in it that he could not have
gotten out of newspapers. On the other hand, it probably makes
him feel good to have someone watching things from the inside. It
seems to me that the author knew nothing of what went on inside
the conclave, that the accounts from the press were more accurate
than the information he had available, and that he is simply reporting the gossip that was going around in the corridors of the Secretariat of State. For example, there is not a mention of the fact that
Giovanni Benelli and Giuseppe Siri canceled each other out the
first day. One has the impression that the author is trying to blame
certain people for the new pope's not being Italian.

First, the report says that the candidacy of Wojtyla was
pushed especially by the West Germans, the English-speaking
North Americans, the English, and the representatives of the
Third World, because these people were against having an Italian
pope, and also because they were against "openings" and compromises, especially any which would lead to the election of
another such "infantile" pope as John Paul I. That some of the
Germans might have thought John Paul I to be infantile is not
beyond believing; that the North Americans, English, or Third
World types (Africans and Asians, I presume) would have thought
the same strikes me as being exceedingly unlikely.

Second, the author of the memo says that in the congregations
leading up to the conclave, North American and German cardinals
complained that they were paying most of the financial cost of the
church and that they were being compromised by the erratic
financial speculation that was going on in the Vatican. That does not
seem to me to be a total impossibility. I don't think such complaints
would have been made on the floor of the congregations, but in the
private consultations there certainly would have been complaints
about the Michele Sindona scandal and other things.

Third, the author says that some of the cardinals were looking
for an "intransigent and conservative" pope who would eliminate
the errors that had occurred since the Second Vatican Council.
Again, doubtless there were such people, but it seems to me that
they supported Siri, not Wojtyla.

Fourth, he observes that many of the cardinals wanted a pastoral pope rather than a curial pope, because a pastoral pope would better understand the difficulties of ordinary people. In particular, he notes, the Germans, the English, the North Americans, and the English-speaking in general had been impressed with the sympathetic and outgoing personality of Wojtyla, whom they had met during his trip around the world. It is also said by the author of the document that the pope had been very close to the young people in his own country and that there is reason to suspect that he will be very sympathetic to young people now as pope. He states that the curial reaction to the election was very negative. He also suggests that the "despot" Benelli will be called back to be secretary of state.

Saturday Afternoon

I've learned that the Latin American cardinals are absolutely delighted with John Paul II, and that Eduardo Pironio is especially pleased. One of the things the pope asked Pironio (he asked everyone this) was "What do you think I should be doing that I'm not doing?" Pironio said he thought the pope ought to preside over the annual monthly "cabinet" meeting of the heads of all the Roman congregations. Pope Paul VI stayed away because he was afraid he would inhibit discussion. Instead, it turned out that nobody discussed anything because there was no point in discussing anything in the pope's absence. Pironio said to the new pope, "I almost had your predecessor talked into presiding over those things, and I would like to try to talk you into it." To which the pope replied, "You don't have to talk me into it, I'll be there." I've also found from a source that he will attend the Latin American bishops' conference in Puebla, Mexico.

Someone also suggested to me today that speculation about John Krol's emerging as the proconsul of the American church was groundless. "Wojtyla is grateful to Krol for the help he has provided Poland, and he would never say an unkind thing about him. Yet nobody in Poland doubts that Wojtyla sees through Krol. You should have seen the look on Wojtyla's face when Krol traveled around Poland in a helicopter provided by a rich friend."

Apparently Cardinal John Cody of Chicago has successfully

played the Polish ethnic card to frustrate attempts by responsible church officials to remove him.

After the election of John Paul II, Cardinal Cody parlayed his past financial contributions to Poland (and some new contributions, according to Chicago sources), the size of the Polish population in Chicago, and his alleged friendship with the pope into a successful counteroffensive against his enemies. John Paul II, according to what the cardinal told visitors in early December, merely offered him a job in Rome, which he declined. The pope, the cardinal intimated, indicated that the matter was thus closed.

Doubtless John Paul II is reluctant to act against a cardinal who helped elect him, though he should have known from the unsuccessful attempts of Cardinal Benelli three years ago to resolve the "Chicago problem" by a Roman appointment that it would not work. He also should know that Cardinal Baggio is not the kind of man to recommend the replacement of a cardinal unless the need for such action is extremely critical.

One must be cautious about turning one's own local concerns into a sweeping judgment of a man's leadership qualities; however, a pope who is not strong enough to deal with the mess in Chicago may not be strong enough to deal with other messy problems in the church. In any initial attempt to evaluate John Paul II, his backing down in face of Cardinal Cody's wheelings and dealings, despite the advice of his own staff, must raise serious questions about personal weakness. One must hasten to add that there are other signs of personal strength. But they don't prevent the lifeblood of the largest archdiocese in the United States from slowly oozing down the drain. I hope to God that this isn't going to be a papal reign in which the wheeler-dealers will inherit the earth.

Two minor points to wind up today. First of all, as best I can find out, the Siri people really thought they were going to win. It was not a ploy, not a trick. Second, a certain ecclesiastic, touring Asia after the August conclave, asked a number of Asian cardinals what they thought about or knew about the new pope—Luciani (John Paul I). At first they reported they didn't know much about him at all, that they knew practically nothing about him. One Asian cardinal said, though, "It is my impression he has very poor health." So at least one cardinal, and probably more, voted for Luciani because he was the person to vote for, even knowing that his health was poor. It is, as I said repeatedly in Rome, a hell of a way to elect a pope.

Similarly, I have to reflect tonight, as I am sitting in my room at the Hilton, reading three books by Jan Pawel, about how many of the people who went in to vote for him had any idea of the material in these books. One is a series of papers, another is a philosophical anthropology book, and the third is a spiritual book called *Sign of Contradiction*. All are fine works, all display a very keen, sensitive, sophisticated mind. But how many of the men who voted for him knew that he had written these books, much less what was in them? Perhaps the leaders of the coalition did, but still one must conclude, on this misty late November evening, that the College of Cardinals seems to have been much luckier than it deserved to be in the men it chose this summer.

Sunday, November 26

I learned this afternoon at brunch at Mickey Wilson's that the pope still moderates doctoral dissertations at the university back in Poland. Indeed, he has already found time among his other work to send back with critical comments two doctoral dissertations submitted since he's been pope. He has read, commented on, and returned to Warsaw two manuscripts! Apparently he plans to have a seminar during the spring with his doctoral students to check up on their work. In addition to being a poet, a playwright, an actor, and a marvelous crowd-pleaser, he also continues to be a college professor.

Monday Morning, November 27—Fiumicino Airport

The clouds have cleared away, the sky is blue once again. My fears of being marooned by a week of rain have dissipated with the clouds. The pope's Angelus talk yesterday was front-page news in the Italian papers. Its theme was sympathy with those who are suffering for the faith in various parts of the world. Eastern Europe was not mentioned explicitly; indeed, he has been careful to avoid specific mention of Eastern Europe. When he talks about religious freedom, he always does so at a general level. After lunch he said mass for the lay leaders of the various Catholic organizations of Rome. This is apparently part of his campaign to integrate himself into the Rome diocese. He met first with the clergy, next the seminarians, and then with the lay leadership. Unfortunately, I think the functionaries have persuaded him to remain in the Vatican and let these people come to see him. It would be much better if he could go out and see them, though I understand the problem of the Italian police and government—150,000 and more people in St. Peter's Square yesterday for the Angelus. If the man ventures forth from the Vatican at all—at least if his venturing forth is announced—the whole city of Rome will get tied up.

The Angelus talk yesterday, the text of which was in this morning's papers, was an impressive enough sermon; but it's really not front-page news—at least not the kind of sermon 150,000 people would normally stop off to hear. So the Papa Wojtyla charisma is red hot in this city.

I had supper last night with Signor Cardinale. He seems in reasonably good health. Despite his operation, he did not look haggard. It was hard to read his reaction to the new pope, though his loyal and dedicated secretary seemed quite positive about Wojtyla.

But there are two shadows. The first, nationalism, and the other, narrowness.

Two Polish priests in Rome before the conclave, when asked about the possibility of a Polish pope, reacted in horror. "Please God, no, we Poles are far too nationalistic to be trusted with the papacy." They did not have Karol Wojtyla in mind and no one asked them specifically about him. There are excellent grounds for Polish nationalism. Poland has a rich, proud, durable culture which has had to fight for centuries to survive. Loyalty—tough, tenacious, powerful—goes hand-in-hand with such nationalism. Nor is there anything unacceptable about such loyalty. Yet it raises some problems.

Indeed, in a touching farewell to his Polish colleagues, he was warned by his seventy-seven-year-old senior, Cardinal Wyszynski, "Now you must embrace not only Poland, but the world." Papa Wojtyla replied to *all* fellow countrymen without exception (including the members of the Communist party), respecting their beliefs and their convictions: "Love of country unites us and must unite us above and beyond all difference. This has nothing in common with narrow nationalism or chauvinism, but springs from the law of the human heart. . . . It is not easy to renounce returning to my homeland, to the fields rich with crops, the hills and valleys, the lakes and rivers, the people who are so loved, to the royal city of Cracow. . . . Do not forget me in prayers at Jasna Gora."

The other problem is related but more subtle. How can one make the enormous leap from Cracow to Rome? In Poland the church has been under siege. It is a garrison resisting a deadly enemy. Loyalty is the most important of virtues. Unity against the enemy is the only sensible strategy. Pluralism is self-destructive and self-critical; long discussion and angry internal confrontation are luxuries which cannot be afforded.

The discipline, the style, the strategies, and the perspectives of the church in Poland are not necessarily appropriate in other countries; undoubtedly John Paul II knows this, and yet the habits, the thought patterns, the responses of a lifetime are hard to shed. The pope now presides over a church in which pluralism is essential, in which free discussion is inevitable, and in which the need for loyalty and for unity may seem oppressive or irrelevant. Karol Wojtyla is going to have to draw back from the attitudes, opinions, and perspectives of a lifetime to be fully effective in his new job.

An example illustrates the problem: some 500 applications for dispensation from celibacy have piled up on his desk. The pope, who apparently never processed a single application for dispensation from the priesthood in Cracow while he was prince-archbishop, is reported to be planning to develop new and presumably tougher norms for those who wish to leave the priesthood. A firm stand against priestly resignations may make sense in a garrison church, but will look like oppression in the rest of the world, especially since there is considerable popular sympathy for men who want to leave the priesthood. Paul VI may have erred in permitting relatively easy resignation, but to reverse that policy now would lead to a world outcry. Will he get the kind of negative feedback on this issue which he needs to avoid a dangerous mistake?

Another example: a lead from a press association dispatch announced, "Pope John Paul II today insisted that priests return to the custom of clerical dress."

I hadn't seen anything like that in the talk, so I dug through it again and found this passage: "We must preserve the sense of our unique vocation, and such uniqueness must be expressed even in our external dress. Let's not be ashamed of it. Yes, we are in the world. But we are not of the world."

The context and the style would indicate that the pope was not laying down rules, not even for the clergy of Rome, much less for the priests of the world, so the press reaction was excessive and unfair.

Nonetheless, this quote illustrates the difference between Cracow and Rome. It seems reasonably clear that as a matter of personal opinion and preference the pope believes that priests ought to wear clerical garb (in Poland they wear cassocks most of the time—they even wear Roman collars when they ski). One might agree with him (and this writer does) that priests should be clearly recognizable as priests and that there is an enormous symbolic power in the identifying marks of priesthood (though, of course, there is room for flexibility in the specifics of these identifying marks). Yet there *are* places in the world where clerical garb is counterproductive. And even in other situations, there is a strong conviction among clergy (not always supported by the facts) that clerical dress sets them so much apart from other human beings that they lose their ministerial effectiveness. The issue is not whether Karol Wojtyla as pope is going to legislate requirements in clerical dress for the whole world. It is unlikely that he will. The issue is whether he can perceive that a strategy for clerical attire that is appropriate and necessary in Poland may be unnecessary and inappropriate in other countries and, further, whether he will come to realize that even passing remarks in addresses to highly specific audiences are going to be seized on as definitive policy statements by the rest of the world.

On specific issues, those who equate progress in the church with the ordination of women and of married men are almost certainly going to be disappointed with John Paul II. At least initially, there will be no change on these matters. The new pope has not come to Rome with strong convictions that such changes are necessary. On the contrary, he has come to Rome with grave reservations about such reforms. If there is sufficient pressure from the bishops of the world and, through the bishops, from the clergy and laity of the world, he can certainly be expected to be willing to listen. The possibility of the ordination of married men in some countries where the shortage of priests is acute certainly ought not to be excluded. One would be completely unjustified in expecting that presently ordained priests in the United States will be permitted to marry. Certainly they will not be so permitted as the result of any unilateral action from the pope (or any pope likely to have been elected by the College of Cardinals as it was constituted in 1978). Doubtless, most American Catholics are in favor of such a reform, but that does not mean that the issue is very salient on their agenda, or that they are likely to push very hard for such a change. Nor does the American hierarchy feel strong pressures to seek either the ordination of married men or permission for presently ordained priests to marry, both of which reforms, by the way, would constitute a modification of rules and not of doctrine.

The ordination of women to the diaconate would also present no problem of doctrine, but there does not seem to be widespread world demand for it, even from Catholic feminist leadership. The ordination of women to the priesthood might present a doctrinal problem (some theologians think it would, others disagree), but outside the United States there does not seem to be a very powerful demand for it. In the United States the demand for women priests does not seem to be strong enough for there to be notable pressure on the bishops to bring the issue to the pope's attention. Again, should there be a worldwide movement to seek the ordination of women, one can expect Pope John Paul II to listen. But the point must be made that presently there is little pressure on him even to listen seriously to such requests and that he himself, coming from a country where clerical celibacy and the ordination of women are not issues that are widely discussed, is certainly not likely to be predisposed to introduce the discussion to the rest of the church (as far as the present writer is concerned, I am in favor of the ordination of women and also in favor of clerical celibacy, a position which I think is reasonably unique).

On sexual issues the best available source is the pope's book on sexuality, written twenty years ago. It is a candid discussion of the problems of frigidity, and it places emphasis on the need for sexual pleasure in marriage—in these regards it was certainly many years ahead of its time. While he accepts, apparently even intellectually, the teaching of *Humanae Vitae* on the need for each act of sexual intercourse to be in some fashion open to the possibility of procreation, he also seems to be very "pastoral" in his approach to the implementation of *Humanae Vitae*, stressing in his talks while he was archbishop of Cracow the need for priests to respect the good-faith decisions of married couples who are under enormous conflicting pressures. *Humanae Vitae*, in other words, seems in his mind to represent the ideal of Christian marriage and birth control, yet there must be tremendous pastoral sympathy for deviation from that ideal, especially when it is a good-faith deviation. Unfortunately for that position, many Catholic married couples, particularly in the West, do not like the implication that their married love is imperfect or second-rate because they are practicing contraception. Nor do they accept the basic premise that every sexual act must be open to procreation. Both in his play, *The Goldsmith Shop*, and in his moral theological writing, John Paul demonstrates his profound insight into the marriage relationship. One wonders if he is going to be able to listen to the experience of married people in a critically important aspect of their lives. Paul VI's most serious mistake lay in his refusing to listen to the married people on his birth control commission while allowing himself to be influenced by frightened curialists. John Paul may not be influenced by scheming curialists, but can he listen to married laypeople and understand what they have been trying to say to the church now for at least twenty years?

For the ordinary Catholic layperson, John Paul's decisions on sexual matters are going to be the most important ones of his pastorate, just as were the decisions on the same subject for Paul VI. If the ordinary Catholic laymen and laywomen do not think the pope is listening to them or understands them or is not sympathetic to their problems, then they will eventually turn him off, just as they did Paul VI. I would have thought, before I began this book, that disillusionment with the papacy and the institutional church could not be any more shattering than it was in the late 1960s. I would have thought that it would be impossible for Catholics ever again to have such euphoric expectations as they had in the days during and immediately after the Second Vatican Council. I'm convinced now that was an erroneous judgment. The euphoria created by the year of the three popes has kindled hope in the papacy once again among the rank-and-file membership of the Catholic church. If they feel let down again, the blow to their confidence in the papacy will, if anything, be even more severe, and the trauma to the church more violent.

I do not intend to suggest that such a disillusionment will occur. I don't think it will; I hope it will not. But honesty and realism compel me not to exclude the possibility. I have discharged all my obligations to such virtues. I have properly hedged my enthusiasm as well as my bet.

CHICAGO

Monday, December 18

The pope sang Christmas carols with children in the Piazza San Pietro last Sunday. A boy from Italy sent him money for poor children in Poland. He walked into the Vatican store the other day to buy a sweater for himself. He listens carefully to the suggestions of visiting bishops—those who have the courage to make them—and asks them for memos on important subjects.

He is reported to look very tired; he has lost five pounds, causing his doctor (a woman, by the way—wonder what the Vatican Press Office makes of that) considerable worry. He admits that he is working too hard and trying to do too much as, like his predecessor, he tries to get a firm grip on the job and put the stamp of his own style on the papacy.

The world press seems to have missed completely the most interesting thing he's done yet: the appointment of his own replacement on the Council of the Synod of Bishops. The new member is George Basil Hume of Westminster—a progressive, an intellectual, and a man with confidence in the future. I take it as an iron rule of politics that anyone who appoints a replacement for himself will choose someone with whose positions and personality he identifies. The naming of Hume to the council of the synod may be the best hint we have of what Jan Pawel has in mind for his papacy.

(According to reliable reports, however, Hume had the highest number of votes among those who were not elected to the Council of the Synod. He was therefore the logical appointment. It is still not without significance that the pope accepted the logic of members when he need not have done so.)

Chorus

And a final word to our pope:

Dear Jan Pawel II: *Niech bedzie pochwalony Jezus Chrystus!*

People are saying that you're the most gifted pope we've ever had. I've gone through the history books of about the last five hundred years and I think they're right. Philosophers we've had before, but not philosophers with enough published articles to guarantee a faculty position at almost any university in the world. Poets we've had; your predecessor Leo XIII wrote lovely sonnets (and did any number of other things about which the Catholic history books are rather silent). A man of great public presence we've had before, but never a man who sparred with the press, kissed babies, and spoke on world television in eleven languages. Heroes of the faith we've had before, and those aplenty, but you're the first one who ever literally risked his life to save Jews from anti-Semitic murderers. In your modesty you would doubtless laugh it off, but the charge of being the most gifted pope in history seems on the record to be irrefutable.

Nor, since you emerged on the balcony of St. Peter's on that gorgeous moonlit evening in October, have you made any wrong moves. From the first "Praise be Jesus Christ" spoken in Italian to a befuddled Roman citizenry, you have with ease and elegance done just exactly the right thing; to express it in American terms, you have pleased the readers both of *Our Sunday Visitor* and of *Commonweal*, the right and the left, almost without exception.

It is now the "honeymoon" time, of course, the beginning of a new administration, when the press and public are automatically enthusiastic about everything a new leader does. This time will not last, and you can expect the sniping criticisms to begin soon. No man, however gifted or adroit, can please everyone all the time. You have tough decisions to make in the days ahead about the organization of the Roman Curia, about the acute financial problems the church faces, about the power of the Synod of Bishops and the various national hierarchies, and about human sexuality. Doubtless you will make these decisions, as you have made all the decisions in your life as a church leader, through consultation, study, prayer, and a careful attempt to build a broad consensus. It is not, however, about these issues that I am writing.

It is rather about the humanity of the papacy that I want to speak. Those of us who were annoyed and then angered by the way the bevy of little monsignors hemmed in and harassed your holy predecessor in his public appearances are delighted at the way you brush them off. We were pleased and touched by your reported visit in a black suit to your close friend, Bishop Andre Deskur, in a Roman hospital. Your informality with churchmen, reporters, and ordinary people has captured the imagination of much of the world. My plea to you in this letter is this: don't let "them" stop you. I do not think "they" are ill-intentioned men. They do their job as they see it. They are trying to protect the majesty and the sanctity of the papal office. What they don't understand and what you apparently do understand is that the majesty and the holiness of the office do not depend on the perpetuation of an outmoded Renaissance court ritual, but on the goodness, the openness, and the hopefulness of the man who occupies the office. Much of the papal style that has lasted through the years seems calculated to deny the humanity of the pope, but this is surely a counterproductive strategy. As Jesus himself well knew, we cannot be inspired by a man who isn't human like us. Hopefulness, courage, and joy are only inspiring when we observe them in somebody in whose rich humanity we see a reflection of our own humanity. Those little monsignors who try to make the pope something more than human in fact often make him somewhat less than human.

There is the rumor that you were married and that your wife was killed by the Nazis. You have denied the rumor (with a smile, I'm told) and I accept your denial, but I cannot understand why an American cardinal characterized the story as scurrilous, offensive, and part of a Communist plot. I fail to see how, even if the rumor were true, it would detract in the slightest from your holiness or your dignity as a pope. We know from scripture that one of your predecessors, a certain Simon Peter, was married (how else could he have had a mother-in-law for the Lord to cure?). The mentality, Jan Pawel II, that denied on a priori grounds the possibility of a pope's being a widower is the enemy of the new papacy that you seem to be striving to create.

So my plea—and I'm sure I speak for millions of other Catholics around the world—is "Don't let them get to you." Keep on climbing the mountains, canoeing the rivers, rushing down the ski slopes, for God made the mountains and the rivers and the ski slopes, and they are good; the pope's enjoyment of them merely reflects God's goodness and makes the whole papacy more luminous, rather than less.

Continue to write your poetry, sing your folk songs, play your guitar, and even write your philosophical articles. What a terrible comment on the church it would be if it forced its leader to shed some of his most admirable and appealing characteristics.

In fact, you might think about sometime singing your religious folk songs on world television. That such a suggestion of a singing pope would shock so many people (and I'm sure it will) merely illustrates how far the process of dehumanizing the papacy has gone. A papal folk-sing would horrify the stodgy, somber, grim-faced people who equate our faith with propriety and dignity instead of joy and hope. I do not want to make too much of this perhaps extraordinary suggestion. I use it as an illustration. Still, it would be one of the most powerful sermons that the world has ever heard in its long history—a song-fest of religious joy and hope in eleven languages presided over by a pope. No one would dare to dismiss Catholic Christianity after something like that.

Don't let them get to you, Holy Father. Don't let them get to you.

With respect and prayers.

The Swiss — the palace guard

Few cardinals mingled with the people or the press before the conclaves. It was a time for prayer and business.

The Carabinieri — Italy's special police were always on guard.

St. Peter's: a place for the sacred, the secular.

Jim Roache presided at the daily press briefing. He was one of the few pros in the Vatican Press Office.

Ballot after ballot, the media — and the world — waited for the smoke. Cameras were always kept trained on an old stove pipe waiting to record a billow of either black or white smoke.

After the election of John Paul II, the
American delegation met the press.
Whether individually or collectively, they
had no power, no influence.

Reporters inspecting the Sistine Chapel.
They concluded that the accommodations
were so bad that the cardinals could not
survive staying in a long conclave.

The Sala Stampa — the Vatican's press hall —
where no news was bad news.

Occasional background
briefings were held at
the USO in Rome.
Here Cardinals
Carberry and Dearden
meet with reporters the
day before entering
their second conclave
in less than two
months.

Through warm brilliant days and cool cloudless nights, hundreds of thousands waited for the smoke signal.

A centuries worn, cast iron stove in the Sistine Chapel was the source of the smoke signal problems.

The computer said Wojtyla

Photo by Tom Drape

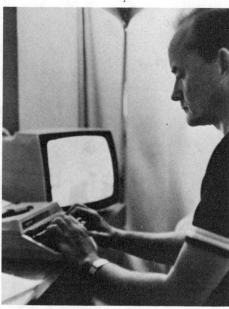

Photo by Tom Drape

The author, and his computer (an IBM 370/165), spent over three years researching and writing this account of the year of the three popes.

Photo by Tom Drape

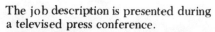
The job description is presented during a televised press conference.

Photo courtesy CBS

The extended mourning period after the death of Pope John Paul I kept the lines inside of St. Peter's long (r.) while outside photographers and television technicians (below) prepared for yet another conclave.

The day on which Pope John Paul II was elected, Jordan Bonfante, TIME's Bureau Chief, who was considered "the best journalist in Rome" was more anxious than most. He needed a cover story in twelve hours.

The days during the October conclave (right) saw larger crowds than were present during the August conclave because most Romans had been on the traditional summer holiday. Yet many did return in August to be met by the long hot sun (below).

A party to which everyone came.

Notes

Overture

1. The tape-recorded diary I kept of my activities of the next three years, edited into presentable English but not altered substantively, is my principal data source for the book.

Prologue
Scene I

1. The Secretariat of State is the central Vatican administrative department. Within its office is the Council for Public Affairs, which handles diplomatic and other relations with civil governments. Casaroli is head of this office and hence responsible for the Vatican Ostpolitik, that is, its attempts to reach accommodations with the Communist governments in Eastern Europe.

2. To be clear at the beginning, I note that there are probably four different Curias:

(a) The *Roman Curia*: This is the central administrative body of the church, made up of congregations and commissions which are presided over generally by a cardinal with a "board of trustees" made up of other cardinals, some bishops, and occasionally other clerics who vote only on major decisions. Beneath the cardinal is a secretary and an undersecretary and a staff of assistants. The cardinal, the secretary, and the undersecretary now are not often Italians. Indeed, in the cardinal "prefect" position there are many more non-Italians than Italians, much to the dismay of many of the resident Italian cardinals who have no major administrative responsibilities. At the junior staff level, however, most of the Curia members are still Italian and tend to a rather narrow Italian ecclesiastical style of thought. The Roman Curia, then, is the church's central administrative civil service, internationalized at the top level but still mostly Italian at lower levels.

(b) The *Curia of Paul VI*: This is the quasi-internationalized Curia that Paul VI had tried to set up, with foreign cardinals presiding over congregations still staffed mostly by Italians: Franjo Seper, at the Holy Office; Bernardin Gantin, at the Commission for Peace and Justice; Johannes Willebrands, at the Secretariat of Christian Unity, for example, as well as the secretary of state. However, the Curia of Paul VI is something less than successful because many of the foreign cardinals—Gabriel-Marie Garrone and Seper, for example—have been figureheads, unable to tame their administrative infrastructures, which, like those in all bureaucracies, resist change.

(c) The *Curia of Giovanni Benelli*: The undersecretary of state, Benelli was originally brought in to aid the mild-mannered Cardinal Jean Villot. However, he in fact quickly became Paul VI's personal chief of staff and, with energy, intelligence, and ruthless efficiency, dedicated himself completely to the service of the pope, organizing in his own office a mini-Curia which supervised the actions of all the other congregations and commissions, often ramming through decisions which these other groups did not want and rejecting decisions which they did want. Benelli plays, in effect, a role like the one Alexander Haig played in the Nixon White House, and H. R. Haldeman before that—the personal chief of staff who bends the bureaucracy to the will of the chief administrator insofar as it is bendable.

(d) The *Italian Curia*: The Italian Curia, not all of whose members are Italian, is that informal group of churchmen who generally support the policy and the perspective of the more conservative Italian cardinals residing in Rome.

Many of the curial cardinals, that is to say, resident Italian cardinals in Rome, bitterly resent the curias of both Paul VI and Benelli because they (men like Antonio Samore, Pietro Palazzini) have, after lifelong service to the ecclesiastical organization, usually in diplomatic service, been excluded from positions of power and prestige. There is also no love lost between the curias of Paul VI and Benelli, because the former looks on the latter as ruthlessly depriving it of its freedom.

Usually, when people speak of the Curia, they mean the Italian civil service, that group which has come out of the civil service, and their allies outside of Rome (like Siri). But even here, one must be careful of terms. Men like Cardinal Sebastiano Baggio, Cardinal Sergio Pignedoli and Archbishop Benelli are Italians, and products of the church's diplomatic service. They are more or less at odds with the traditionalists in the Curia who would look northward to Siri for leadership. To make matters even more confusing, many of the Italian residential bishops—Michele Pellegrino, for example, the red bishop of Turin (who resigned in 1977); Salvatore Pappalardo, the archbishop of Palermo; Antonio Poma, the archbishop of Bologna; and Albino Luciani, the archbishop of Venice (who apparently avoids Rome as though it were a contagious disease)—are far more open-minded than their curial compatriots and far more likely to think that the Vatican Council was a good idea.

3. Ernie Primeau, my high-school French and mathematics teacher, former bishop of Manchester in New Hampshire, rector of Villa Stritch, the residence house for American priests working in Rome, and one of the most colorful, insightful, and generous men I have ever known.

4. Pericle Felici is described as a witty but cynical man, quintessentially curial in his style, with some faintly humanizing characteristics, such as an interest in poetry and photography. Vagnozzi was the papal delegate to the United States who shot his mouth off more during his term of office than all the other apostolic delegates put together and is responsible for some of the worst appointments in the American church. Samore got to be an important diplomat mostly because he was an effective typist and virtual slave to the once powerful Cardinal Tardini—he is one of the coldest authoritarians among the curial officials.

5. The Congregation for Bishops does not make nominations in the countries where there is a formal treaty or concordat with the Holy See or in the 850 mission dioceses, or in the oriental Catholic dioceses. Nominations for the first group are made by the Secretariat of State, for the second by the Congregation for the Propagation of the Faith, and for the third by the Oriental Congregation.

6. In retrospect, there were two mistakes in my initial impression of Cardinal Baggio. I missed the point that he is an extremely efficient administrator, one of the best in the Vatican, a quality which is concealed by his pleasant, easygoing smile. Second, I also did not understand how badly factionalized the Curia was and how much opposition to Baggio there would be from other curial officials. If the Curia had rallied behind Baggio, they probably could have elected him in August of 1978 with little trouble. As it turned out, Baggio was instrumen-

tal in the election of the archbishop of Cracow in October, enjoys Jan Pawel's full confidence, and may eventually become his secretary of state.

7. Two reasons were given for Bertoli's resignation. One was that he resented Benelli's pushing for more canonizations to beef up the Holy Year, and the other was that he resented an undersecretary's having been appointed without his consultation. In either case, resigning as head of a congregation is an unheard-of thing to do in Rome; especially when there are so many deserving Italian cardinals (most of them former diplomats) sitting around Rome without a congregation to head.

8. Table 1: RECORD OF VOTING DURING THE 1958 CONCLAVE

Cardinal	1st Ballot	2nd Ballot	3rd Ballot	4th Ballot	5th Ballot	Final Ballot
Roncalli	7	7	8	15	20	38*
Ottaviani	2	5	8	16	15	9
Ruffini	17	17	15	5	5	1
Agagianian	13	13	12	8	6	1
Masella	5	6	4	3	2	1

*Enough to win

9. Consistently throughout my investigation, I underestimated the likelihood of the non-Italian cardinals' being organized and overestimated the probability that the curial cardinals could get their act together. My mistaken assumption about the foreigners resulted from my not realizing how well they had learned the tricks of organization at the council and the various synods. My mistake about the Italians derived from my failure to realize that the forcefulness of the Benelli personality had fractured curial unity. I was also, incidentally, patently wrong about the bugging of the conclave. I guess I overestimated the industry of the Italian journalists.

10. I have received so many questions, both in Rome and subsequently, about the role of the Holy Spirit in papal conclaves that I sought out a theologian friend of mine (quite orthodox, quite moderate) and interviewed him:

Question: Who is the Holy Spirit?

Answer: He is that personality in God or, if you prefer to think of it differently, that dynamism, that energy, that personified power which is revealed in the world by the variety, the diversity, the creativity, the spontaneity of the forces of the universe and particularly the actions of human beings.

Question: Huh?

Answer: St. Peter says that the Spirit speaks to our spirit. By that he means that the creative energies of God speak to the most creative energies in the human personality. The Holy Spirit is God calling us to do that which is most generous, most open, most unique, most authentically good in our personalities.

Question: That sounds like existentialism.

Answer: It's Thomas Aquinas, friend, put in slightly modern language. The Holy Spirit is the spirit of God's love. If you want it put more simply, he calls us to love and when we love we are most uniquely ourselves. Will that do?

Question: I guess so. How does the Holy Spirit work in the world?

Answer: (sigh) The standard Catholic teaching is that God operates in the world through secondary causes; almost all the time, he works on us through the events of ordinary life, and particularly he challenges and comforts us, he calls us to love and generosity through the behavior of other human beings.

Question: Then he doesn't reveal things directly in moments of special revelation?

Answer: Since Thomas Aquinas refuted the doctrine of Peter Lombard, it has been accepted Catholic teaching that the special revelation of the Holy Spirit is rare indeed and that one ought not to live one's life or do one's work counting on such a special revelation.

Question: How does the Holy Spirit work in conclaves?

Answer: Sometimes he doesn't seem to get much chance to work at all. Do you want to make him responsible for Alexander VI, the Borgia pope, or for the conclaves that young Cesare Borgia controlled through bribery and poison? No, at some conclaves the Holy Spirit isn't working at all or, if he is, he doesn't have many votes.

Question: How can the cardinals best cooperate with the Holy Spirit in preparing for a conclave?

Answer: The conclave is an election process. The Holy Spirit will work best with those cardinals who are best prepared for the election process. A cardinal can prepare for the conclave most effectively by familiarizing himself with the issues and the candidates and working hard together with other cardinals to clarify the kind of pope they need and what the church needs and what sort of man is likely to be that kind of pope.

Question: That sounds like politics.

Answer: You're from Chicago, you ought to know politics when you see them.

Question: You mean the Holy Spirit is involved in the political process of a conclave?

Answer: If there isn't any political process, that isn't an election. Where else can the Holy Spirit get involved in elections save working through and with human beings who are doing the electing?

Question: But isn't politics something unworthy of God?

Answer: You should know better than that. Both Aristotle and Aquinas said that politics was among the most noble of human arts. Why shouldn't the Holy Spirit be involved?

Question: Then you mean it is not enough for the cardinals to just sit around and wait for the Holy Spirit to inspire them?

Answer: Even Cardinal Siri has said that the Holy Spirit only works when we do our part.

11. The theology of the *sensus fidelium* is not very well developed, but the basic notion is that the ordinary, devout, believing Catholic people as a collective know what is the authentic tradition of the church. Indeed, for the first thousand years of Christian history, almost all solemn, papal, or episcopal pronouncements contained within them a statement like "with the consent of the whole Christian people," indicating that in those years it was taken for granted that nothing had been validly done unless the believing faithful had made some kind of contribution, at least to the extent of accepting the teaching without protest.

Scene II

1. For two hundred years the Roman Catholic church as an institution has been wrestling with how to adjust to the world that emerged from the multiple revolutions at the end of the eighteenth century—political, industrial, scientific. Three main issues have characterized this struggle: political democracy, modern methods of scholarship, and the role of the Roman pontiff.

Repeatedly since 1800, loyal and dedicated Catholics have argued that, far from being opposed to modern science and scientific methods, the Roman Catholic tradition ought to be open to them, because traditionally the church has been not only responsive to the quest for knowledge but a leader in it. They have also argued that, far from being opposed to political democracy, the church, which for the first fourteen hundred years of its history was organized essentially on democratic lines, ought to be most sympathetic to the democratic revolution. (Bishops, abbots, and religious superiors almost always were elected by all of their subjects—to such an extent that other methods of selection were repeatedly denounced as "grievously sinful.") Finally, the "liberal" Catholics have suggested that the pope ought to be the leader in the church's rapprochement with the modern world.

Solidly opposed to this position have been those who in the nineteenth century were called "the intransigents." Sometimes they were prepared to concede the theory that the church once used democratic methods of selecting leadership and once was allied with scholarship and the search for knowledge. The intransigents argued that the modern world was too sinful, too evil, too pagan, too antireligious for the church to trust and that the only proper reaction to the modern world was the same reaction the church displayed to the Reformation: dogged determination to resist it at every turn with the serene confidence that the church would outlive its enemies as it had done repeatedly in the past.

Without a doubt the "liberals" have included some of the great Catholic thinkers of the last two centuries—the Frenchmen, Lacordaire, Lamennais, Montalembert, Dupanloup, and, more recently, de Lubac, Rousselet, and Teilhard de Chardin; the Germans of the famous Tübingen school from Klee in the nineteenth century to Hans Küng in the twentieth; Englishmen like John Henry Newman, Lord Acton; and even Italians like the great philosophers and political thinkers Antonio Rosmini, Gioberti, and Manzoni.

Most of these great men were open in one way or another to modern scholarship, supportive of political democracy, and eager for a reformed, modernized papacy. If most of the church's best thinkers were on the side of the liberals, it must be said that the administrative structure of the church was usually on the side of the intransigents. To make matters worse, intermittent popes would lean in the liberal direction (Pius VII in the early nineteenth century, Leo XIII in the latter part of that century, Benedict XV in this century, for example), to be followed by stern reactionaries. Leo XIII permitted the flowers of liberty, democracy, and serious scholarly research to bloom toward the end of the nineteenth century; he was followed by Pius X, who for all his simplicity and holiness, presided over the most ruthless reign of terror the church had known since the time of the Inquisition. No one was executed or imprisoned, but freedom of thought and expression were utterly and completely suppressed in the name of resisting the so-called modernist heresy.

Furthermore, while undoubtedly the positions denounced by Pius X in his antimodernist encyclical were false to the Catholic teaching, it is not clear that very many of the modernists actually held the positions attributed to them by the encyclical. The encyclical was based on the work of an Italian theologian in Rome who developed an elaborate, systematic, "modernist" theory, which he claimed penetrated to the "real" thought of modernists, a systematic thought which he claimed was latent in their writings. Actually, no modernist writer ever expressed such a system.

Some men's lives were destroyed by the alternation of liberals and intransigents on the papal throne. Others, like Alfred Loisy and the Englishman George Tyrrell, were driven from the church. Tyrrell remained loyal in his own way, Loisy gradually drifted off into what was certainly heresy—though it is less than clear that their positions when condemned were heretical. Still others, the French philosopher Maurice Blondel, the English Baron von Hugel, the Frenchman Teilhard de Chardin, and the French genius Montalembert, were forced to live out their lives endlessly harassed by narrow-minded, inquisitorial reactionaries.

After the reign of Pius X, there was a brief respite in the reign of Benedict XV, who ended most of the witchhunts of the reign of his predecessor under the auspices of Cardinal Merry del Val. Both Pius XI and Pius XII continued the generally repressive approach toward both scholarship and political democracy. The founder of the precursor of the Christian Democratic party in Italy, the brilliant Sicilian priest, Luigi Sturzo, was driven into exile, and until World War II, Catholic historical and scriptural scholars labored under enormously complex restrictions and restraints.

In the years immediately after the war there was a brief flowering in France and Germany which was halted abruptly by Pius XII in the encyclical letter *Humani Generis*. However, the reactionaries who sent Pius XII on the witchhunt made a major strategic blunder. Their real enemies were not the French Dominicans like M. C. Chenu and Yves Congar and the French Jesuits like Henri de Lubac and the younger Jean Danielou; their real enemies were the German Karl Rahner and the Canadian Bernard Lonergan, whose "transcendental" Thomism represented a dramatic break with traditional Catholic thinking. The conservative Thomists, led by Reginald Garrigou-Lagrange, carried the day in the *Humani Generis* condemnation but lost the war. Catholic philosophical and theological thought in most countries of the world today is shaped not by traditional Thomism but by the existential or transcendental Thomism of Rahner and Lonergan (whose theological teaching rules absolutely supreme in Catholic seminaries and universities in America, for example).

It can be argued, of course, that the intransigents were resisting much that was worth resisting in the modern world—the claims, for example, of the state under Bismarck in Germany or Cavour in Italy to completely dominate religion, the claims of the liberal revolution to be able to take away the rights of minorities in the name of the people, the easy scientific optimism that was wiped out at Hiroshima. In other words there was much in the nineteenth and twentieth centuries that deserved to be resisted.

But few of these political and theological thinkers were unnuanced worshipers of the modern world. They argued more for dialogue and conversation than they did for surrender. They were consistently beaten, for the most part, humiliated, broken, and in some cases, virtually driven out of the church.

If, as the modernists claim, they were more interested in the methods of scholarship than in specific conclusions, then it surely has to be said that while many of the conclusions they drew and certainly the underlying system which the Vatican claimed to have found in their thought (but which they denied was there) would not be taken seriously by contemporary Catholic thinkers, virtually all the historical methods advocated and followed by the modernists are now taken for granted in the church. Similarly, the church's acceptance of democracy, advocated at considerable peril by nineteenth-century thinkers such as Montalembert and Rosmini, is also taken for granted. It must be left to the scholars of the future to determine whether good men were needlessly ground into the dust by a harsh, insensitive, centralized papal bureaucracy which—doubtless with good faith— condemned men for positions that they never really held—at least not in the sense in which they were condemned. This went on from the time of Lamennais in 1830 to the time of Teilhard de Chardin in the 1950s.

John XXIII was a liberal pope in the tradition of Leo XIII, Benedict XV, Pius VII, or the younger Pio Nono (Pius IX), though he was a much more spectacularly successful liberal pontiff. As recently as 1965, E. E. Y. Hales could raise the question of whether the movement started by Pope John's revolution was indeed irreversible. "We are told that the movement now started is irreversible, but it is hard to see why. . . . An able and experienced civil service such as the Curia could circumvent it. A few small steps have been taken toward ecumenism, but they might only lead out into the sand. A new and more generous mood exists, but like all moods it is subject to reaction" (*Pope John and His Revolution* [London: Eyre and Spottiswood, 1965], p. 205).

Ten years later, it would appear that basically Pope John's revolution is irreversible and that it is the major achievement of Paul VI to have made that revolution irreversible. There will be no more white terrors of Pius X, no more blind reactions of Pio Nono, no more ruthless repressions of the *Humani Generis* variety. It is true that the same old curial techniques are still at work. Men's work is investigated and frequently distorted out of meaning and open to condemnation. Some men have lost their jobs, a few have left the church; but the greatest critic of the 1970s, Hans Küng, has not left the church, has not been driven out, has not lost his job, and has only been treated with mild reproof, even though his peace of mind has been assaulted and his integrity viciously questioned—more so, in fact, by German rivals than by papal authorities (though the Germans were undoubtedly egged on by the papal authorities). Paul VI's major achievement was the confirmation of the Johannine reforms. The struggle of the last two centuries is finally ended with the victory of the liberals over the intransigents, an extraordinarily successful victory, one might add, as evidenced by the fact that someone like me, who has done research on the effect of the birth control encyclical and who has openly criticized his archbishop for years, is still a priest in good standing and uncondemned. Seen from this perspective, Pope Paul liberated the church from its vicious cycle of liberal pope followed by intransigent pope. For while he was not as liberal, at least in his style and his enthusiasm, as his predecessor (and what a hard act to follow that was!), and while he did permit himself to be intimidated repeatedly by the Curia and its allies, such as Cardinal Siri, nonetheless he institutionalized the Johannine reforms up to a point. Indeed, he institutionalized them so much that they are now virtually untouchable. The last set of appointments to the College of Cardinals seems to have guaranteed that while the Curia may have the veto power on the next pope, that is all it will have.

We'll probably see Pope Paul VI as the man who solidified and guaranteed the reform impulses which began after the Second World War and which produced the Second Vatican Council and made possible the open window of Pope John. As one progressive Vatican official said to me, "If he had resigned at the age of seventy-five, as he requires other bishops to do, and if he had not written *Humanae Vitae*, he would go down as one of the greatest popes in the church's history." For all my criticisms of the way the Vatican has operated in the last several years, I must completely agree with that judgment.

2. It was a very accurate observation. As will be noted later, it was apparently the Germans who were most enthusiastic about Karol Wojtyla when the October conclave deadlocked.

3. Much of the material here is gathered from Giancarlo Zizola, *Quale Papa* (Rome: Borla Publishing House, 1976).

In 1903, the leading candidate was Cardinal Rampolla, the secretary of state to Leo XIII, who would have continued Leo XIII's liberal or quasi-liberal policy. He led during the first days but by the fourth ballot had only thirty of the forty-two votes he needed. The Austrian vote apparently blocked his obtaining the other twelve votes. He was also faced with a well-organized group of five implacable opponents who voted for Giuseppe Sarto (later Pius X), the patriarch of Venice. Supporters of Gotti, who was the principal opponent, and Sarto made up more than one-third of the votes. The Gotti forces threw their votes to Sarto and he was elected as apparently a compromise candidate between the liberal Rampolla and the intransigent Gotti. In fact, he turned out for all his personal holiness (he is known as St. Pius X) to be even more reactionary in his attitude toward modern scholarship and culture than Gotti. The antimodernist reign of terror would blight church thought and scholarship for four decades.

In 1914, just as World War I was starting, the cardinals met to elect another pope. Cardinal della Chiesa represented Leo XIII's forces while Cardinal Maffi represented the progressives and Cardinal Merry del Val represented the intransigents. Della Chiesa was opposed on the grounds that he was mediocre and that his election would be an insult to Pius X (he worked for Rampolla, secretary of state to Leo XIII, and he had been exiled because he kept alive the Rampolla tradition).

The Austrian/Hungarian cardinals supported della Chiesa because they thought he would favor Austria in the war that was about to begin. But the curialists supported Merry del Val and then Serafini to block della Chiesa. As one can see from the table, the Pompili and Merry del Val votes drifted eventually to Serafini and the Maffi votes to della Chiesa. The issue was Pius X versus Leo XIII, represented respectively by Serafini and della Chiesa. The intransigents lost, but they humiliated della Chiesa by accusing him of voting for himself and demanding that his ballot be inspected. A complex system enabled the check to be made; in fact, della Chiesa had not voted for himself and became Pope Benedict XV. Even though he was elected at age sixty, he died only four years after the end of the war, but was one of the more open, intelligent, and liberal popes the church had seen since the time of Napoleon.

In the conclave of 1922, there was a substantial party who thought that after the regime of Benedict XV the time had come to be even more universal in their viewpoint and elect a non-Italian pope. However, they didn't have the votes, and so they agreed to support Gasparri, who had been Benedict's secretary of state, while the Pius X supporters in the conclave supported La Fontaine and Merry del Val, who had been Pius X's secretary of state. The Merry del Val votes flowed to La Fontaine and most of the other votes went first to Gasparri and then, when Gasparri could not obtain the required two-thirds majority, to Achille Ratti. The Merry del Val forces tried to make a deal with Ratti to promise him their votes before Gasparri shifted his votes, thus, it is alleged, incurring automatic excommunication. It is interesting that Ratti accused young Angelo Roncalli (later to be Pope John XXIII) of modernism. The conclave was one of the most bitter of recent centuries. It seemed that Ratti's election and Gasparri's appointment as secretary

Table 2: Record of Voting During the 1914 Conclave

Candidate	September 1 Ballot No.				September 2 Ballot No.				September 3 Ballot No.	
	1	2	3	4	1	2	3	4	1	2
Maffi	12	16	16	15	13	7	2	—	—	—
della Chiesa	12	16	18	21	20	27	31	32	34	38
Pompili	9	10	9	9	6	2	—	—	—	—
Merry del Val	7	7	7	6	2	—	—	—	—	—
Serafini	4	2	2	2	10	17	21	21	22	18
Ferrata	2	2	1	1	—	—	—	—	—	—
Bacilieri	2	1	—	—	1	—	—	—	—	—
Gasparri	1	—	—	—	—	—	—	—	—	—
Falconio	1	—	—	—	—	—	—	—	—	—
Agliardi	1	—	—	—	—	—	—	—	—	—
Ferrari	1	—	—	—	—	—	—	—	—	—
Gotti	1	—	—	—	—	—	—	—	—	—
de Lai	1	1	2	1	1	1	1	1	1	1
Richelmy	—	—	—	—	1	1	1	1	1	1
Francisca Nova	1	—	—	—	1	—	—	—	—	—
Van Rossum	—	—	—	—	1	—	—	—	—	—

of state was a mild victory for the supporters of Benedict XV and a more liberal attitude toward the world.

In fact, when Gasparri died and Pius XI was free to follow his own instincts, the policies of the church turned sharply back to those of Pius X. Oppression smothered scholarship, and cooperation with the Fascist regimes of Mussolini and later Hitler became Vatican policy (though still later Pius XI would condemn both Fascism and Nazism).

In 1939, Eugenio Pacelli was elected Pius XII, but contrary to the report that spread afterward (perhaps with his encouragement), he was not elected unanimously. He received only forty-eight of the sixty-three votes on the third ballot. However, Pacelli, who had traveled widely through the world as Pius XI's secretary of state, had the overwhelming support of the foreign cardinals, although several Italian cardinals supported Elia dalla Costa, the archbishop of Florence, a spiritual, pastoral, "religious" man who was considered by most electors unacceptable in light of the political needs of the time, particularly the threat of war in Europe. The cardinal vicar of Rome, Cardinal Selvaggiani, would later say, "If the angels had votes they would have elected dalla Costa, if the demons had voted they would have elected me. Unfortunately, it was men who voted."

Finally, the election of Cardinal Montini in 1963 was by no means as easy as it appeared on the outside. Eighty electors, more than ever before, gathered in the Sistine Chapel on June 19, 1963. Twenty-nine of them were Italians, a lower proportion than before but still enough to control the outcome of the election. Montini was the favorite, but it still took six ballots to elect him. A very strong opposition was led by blunt-spoken, tempestuous Giuseppe Siri, cardinal archbishop of Genoa, the witty but reactionary Cardinal Alfredo Ottaviani, the nearly blind prefect of the Holy Office, and the conservative, anti–Vatican Council group who wished to end the madness that Pope John had started. At the end of the second ballot, Montini had thirty votes; Ildebrando Antoniutti, the candidate to whom Siri had turned with his votes, had twenty; and supporters of the progressive and deeply spiritual Cardinal Lercaro of Bologna had scraped together twenty votes, representing a group even to the left of the Montini faction. Even though Lercaro votes went to Montini at the urging of Belgium's Leo Suenens, he was still several votes short of victory. When ballots were being distributed for the fourth vote, Cardinal Gustavo Testa—a close friend of John XXIII who reopened the links between the Vatican and the patriarch of Moscow—who was a reluctant supporter of Montini because he did not trust the cardinal of Milan's steadfastness or consistency, lost his temper and told two cardinals close to him, Confalonieri and di Jorio, that it was time for the Curia to give up their maneuvers and plotting and find an agreement for the general welfare of the church. Siri hit the ceiling, but Montini picked up more votes on the fourth ballot, though he was still two to three votes short of the required fifty-four. That evening he apparently agreed, indirectly of course, that the aging conservative Cardinal Amleto Cicognani would remain as secretary of state. The curial faction now was split. Some, like Ottaviani, were willing to accept a compromise; others, like Siri, rejected it. The next morning, on the fifth ballot, Montini picked up two more votes, Ottaviani's and Cicognani's—still not quite enough. Finally, on the sixth ballot, four more votes from the curial camp, probably recuited by Ottaviani and Cicognani, moved to Montini and he won with fifty-seven votes, three more than necessary.

However, both during and after the election (but still in the conclave), the Siri crowd was rude and insulting in its behavior toward Montini; the scars of the conclave would remain on Pope Paul through most of his pontificate. He feared

Table 3: Record of Voting during the 1922 Conclave

Candidate	February 3 Ballot No.				February 4 Ballot No.				February 5 Ballot No.				February 6 Ballot No.	
	1	2	3	4	1	2	3	4	1	2	3	4	1	2
Merry del Val	12	11	14	17	13	7	1	—	—	—	—	—	—	—
Maffi	10	10	10	9	1	—	—	—	—	—	—	—	—	—
Gasparri	8	10	11	13	21	24	24	24	24	19	16	2	1	9
La Fontaine	4	9	2	1	7	13	22	21	18	8	23	22	18	9
Ratti	5	5	6	5	5	4	4	5	11	14	24	27	30	42
Van Rossum	4	—	—	—	—	—	—	—	—	—	—	—	—	—
Bisleti	3	1	4	4	2	2	1	1	—	—	—	—	—	—
de Lai	2	2	1	—	1	1	—	1	1	—	—	—	—	1
Pompili	2	1	1	1	1	—	—	—	—	—	—	—	—	—
Mercier	1	—	—	—	—	—	—	—	1	—	—	—	—	—
Laurenti	2	4	3	2	2	2	1	1	3	5	4	3	4	2
Lega	—	—	1	1	—	—	—	—	1	1	—	—	—	—
Giorgi	—	—	—	—	—	—	—	—	1	1	—	—	—	—
Granito di Belmonte	—	—	—	—	—	—	—	—	—	8	—	—	—	—
Sbarretti	—	—	—	—	—	—	—	—	—	1	—	—	—	—

the Siri faction; while he did not give them organizational power in the church, he still permitted himself to be unduly influenced by their pressures. Many of the more cautious restrictions he imposed on the final three sessions of the Vatican Council were undoubtedly aimed at placating the Siri-curial crowd. Cardinal Leo Suenens of Brussels, one of Paul VI's great supporters in the conclave and the man responsible for persuading the Lercaro supporters to switch their votes to Montini, was apparently considered for secretary of state but was rejected because of the opposition of Siri; he later would fall from favor because of mild criticisms of Paul's failure to implement the Second Vatican Council. And Paul said to Cardinal Lercaro, "You see how life is, Eminence, you should be here in my place." Later Lercaro was removed as archbishop of Bologna on trumped-up charges about financial maladministration. Paul VI, in other words, was unduly diffident to his conclave enemies and unduly harsh to his conclave friends.

What conclusions can be gathered from this brief investigation of the dynamics of the twentieth-century conclaves? The battle between the new and the old, between the curial and the pastoral, between those who trusted the modern world and those who distrusted it, has marked every conclave since 1903 with the single exception of 1939. Both sides have had to accept "compromise" candidates. In 1922, the compromise candidate seemed to represent a victory for the progressive forces; in fact, he turned reactionary once the progressive secretary of state died. In the election of Roncalli (John XXIII), what had appeared a curial victory turned out to be the most dramatic victory the liberals could have imagined. Compromise candidates, in other words, end up by disappointing one side or the other and, not infrequently, the side which supported them.

Second, built into the compromise process inevitably are mechanisms which might be called "arrangements," but which in papal elections are called "assurances." Such "assurances," if not exactly commitments, still fit the same function in papal politics as do promises in other political systems. Sometimes, these assurances are about as well kept as other campaign promises too.

Third, while caucuses and blocs may not exist formally, it is not hard for the cardinals to find out for whom people who agree with them are voting. The "great electors"—the influential leaders to whom others turn for signs and cues—play a role not unlike "whips" in parliamentary bodies or ward committeemen in American urban politics.

Fourth, popes often surprise those who elect them. No one thought that Giuseppe Sarto (Pius X) would be a witch-hunting reactionary despite his holiness. The spiritual vision of Papa della Chiesa (Benedict XV) amazed even his supporters. The authoritarianism of Papa Ratti (Pius XI) came as a surprise to Gasparri and the other progressives who elected him. John XXIII was one of the biggest surprises in history. While Siri and Ottaviani and the other curialists were able to intimidate and harass Paul VI, they did not prevent him from institutionalizing irrevocably the reforms of the Second Vatican Council.

Fifth, the conclave is a highly unpredictable mechanism for selecting a pope. The pressures of time and place often force the cardinals into a hasty decision which, if there were more time for discussion and preparation, would not occur. The secrecy which inhibits preconclave debate and discussion increases the possibility of impulse voting and sudden choices in the highly charged emotional atmosphere of the Sistine Chapel.

Scene IV

1. The conclave came too soon for us to have the statement sold in advance as planned but copies were distributed both in Italian and English to the College of Cardinals. I also wrote a paper providing the sociological rationale for the job description. The latter statement is reprinted in Appendix I. I expect many of the cardinals threw the papers into the wastebasket. Nevertheless, it doesn't seem out of place to suggest here that if ever a sociological theory was overwhelmingly supported by evidence, the summary job description of "a hopeful holy man who can smile" was confirmed by the September papacy of Papa Luciani. My two papers had hypothesized a hopeful, smiling holy man—and Luciani did indeed capture the hearts of humankind and did indeed become the first worldwide religious leader that we've ever had. Indeed, so powerful was the impact of John Paul I that the cardinals had no choice but to try to elect someone just like him, even if, to do that, they had to end the four-and-a-half-century tradition of the Italian papacy by electing Karol Wojtyla of Cracow.

Act One

Scene I

1. The correspondent lost the tape and CBS had to reinterview me the next day. So the afternoon caper had been a waste of time, much to the dismay of the small-fry.

2. Even then, Koenig was thinking of Karol Wojtyla.

3. The eight cardinals who voted in the Montini election and were back for their second conclave were José Maria Bueno y Monreal, Spain; Franz Koenig, Austria; Bernard Alfrink, Holland; Laurean Rugambwa, Tanzania; José Quintero, Venezuela; Juan Landázuri Ricketts, Peru; Henríquez Raúl Silva, Chile; and Leo Josef Suenens, Belgium. Some of these are "veterans"; Koenig, Alfrink, and especially Suenens would have extraordinary impact on the outcome of the conclave.

4. The italicized segment of this part of the narrative attempts to reconstruct, on the basis of evidence available to us, the events which led to the election of the pope. For example, that Felici made phone calls from the couch of his apartment is certain, as is the meeting between him and Rossi. That Felici earlier suggested Luciani and brought some curial voters to the Luciani side is also certain. Much more speculative, however, is the question of Felici's motives, though the promulgation of his "fundamental law" seemed to many Roman observers to be an excellent reason. Felici and Luciani were close friends, and the former could be expected to have considerable influence in a Luciani papacy. Similar rubrics should be applied to all the reconstructions contained in italics through the rest of this book. The basic outlines of what happened are factual; but one must guess at the thoughts and the motivations and, occasionally, the communication links.

The Making of the Popes 1978

Scene II

1. Benelli had put together a grand coalition, but it was a coalition that had been constructed subtly, delicately, indirectly, and so casually that one is hard-put afterwards to find anything but faint traces of it. There are two principal reasons for the thinness of the links:

(a) The regulations governing the conclave require a subtle and indirect approach.

(b) It is simply good politics to respect the freedom of the individual voter. No one tells anyone else how to vote, and no one is really a parliamentary "whip" casting blocks of votes. No voter goes along with a group of other voters because of irrevocable commitments to his own voting bloc. One manipulates atmosphere and environment by hints and casual words dropped here and there, rather than by blunt and direct political maneuvering. The processes are similar to the processes of any election, of course. There are blocs, there are strategies, there are whips, but their style is necessarily delicate, gentle, indirect.

2. In fact, the three thousand employees of the Vatican did not get a month's salary in the election of John Paul I, but a flat $210 bonus—which amounts to $630,000. Added to the average $500 bonus at the death of Paul VI, this means that about a little more than $2 million were spent on extra Vatican salaries. John Paul II restored the practice of paying a full extra-month's salary to all Vatican employees when he was elected. Perhaps he figured that if the Vatican did go into insolvency, it would not be for the extra $1.5 million added to the wretchedly bad pay of its employees.

3. More information on Vatican finances.

There are no secondhand marketplaces where you can sell used Renaissance churches. Who would buy St. Peter's? Indeed, who would accept it as a gift? It doesn't bring in any income and, indeed, it costs money to maintain. St. Peter's produces no income and has no resale value. Estimates of its worth are irrelevant when it comes to the actual financial situation of the Vatican. Similarly, it would appear that the Vatican Museum is just about able to pay for itself each year through its ticket income. Suppose you tried to sell the Vatican Museum. Who would buy it? How much money would you make if you did sell it, especially since a lot of the works that are in it probably would go begging in the open marketplace? To give away the proceeds of a sale of the Vatican Museum would be a splendid gesture but would make little dent in the poverty of the world. You could always invest your profit from the sale, but how much annual income would that provide you? The same comment could be made about the jeweled chalices in the Vatican treasury which so scandalize the good Protestant visitors to Vatican City. Individual agencies of the Department of Health, Education, and Welfare spend more money every day than the total worth of the Vatican treasury.

The Vatican makes some money on its stamps, perhaps half a million dollars from the sale of stamps at the time of a funeral and a conclave. Beyond that, there is little income-producing or resale property anywhere within the walls of the Vatican. You can put whatever book value you want on the property, it is still worthless as far as paying yesterday's bills is concerned. If you wanted to make Vatican City income-producing, about the only thing you could do is tear down the papal palace, the Vatican Museum, and St. Peter's, and build high-rise apartments on the vacant land.

To those enthusiasts who want to give away the Vatican wealth one could reply by asking how you give away the Sistine Chapel; or, if you could find someone interested in the chapel, how would you give away Michelangelo's *Last Judgment*? To the people who are always estimating the "fabulous Vatican wealth" one could ask, "What's the book value of Michelangelo's *Last Judgment*? How much income does it produce; what's its resale value?"

The poverty in the Vatican is not new. When Benedict XV died in 1922, the Vatican had to borrow $100,000 from a Rome bank to cover the expense of his funeral and his conclave.

This time they will probably have to borrow even more.

What about all the money the Vatican got from Mussolini at the time of the Lateran Treaty in 1929, when the Vatican City was established and the papacy made its peace with modern Italy?

All that money wasn't all that much, a mere $80 million for all the lands confiscated by the Italian government. Under the administration of a very shrewd layman, one Bernardino Nogara, this money was increased by investments in Italy and in foreign companies and by speculation in gold, so that by the time of Pius XII's death in 1958, its value had reached $500 million. In the ensuing twenty years, this fund, the Vatican's only income-producing resource, has grown to somewhere between $1.5 and $2 billion dollars, depending on what source you believe. (My guess is that it is substantially closer to the lower figure and maybe even lower than that.) This is not a bad performance by any financial measure. The Vatican investment administration has handled its monies in such a way that it has managed to combine a 5 percent annual compound interest with a capital gain commensurate with the change in the Dow Jones since the time immediately after the Lateran Treaty, as though it had gained stock and bond income on the same money at the same time. As James Gollin says in his careful study of ecclesiastical finances, *Worldly Goods* (New York: Random House, 1971), "By the standards of the professionals this is an excellent record, a well-managed, medium-sized investment operation." Or, as a stockbroker friend of mine put it, "It's a helluva lot better than Morgan Guaranty did in the same half-century." (There is reason to believe that speculations in gold, certainly illegal in canonical law and perhaps in civil law, too, were responsible for much of the success of the Vatican investment in the 1930s and 1940s.)

The income-producing holdings of the Vatican are perhaps a little larger than the endowment of Harvard University and substantially smaller than the book value of the Ford Foundation. A tidy sum of money, perhaps, but scarcely fabled wealth. If one assumes a 6 percent earning on investment (which earning is not plowed back into increasing one's capital resources), the income of the Vatican from its investments and holdings is somewhere around $90 million a year, a little more or a little less than its annual budget, depending on which figure you take seriously as a budgetary estimate. Since the Vatican has other expenses (overseas commitments, charities, special expenses of the pope) which are not in its annual budget, one has to conclude that there is basic agreement that the Vatican budget is relatively small compared to that of most other major world institutions, but is still somewhat larger than its even smaller annual income.

But what about the "Peter's Pence," the annual contributions of Catholics all over the world to the support of their church?

The Peter's Pence has declined substantially since the time of Pope John. According to some people, it is only one-quarter of what it used to be—and that is even without taking inflation into account. One Vatican source told me it was not more than $10 million a year.

Ten million dollars a year from 700 million Catholics? There has to be something wrong with such a financial operation, you say?

You've noticed it, too.

The truth is that, far from being fabulously wealthy, sleek international financiers, the people responsible for Vatican finances are running what, by the standards of many Protestant and Jewish fund-raising enterprises in the United States, would be considered a penny-ante affair. (One of my sources told me that until last year the Vatican was able to finance its operations out of the income from investments. Last year, however, they had to dig into capital. Presumably this year it will be worse.)

But what about all the money lost in the Michele Sindona scandal? The Vatican's loss in that unsavory affair seems to have been around $100 million, a sharp setback indeed, but no worse than that suffered by many investment portfolios. Whether or not the Vatican ought to have been involved with Sindona may be an appropriate question, but in terms of the funds actually lost, the harm done to the Vatican's portfolio was substantially less than that done to the book value of the Ford Foundation or of many big American universities by the bear markets of the 1970s. It is not my intention to make a case for either the integrity or the financial acumen of the Vatican financiers. I am merely contending that the Vatican doesn't have much money today because it didn't have much money to start with, and not because of mistakes, scandals, or even incompetence.

A roadmap is needed to get through the tangle of institutions within the Vatican which have financial responsibility. The Prefecture of Economic Affairs (PAE) is allegedly a supervisory agency which coordinates all Vatican finances. Presided over by a cardinal president (Cardinal Egidio Vagnozzi), the PAE is largely a paper tiger with very little control over the institutions it supervises.

In addition to such independent, relatively minor groups as the Congregation for the Evangelization of Peoples and the "Fabric of St. Peter's" (the office responsible for the maintenance of St. Peter's), which have their own budgets, the principal operating agencies for Vatican finance are the Administration of the Patrimony of St. Peter (APSA), the government of the State of Vatican City, and the Institute for the Works of Religion (IOR, or the "Vatican Bank"). The APSA is divided into two sections, the "ordinary," which together with the government of the State of Vatican City is responsible for Vatican spending, and the "extraordinary," which oversees the Vatican's investment policy (with its principal task being to oversee the investment of funds originally derived from the Lateran Treaty settlement with Mussolini). The IOR was founded in 1942 to facilitate the transfer of funds from fascist Italy to the various religious orders all over the world. It is in effect a bank set up for religious orders, Vatican organizations, lay groups connected with the church, and diplomats of the Vatican to rely on for ordinary banking services. In addition, apparently some Italian laymen deposit their funds in it; it has connections with the supersecret Swiss and Caribbean banking systems.

There are two principal charges leveled against the IOR. First of all, it has been accused of being a channel by which wealthy Italians funnel lire out of Italy into a foreign bank and thus increase the drain on Italian currency. It has also been accused of investing in "capitalist" enterprises. The former charge is undocumented, the latter is absurd. What other enterprises does one invest in but capitalist enterprises if one is seeking a return of income on one's funds?

It may well be that the IOR has been used by some of its clients for actions that would be illegal in Italy. It may also be that either the IOR or the extraordinary section of the APSA has invested money in drug firms that make contraceptives, in gambling casinos, and in munitions companies. One has no way of knowing because, like everything else in the Vatican, the investments of the IOR and the APSA are carefully guarded secrets, thus virtually guaranteeing spectacular rumors. However, to say that the Vatican "owns" the Monte Mario region (whereon stands my beloved Rome Hilton) or "owns" anything is like saying that someone who has a thousand shares of common stock in General Motors owns General Motors. James Gollin estimates that the Vatican stock portfolio in Italian companies in 1968 amounted to about $200 million, and points out that the Swiss, German, and American investments in Italian industries were worth more than five times that much. The myth of Vatican control of the Italian economy or even of any major corporation, according to Gollin, ought not to be taken seriously. Its biggest investment in Italy (since liquidated) was the 15 percent interest in the real-estate and construction company Società Generale Immobiliare (SGI). The Vatican, in other words, owned the land on which stands the Rome Hilton, only in the sense that it had a minority investment (worth about $25 million) in the company which owned that land, as well as many other Italian properties.

According to Gollin, Paul VI was dismayed by even the relatively minor influence the Vatican had on the Italian economy. The Vatican's interest in the SGI was liquidated in a sale to a French syndicate in 1969. According to Gollin, the go-between in the transaction was the Sicilian financial wizard, Michele Sindona.

Later, of course, Sindona would be involved in the Franklin Bank bankruptcy scandal, and the Vatican, as well as many other investors who had trusted him, would be taken to the cleaners. It is well to note, however, that the original impulse which brought Sindona into Vatican affairs arose from the desire to improve the ethical posture of Vatican investing. Bishop Paul Marcinkus, an American who is the president of IOR, has been blamed by the press for the Sindona losses.

Marcinkus's friends in Rome say that the attacks on him are an attempt by Italian curialists to oust a non-Italian from the very important post he holds. They argue that it was not the IOR that arranged the transfer of the SGI to Sindona, but the "extraordinary" section of the APSA. They insist that the Vatican losses in the Sindona affair were limited almost entirely to the collapse of the remaining Vatican stock in SGI and had nothing to do with Marcinkus's investments. They claim that some of the press are deliberately exploiting the complexity of Vatican finances in order to blame Marcinkus for decisions over which he had no control and policies which he did not initiate. His friends also say that he was made a scapegoat for the mistakes made by others in dealing with Sindona. "Paul was the one who had to take the heat," remarked one inside source to me. For whom did he take the heat? The most obvious answer to the question is that there was only one man in the world for whose mistake Paul Marcinkus would take the heat and that was Pope Paul VI. James Gollin backs this up.

Il Mondo blasted away at Italian finances and especially at the IOR and Bishop Marcinkus; in the month of September, it called world attention to the rumors of dubious dealings in Vatican financial affairs and in the Sindona miscalculation. Having maintained the cloak of secrecy over its financial doings, the Vatican was in no position to refute or even respond to the *Il Mondo* charges. (John Paul I was deeply disturbed by the liquidations made necessary by the Sindona affair, and had determined on his own to organize a systematic review of the Vatican financial operation. Such a review is certainly imperative, if only to re-establish the credibility of Vatican finances, which has been badly shaken by the charges of the world press. However, even if the Vatican adopts a policy of full and public accountability for its financial affairs, such charges can easily be repeated.)

There is simply not enough information available at the present time to make any definitive judgments either on the functioning of the IOR or the Vatican's involvement in the Sindona affair. Three comments do seem to be in order, however, about the state of Vatican finances:

(1) Financial administration of the Vatican seems to be confused and disorganized; the overlapping responsibilities of interlocking directorates make it difficult to tell precisely who is responsible for what.

(2) The secrecy surrounding Vatican finances is counterproductive, because it enables the enemies of the church to make outlandish charges (such as the $25 or $50 billion of wealth that the Vatican is alleged to have) or accusations of corruption which cannot be refuted in the absence of full and public accountability.

(3) But the most serious problem with the Vatican is neither secrecy nor confusion nor corruption nor speculation; it is poverty. The Vatican does not have enough money to meet its expenses. Expenses are going up and income is going down. The Holy See is now living off its capital, which is very modest given its worldwide organizational responsibility. One of the disadvantages of an impoverished Vatican is that the church is forced to pay its help poorly, thus leaving many of them open to the influence of generous patrons who shower them with gifts (Cardinal Cody is a lavish giver). The distinction between gifts (such as a $1,000 stipend, for example) and bribes is often hard to make. The new pope is not only going to have to establish some order in the confusion of the Vatican finances and eliminate the counterproductive secrecy, he is going to have to discover much more broadly based sources of income. It is ridiculous for the Roman Catholic church to continue to try to finance its central administration out of the pathetically small Peter's Pence or an income on investments which is not much larger than that of many American universities and is smaller than those of many of the world's major philanthropic foundations.

The next pope will inherit an institution which is, if not insolvent, at least living off its capital. One of my Vatican sources summarized the state of the Vatican finances very neatly when he said, "Thank goodness we are not going to have another conclave for a while."

The Vatican exercises very little control over the financial administration of a national hierarchy, such as the one in the United States, and a national hierarchy in turn exercises little control over what a local bishop may do in his own diocese. Thus, in recent years new bishops in such prominent dioceses as Boston, Newark, Santa Rosa, California, and New Orleans have discovered to their horror that they have inherited enormous indebtedness from their possibly well-meaning but incompetent predecessors. One such bishop told me that the attorney general of the state was waiting for him upon arrival, prepared to foreclose on diocesan property (his predecessor has been promoted to a larger diocese, where he continues to spend money recklessly). Another bishop said that it took him a year merely to find all the sources of financial hemorrhage in his diocese. "The thing that shakes me," he said, "is that I'm sure that there are several other places in the country where the same thing is going on, and nobody can do anything about it until the man is replaced." The problem in such dioceses is not corruption or malfeasance but incompetence and absence of any outside accountability or control. A local bishop may do just about anything he wants with the income of his diocese. Even though some of his actions may violate canon law, there is no one who can be sure that canon law is being violated unless the Vatican chooses to intervene and demand an accounting; the Vatican in its turn is in no position to do this unless the volume of denunciations—which are, for the most part, necessarily undocumented, since nobody has access to the documentation—becomes so large that it simply cannot be ignored. Both in Rome and in the American church there is not yet a recognition that in the absence of full and public accountability, the credibility of Catholic financial administration will rapidly vanish. Nor ought the annual reports that many dioceses issue necessarily be taken seriously. In some dioceses, for example, all funds are audited and the auditing is done by stern and careful accounting firms. In other dioceses published reports are routine checks of only those books that the diocese makes available to the auditors and only those aspects of the administration which are submitted for auditing. Thus in the archdiocese of Chicago it is alleged that there are $60 million of parish funds on deposit with the chancery office. There is no public accounting of the use made of such funds. One pastor in Chicago admitted to a group of friends that he has $300,000 in private accounts to keep the money out of the cardinal's hands. He is afraid if he gives the cardinal the money it will go down the drain in one of the cardinal's financial ventures. He estimates that most of the other pastors in the city who do not have deficit parishes do the same thing, suggesting that there may be tens of millions of dollars kept in secret accounts to protect them. When asked what would happen to the money if he and his curate (who also knows about the account) should die in the same auto accident, the pastor twisted uncomfortably in his chair and said, "That's too bad for God. He's responsible for that crazy son-of-a-bitch being here, not me."

Scene III

1. The numbers are approximate. Various sources indicate slight variations in the numbers.

2. "May God Forgive. . . ." The quotation was a slightly modified version of the letter St. Bernard wrote when one of his monks was elected Pope Eugene. Thoroughly displeased with the younger man's accepting the papal office because he was convinced this could only mean trouble for the monastic orders, he had written, "May God forgive you for what you have done in this regard." Luciani's prodigious memory was a storehouse of such quotes, and he could not resist using them even on the most solemn and important occasions. Later he would apologize to the cardinals, explaining that he had not meant to be rude to them, but of course they knew he was referring to St. Bernard's letter to Pope Eugene. *Sure they knew*.

3. Later it would be explained that the cardinals were burning their own personal notes and that somehow, by mistake, some of the black smoke flares got mixed in.

4. I said I'd admit my mistakes, didn't I?

5. *Little did I know then about their activity!*

6. The tracing down of that clue is reported in the reconstruction of the conclave in the italicized sections of this book.

The Making of the Popes 1978

Act Two

Scene I

1. Here is the questionnaire we used:

CARDINAL'S NAME: ——————

Place an X in the place on the seven-point scale which most accurately reflects where each cardinal normally is.

	1	2	3	4	5	6	7	
Confident about the future of the church	—	—	—	—	—	—	—	Worried about the future of the church
Authoritarian in his dealings with his clergy	—	—	—	—	—	—	—	Collegial with clergy
Would favor a reappraisal of the birth control issue	—	—	—	—	—	—	—	Feels the birth control issue is settled
In touch with recent theological developments	—	—	—	—	—	—	—	Uninformed about recent theology
Approves the governing style of the Roman Curia	—	—	—	—	—	—	—	Skeptical about the Curia's power
Would like to see the power of the Synod of Bishops expanded	—	—	—	—	—	—	—	Satisfied with the powers of the synod
Favors election of the pope by the College of Cardinals	—	—	—	—	—	—	—	Favors an expanded electoral body
A pastor rather than a politican or diplomat	—	—	—	—	—	—	—	A politician or a diplomat; not a pastor
Uneasy with the currents of change in the church	—	—	—	—	—	—	—	Sympathetic with the currents of change
In close touch with the feelings of ordinary people	—	—	—	—	—	—	—	Does not understand problems of ordinary people
Against expanded role for women in the church	—	—	—	—	—	—	—	In favor of expanded role for women
Known for his personal piety	—	—	—	—	—	—	—	Not known for his personal piety
More an "administrator" than a "scholar"	—	—	—	—	—	—	—	More a "scholar" than an "administrator"

Would support a
requirement for papal
retirement   — — — — — — —

Would oppose a
requirement for papal
retirement

Act Two

Scene II

1. The "Street of the Covered Shops" is now a broad through street, but in medieval Rome it was as narrow as the "Street of the Poles" and the covered shops were places where various medicines could be purchased. Next to St. Stanislaus on the Street of the Covered Shops, just around the corner (the Street of the Poles), are the headquarters of the Italian Communist party and the place where Aldo Moro's body was found.

2. Wadowice is not far from Auschwitz, the worst of all Nazi death camps. The measure of the Wojtyla personality is that he has repeatedly said mass there and has done his best to keep the horrors of Auschwitz alive in the minds of people of Poland and the world. He went to school with Jews and had many close Jewish friends in his childhood and young adulthood. He has been warmly sympathetic to the remnant Jewish community in Cracow, has denounced anti-Semitism in his diocesan newspaper, and has attacked the Polish government for tolerating and even encouraging anti-Semitism. On the other hand, he took the lead in the spring of 1978 in calling for a reconciliation between the Polish and the German church, asking the Germans for forgiveness for any of the offenses for which the Poles might have been responsible (in particular, the appropriation of ancient Polish land, which had been German for centuries, after the end of the Second World War). As many Polish Catholics as Polish Jews died at Auschwitz. His taking the lead in reconciliation with the Germans while at the same time refusing to forget the horrors at Auschwitz indicate an extraordinary man.

3. In the 1970s Suenens became one of the leaders of the moderate faction of the Catholic pentecostal movement.

4. *Znak* rejects 90 percent of the poems submitted. Doubtless, once it found out who Andrzej Jawein was, it was more than a little eager to publish his long, free-verse compositions, many of which are not explicitly religious, but he got into the journal the first time on his own. Andrzej Jawein, by the way, was a character in a World War II Polish novel who lost his faith, recovering it after the war. Whether there is anything autobiographical in the choice of names, only Wojtyla himself could say.

Two samples of Wojtyla's poetry

from "Before I Could Discern Many Profiles"

I

A profile among trees, different among pillars
and different again in the street, melting into its wet surface.
Different is the profile of a man standing at his own door;
different a victor's profile: a Greek demigod.
I know the Cyrenian's profile best,
from every conceivable point of view.

The Making of the Popes 1978

The profile always starts alongside the other Man;
it falls from his shoulders
to break off exactly where
that other man is most himself,
least defenseless

(he would be defenseless if
what is in him and of him
did not form a vertical line, but gave way).

Life tells me unceasingly
about such a profile, about that other man.
(Profile becomes cross-section.)

2

Feet search the grass. The earth.
Insects drill the greenery, swaying the stream of the sun.
Feet wear down cobbles, the cobbled street
wears down feet. No pathos. Thoughts in the crowd,
   unspoken.

Take a thought if you can—plant its root
in the artisan's hands, in the fingers
of women typing eight hours a day:
black letters hang from reddened eyelids.

Take a thought, make man complete,
or allow him to begin himself anew,
or let him just help You perhaps
and You lead him on.

3

Why is it not so, Magdalene, Simon of Cyrene?
Do you remember that first step which you are still
taking all the time?

4

Grass waving, a green hammock, a breezy cradle of bees.
Stone slabs stand, split by a vertical ray.
You had better walk with the wave. Walk the wave—
   don't hurt your feet.

In the wave's embrace you never know you are drowning.

5

And then He comes. He lays his yoke
on your back. You feel it, you tremble, you are awake.

"Children"

Growing unawares through love, of a sudden
they've grown up, and hand in hand
wander in crowds (their hearts caught like birds,
profiles pale in the dusk).
The pulse of mankind beats in their hearts.

On a bank by the river, holding hands—
a tree stump in moonlight, the earth a half-whisper—
the children's hearts rise over the water.
Will they be changed when they get up and go?

Or look at it this way: a goblet of light tilted
over a plant reveals unknown inwardness.
Will you spoil what has begun in you?
Will you always separate the right from the wrong?

A man reveals far more of himself in poetry and fiction than he does in prose. Wojtyla the poet is a deep, complicated, anguished, hopeful, and affectionate man. Wojtyla the playwright is even more interesting. His *The Goldsmith Shop*, which appeared in *Znak* in 1960, was written (again under the pseudonym of Andrej Jawien) for an attempt in the late 1950s to revive the Rhapsody Theater of his good friend Mieczyslaw Kotarczyk. The Rhapsody Theater, if one is to judge from *The Goldsmith Shop*, tended toward symbolic, metaphysical, and poetic presentation and was very "modern" in its approach to stagecraft. The story deals with three marriages. The first two, those of Theresa and Andrew and Anna and Stephan, are broken, in the former case by the death of Andrew in the war and in the latter case by the breakdown of love between the two spouses. The third act describes the beginnings of the love of the children of these first two marriages, Monica and Christopher. The author of the play has a profound insight into the dynamics of human relationships, and in particular, a very sensitive grasp of the things that can go wrong in a marriage. The account of the deteriorating relationship between Stephan and Anna is a subtle and complex psychological portrait.

One cannot help noting that the husband in the first marriage who is killed in the war is called Andrew, the same name as the one that Wojtyla chooses for the author of the play. Did he identify with the first husband? Is there some hint of a love of his own that was destroyed by the war? That these questions should arise is inevitable, but they cannot be answered, both because they might pertain to Karol Wojtyla's own personal life, which is not anyone's business, and because it is simply not fair to attempt to read literal autobiography into fictional work. Minimally, one has to say however, that Wojtyla has a perceptive and sympathetic understanding of human love. You do not, however, have to be married or to have been "in love" to have such understanding. One of the more beautiful passages in *The Goldsmith Shop* portrays Andrew and Theresa standing in front of the window of the shop, symbolically exchanging rings. Theresa says:

"Look, we are reflected in the window as in
the mirror of the future
Andrew takes one of the rings
I take the other, we put them on each other's hands
My God how simple!"

5. There have been three dramatic revolutions in Poland during the Communist regime. The first, in 1956 (brought about by riots in Poznań), led to the ousting of a Stalinist regime and the expulsion of the Russian field marshal who was Polish defense minister. Wladyslaw Gomulka came to power and ruled for fourteen years, trying to steer a middle course between Polish nationalism and the Russian army still present in the country. In 1970, there was yet another revolution (caused by riots in Gdańsk and Szczecin). Gomulka was ousted and Edward Gierek, the present party leader, came to power. In 1976, Gierek tried to impose price increases and found (after violence in Radom, Plock, and Ursis) yet another

revolution on his hands. Unlike his predecessors, he quickly backed off and made peace with the angry workers. In each case, the revolutionaries were skillful and restrained in their demands. They did not try to achieve the total independence the Hungarians sought in 1956 and the Czechs in 1968. Russia's fear of Poland is too old and too well-founded to allow the Poles to take such a chance. The striking workers demanded a change and a liberalization of the Communist party itself. The leadership of the party continues to govern, knowing that it can neither yield too much freedom to its passionately patriotic people for fear of the Russians nor accept too much control from the Russians for fear of its own people. Under such circumstances, as one Polish intellectual said to me, "The church and the party are locked in mortal combat, two aging giants wrestling with one another but also leaning on each other for support."

On the feast of Corpus Christi in Warsaw, half a million people march out of the old city and down the main street in solemn religious procession, with Cardinal Wyszynski himself carrying the Blessed Sacrament under the warm spring skies. Three times the procession pauses, the final time in front of the home of the prime minister. Each year the church must ask permission for the procession. Each year the government, with a show of reluctance, yields permission, and each year the church has more people in its procession than the party has in the May Day parade. "It's 50 percent religion, 50 percent folklore," a Polish sociologist explained to me, "and 100 percent politics."

The government endlessly harasses the church—customs guards even seized the luggage of Wojtyla when he returned from Rome. The church, for its part, relentlessly insists on full rights: to construct places of worship; to educate the young along Christian lines; to ensure equality in the state for believers; and to have the appointment of bishops free from state interference. The conflict between church and state in Poland, then, is ceaseless, neither side daring to yield too much to the other, and both sides afraid to push the other beyond its last defenses. The church flourishes. Seminaries have to turn away applicants. The parishes are filled on Sunday, even with unbelievers, who know that the churches are the links in the national underground communication network. Even many party members secretly have their children baptized and the Warsaw Academy of Catholic Theology is financed by government money. (One needs both party and church permission to lecture at the Theological Academy. I was rejected by both sides, and ended up speaking for *Kit*, the club of Catholic intellectuals which is closely related to Znak, the publishing company whose magazine carries Wojtyla's poems.)

One can find dedicated Marxists who are anti-government and anti-party arguing vigorously in support of the ecclesiastically conservative policies of Cardinal Stefan Wyszynski on the grounds that only a reactionary church can deal with a reactionary party. Those progressive Catholics who would support more rapid modernization of the church do exhibit some anxiety, for modernization can mean fragmentation. And a church under siege, they will tell you, can scarcely afford the luxury of internal conflict. Wojtyla is much more progressive personally and religiously than the authoritarian Cardinal Wyszynski, but he reveres Wyszynski as a leader and a martyr and differs with him not in the slightest in his opposition to Marxism, though as an intellectual, he is able to bait the Marxists from within their own philosophical framework.

The Poles survive as free people in an unfree nation, in part because of their faith and in part because of their humor: "The Russians are not our friends, they are our brothers; you get to choose your friends." "The Stalin Palace [a huge government skyscraper in the center of Warsaw] has the most beautiful view in the city. Why? Because from the top of it you cannot see the Stalin Palace."

The struggle, the compromise, the accommodation between church and party have been characteristic of the Poland to which Wojtyla returned in 1946. For the last three decades, the church has survived, has flourished, has won more and more concessions from the Communists. It continues to be the center of Polish patriotism and Polish cultural life and has paid the perhaps necessary cost by repressing some of the internal ferment that has occurred in the rest of the world. The international Catholic review *Concilium* is banned in Poland because Cardinal Wyszynski thought it a threat to the unity of Polish Catholics against the party. Wojtyla has discreetly smoothed the ruffled feathers of Catholic intellectuals and provided a rallying point for more religiously progressive Catholics in Cracow, while at the same time maintaining complete unity with Wyszynski against the party and against the kind of ecclesiastical innovations that might weaken the church in its conflict with the party.

Scene IV

1. "Basta," the functionary said—enough. The pope ignored him, as he would continue to ignore other functionaries in the days ahead.

2. Tanner repeated his "analysis" in a piece which appeared in the *Arizona Daily Star* on January 13, 1979.

Appendix A

Sociological Rationale for Papal Job Description

Sociologists in general, even those who have no personal religious belief, recognize that religion exerts a powerful influence on human life and that at certain critical times a religious and moral leader can have far more impact on human behavior than political and administrative leaders. Pope John XXIII, for example, was the kind of man whose worldwide influence could have been brought to bear to avert a nuclear holocaust, had such a situation threatened during his papacy.

Even apart from the possibility for such dramatic action, a religious and moral leader has great power over human events precisely because he speaks—or is supposed to speak—to that which is most generous, most open, and most noble in human nature. Even though religion can be corrupted into dangerous fanaticism, at its best it becomes a challenging, reconciling, ennobling force. That's why so many representatives of the world press are in Rome; editors all over the world know that religion is news, and not merely to religious people. The election of the leader of the Catholic church is a matter of great interest to the public at large because even those who do not take religion seriously acknowledge the impact religion can have on human life and understand the immense possibilities open, particularly in our age, to the religious leader who is able to react sensitively to the aspirations and hopes of mankind. Hence, in the modern world, a sociologist studying the papacy is forced to think about the "public image" of the pope.

When a sociologist looks at a particular organization, he wants to find out in what ways it may be similar to other organizations and in what way it may be distinct. When he looks at a church, the first thing he sees is that the church is concerned about religion, that is, about the meaning of human life and human death. He therefore concludes that the most distinctive thing about the leader of a church is that he is a religious worker. The religious leader may share with other leaders the responsibilities of administration and diplomacy, of finance and conflict resolution, but the unique thing about him is his religious function. The sociologist must judge that if the head of a church is a superb administrator, a brilliant diplomat, a dazzling financier, and a Solomon at conflict resolution but is not effective in the religious dimension of his job, then he has failed as a leader.

I must insist that any sociologist would arrive at this conclusion, even one who rejects absolutely the goals of religion. Indeed, when I put on my sociologist's cap and began thinking systematically about a papal "job description," I realized how much my own thinking had been focused on organizational and political issues, which, while they may be important—indeed, critically important—do not necessarily have much to do with the specifically life-and-death issues which are the essence of religion.

Some of us who are on the "inside" of the church organization—priests, intellectuals, involved laity—can become deeply concerned about such organizational issues as celibacy and the ordination of women. We perhaps fail to recognize that while these matters are important enough in themselves, they mean relatively little to ordinary men and women, whether they be Catholic or not, who are passionately and poignantly searching for something to give a shred of meaning and purpose to their lives and a shred of dignity and hopefulness to their deaths.

I do not intend to sound pious. Again, I must insist that any sociologist would make exactly the same observations: a church which functions brilliantly as an organization but fails to meet its members' deepest religious need, the giving of purpose to life and death, is an unsuccessful church. A church leader who is unable to inspire purpose and hope is a failed religious leader.

In recent years two unrelated historical developments have served to emphasize the central importance of the strictly religious function of the papacy: the decline of the temporal political power of the Vatican, and the emergence of a worldwide mass-media culture.

For centuries the pope played, probably necessarily, a major political and diplomatic role on the world stage, or at least on the European stage. Often this role was performed brilliantly—and almost always skillfully. Since the end of the papal states a hundred years ago and the resolution of the Roman question fifty years ago, the diplomatic role of the papacy has diminished in importance. I do not suggest that it is unimportant, but that the pope is no longer the temporal political leader he used to be.

Still the diplomatic role has continued to receive heavy emphasis in papal activity and in the evaluation of papal candidates. Concordats, participation in world conferences, delicate negotiations with countries that are anti-Catholic if not antireligious must, of course, continue. Perhaps because the last three popes were skilled diplomats (one of them, Pope John, a very special kind of diplomat), the political-diplomatic emphasis has continued to consume vast amounts of time and attention. It seems at least arguable that this emphasis ought to be modified somewhat since most of the major world powers do not seem disposed to consider the papacy an important mediating or diplomatic force in the world. Furthermore, in an instructive paradox, it was precisely the pope who almost carelessly tossed aside the traditional diplomatic-political role who seemed to end up with the most influence on the political leaders of the world. In a curious twist, religious leadership, pure and simple, turned out to have an enormous political impact.

The reason for this, I would submit, has to do with the second development referred to above: in the age of mass media, the pope has become a media personality—one might even say, at least potentially, a media personality par excellence.

Most Catholics in the course of the history of the church would have had no idea of what their pope looked like; many perhaps didn't even know his name. I would imagine that as recently as 1930, few Catholics had seen anything but a painting or a still-life photo of the pope. Even Pius XII could be seen in movement only in an occasional newsreel or documentary, and although his Christmas message was broadcast live, it was heard by relatively few people. Now the TV camera follows the pope wherever he goes. His personality has become critically important, and by that I mean his *religious* personality, the vision of the meaning of life and death he incarnates in the way he smiles, the way he talks, the way he walks, and the way he treats people around him. I would argue that this is true whether or not the pope wishes it to be. His "media image" will have a profound effect for good or ill on his own followers and on others, regardless of whether he knows it or approves of it.

One of the aspects of a public figure's personality that is most clearly revealed in the mass media is the extent of his trust in people, particularly his colleagues and subordinates. Nothing can turn ordinary people off more quickly than the sense that a leader, political or religious, is a narrow, suspicious man who is afraid to trust others and must hoard all power for himself.

I am not suggesting that the papacy is a "public relations" position in the pejorative sense of those words. Nor am I suggesting that the papal image should be "manufactured" or "created." Indeed, the failure of successive waves of "image merchants" to upgrade the image of various American presidents shows that people are not deceived by media-manipulated phoniness. A good and virtuous man may not appear so at first on TV because of nervousness or shyness, but with time that will pass. A less than good man will fool people only for a very brief period of time.

The next pope will, within a week, be in the homes of most families in at least the First and Second Worlds and will be seen "personally" by many more families in the Third World. He will have a platform unlike that available to any previous religious leader in human history. Willy-nilly, he will use that platform—either to teach faith by what he says and who he is or, by the same means, to discourage faith. Purely as a sociologist, I have to say that transparent virtue and authentic holiness have become essential to the papacy. The degree to which the next pope possesses, or does not possess, these qualities will be perceived by more people and will have a greater impact on them than ever before.

The modern pope then is front and center on the world religious stage at every moment. The modern conclave must consider whether the man they select can occupy that stage in such a way as to persuade, attract, win, reassure, encourage, challenge those who are watching. John XXIII, perhaps by instinct, perhaps by innate shrewdness, most likely by a marvelous blend of both, was the first modern pope. He demonstrated what the pope as a world religious leader, indeed, the most important world religious leader, can achieve.

I am not suggesting that the Papa Roncalli approach is the only effective one, I am rather suggesting using him as an illustration of my point: the religious leadership function is the essential one for the modern papacy, and, given the successful exercise of that function, the other roles are much easier to deal with—if, indeed, they don't tend to take care of themselves.

Do not misunderstand me: I am not a simplist saying that administration, diplomacy, finance, and conflict resolution are unimportant. I am not suggesting that issues like celibacy and the ordination of women, much less a Christian vision of the importance of sexuality, are unimportant. I am saying rather that they are not as important, not nearly as important, as the radiant faith and hope, the confidence and the joy of the man who sits on the chair of Peter the Fisherman.

Appendix B

Acceptance Messages of John Paul I and John Paul II

Acceptance Message of John Paul I

On the occasion of the mass at 9:30 A.M. in the Sistine Chapel, in which all of the cardinals concelebrated, the pope presented in Latin the following message, 27 August 1978.

Dear Brothers!

My dear sons and daughters throughout the entire Catholic world!

Having been called through a mysterious yet loving Father, to this awesome responsibility of the papacy, we extend to you our greetings. At the same time we greet everyone in the world, all who hear us. Following the teachings of the Gospel, we would wish to think of you as friends, as brothers and sisters. To all of you, I wish good health, peace, mercy, and love: "May the grace of our Lord Jesus Christ and the love of God and the fellowship of the Holy Spirit be with you all."

We are still overwhelmed at the thought of this tremendous ministry for which we have been chosen: as Peter, we seem to have stepped out on dangerous waters. We are battered by a strong wind. So we turn towards Christ saying: "Lord, save me" (Mt. 14:30). Again we hear his voice encouraging and at the same time lovingly reminding us: "Why do you doubt, oh you of little faith." If human forces alone cannot be adequate to the task before us, the help of Almighty God, who has guided his church throughout the centuries in the midst of great conflicts and opposition, will certainly not desert us, this humble and present-day servant of the *servants of God*. Placing our hand in that of Christ, leaning on Him, we have now been lifted up to steer that ship which is the church; it is safe and secure, though in the midst of storms, because the comforting, dominant presence of the Son of God is with it. According to the words of Saint Augustine, an image dear to this Father of the Church, the ship of the church must not fear because it is guided by Christ and by his vicar: "Although the ship is tossed about, it is still a ship. It carries the disciples and it receives Christ. Yes, it is tossed on the sea but without it, one would immediately perish" (Sermon 75:3; PL 38, 475). Only in the church is salvation: *without it one perishes!*

We proceed then with this faith. God's assistance will not be wanting to us, just as he has promised: "I am with you always even to the end of the world" (Mt. 28:20). The common response and willing cooperation of all of you will make the weight of our daily burden lighter. We bind you to us in this awesome task, realizing the uniqueness of the Catholic church. Its tremendous spiritual power is the guarantee of peace and order, as such it is present in the world; as such it is recognized in the world. The echo of its daily life gives witness that, despite all obstacles, it lives in the heart of men, even those who do not share its truth or accept its message. As the Second Vatican Council (to whose teachings we wish to commit our total ministry, as priest, as teacher, as pastor) has said: "Destined to extend to all regions of the earth, the church enters into human history, though it transcends at once all time and all racial boundaries. Advancing through trials and tribulations, the church is strengthened by God's grace, promised to her by the Lord so that she may not waver from perfect fidelity, but remain the worthy bride of the Lord, until, through the cross, she may attain to that light which knows no setting" (*Lumen Gentium* 9).

According to God's plan: "All those who in faith look towards Jesus, the author of salvation and the principle of unity and peace, God has gathered together and established as the church, that it may be for each and everyone the visible sacrament of this saving unity" (ibid).

In that light, we place ourselves interiorly, turning all of our physical and spiritual strength towards the service of the universal mission of the church, that is to say, at the service of the world. In other words, we will be at the service of truth, of justice, of peace, of harmony, of collaboration within nations as well as rapport among peoples. We call especially on the children of the church to better understand their responsibility: "You are the salt of the earth, you are the light of the world" (Mt. 5:13). Overcoming internal tension which can arise here and there, overcoming the temptation of identifying ourselves with the ways of the world or the appeal of easily won applause, we are rather united in the unique bond of love which forms the inner life of the church just as with its external order. Thus, the faithful should be ready to give witness of their own faith to the world: "Always be prepared to give a reason for the hope that is in you" (1 Pet. 3:15).

The church, in this common effort to be responsible and so respond to the pressing problems of the day, is called to give to the world that "strengthening of the spirit" which is so needed and which alone can assure salvation. The world awaits this today: it knows well that the sublime perfection to which it is enjoined by research and technology—in which it is just to recognize the fulfillment of the first command of God: "Fill the earth and make it subject to man" (Gen. 1:28)—has reached a height at which dizziness occurs. It is the temptation of substituting for God one's own decisions, decisions that would prescind moral law. The danger for modern man is that he would reduce the earth to a desert, the person to an automaton, brotherly love to a planned collectivization, often introducing death where God wishes life.

The church, admiring yet lovingly protesting against such "achievements," intends rather to safeguard the world, which thirsts for a life of love, from dangers that would attack it. The Gospel calls all of its children to place their full strength, indeed their life, at the service of mankind in the name of the charity of Christ: "Greater love than this no man has than that he would lay down his life for his friends" (Jn. 15:13). In this solemn moment, we intend to consecrate all that we are and all that we can achieve for this supreme goal. We will do so until our last breath, aware of the task insistently entrusted to us by Christ: "Confirm your brothers" (Luke 22:32).

He helps then by strengthening us in our difficult challenge. We remember the example of our predecessors, whose lovable, gentle ways bolstered by a relentless strength provide both the example and program for the papacy: we recall in particular the great lessons of pastoral guidance left by the most recent popes, Pius XI, Pius XII, John XXIII. With wisdom, dedication, goodness, and love of the church and the world, they have left an indelible mark on our time, a time that is both troubled and magnificent. Most of all, the pontifical pastoral plan of Paul VI, our immediate predecessor, has left a strong impression on our heart and in our memory. His sudden death was crushing to the entire world. In the manner of his prophetic style, which marked his unforgettable pontificate, he placed in clear light the extraordinary stature of a great yet humble man. He cast an extraordinary light upon the church, even in the midst of controversy and hostility these past fifteen years. Undertaking immense labors, he worked indefatigably and without rest. He extended himself to carry forth the Council and to seek world peace, the *tranquility of order*.

Our program will be to continue his; and his in turn was in the wake of that drawn from the great heart of John XXIII.

We wish to continue to carry forth the heritage of the Second Vatican Council. Its wise norms should be followed out and perfected. We must be wary of that effort that is generous perhaps, but unwarranted. It would not achieve the content and meaning of the Council. On the other hand, we must avoid an approach that is hesitant and fearful—and thus would not realize the magnificent impulse of the renewal and of life.

We wish to preserve the integrity of the great discipline of the church in the life of priests and of the faithful. It is a rich treasure in history. Throughout the ages, it has presented an example of holiness and heroism, both in the exercise of the evangelical virtues and in service to the poor, the humble, the defenseless. To achieve that, we place a priority on the revision of the two codes of canon law; that of the oriental tradition and that of the Latin tradition, to assure the blessed liberty of children of God, through the solidarity and firmness of juridical structures.

We wish to remind the entire church that its first duty is that of evangelization. Our predecessor, Paul VI, presented the directions for this in his memorable document: animated by faith, nourished by the Word of God, and strengthened by the heavenly food of the Eucharist, one should study every way, seek every means "in season and out of season" (2 Tim. 4:2), to spread the word, to proclaim the message, to announce that salvation which creates in the soul a restlessness to pursue truth and at the same time offers strength from above. If all the sons and daughters of the church would know how to be tireless missionaries of the Gospel, a new flowering of holiness and renewal would spring up in this world that thirsts for love and for truth.

We wish to continue the ecumenical thrust, which we consider a final directive from our immediate predecessors. We watch with an unchanging faith, with a dauntless hope, and with endless love for the realization of that great command of Christ: "That they might all be one" (Jn. 17:21). His heart anxiously beat for this on the eve of his sacrifice at Calvary. The mutual relationships among the churches of the various denominations have made constant and extraordinary advances as anyone can see; yet division remains a cause for concern, and, indeed, a contradiction and scandal in the eyes of non-Christians and nonbelievers. We intend to dedicate our prayerful attention to everything that would favor union. We will do so without diluting doctrine, but, at the same time, without hesitation.

We wish to pursue with patience, but firmness, that serene and constructive dialogue that Paul VI had at the base of his plan and program for pastoral action. The principal theme for this was set forth in his great encyclical *Ecclesiam Suam*. It called for a mutual knowledge, man to man, also with those who do not share our faith. We must always be ready to give witness of the faith that is ours and of the mission that Christ has given to us, "that the world might believe" (Jn. 17:21).

We wish finally to express our support for all the laudable, worthy initiatives that can safeguard and increase peace in our troubled world. We call upon all good men, all who are just, honest, true of heart. We ask them to help build up a dam within their nations against blind violence, which can only destroy and sow seeds of ruin and sorrow. So, too, in international life, they might bring men to mutual understanding, to combining efforts that would further social progress, overcome hunger of body and ignorance of the mind, and advance those who are less endowed with goods of this earth, yet rich in energy and desire.

Brothers and dearest sons and daughters, in this awesome moment for us, yet a moment enriched by God's promise, we extend our greeting to all of our sons and daughters: we wish we could see all of them face to face, embrace them, give them courage and confidence, while asking their understanding and prayers for us.

To all then, our greeting:

—To the cardinals of the Sacred College, with whom we have shared this decisive hour. We depend upon them now, as we will in the future. We are grateful to them for their wise counsel. We appreciate the strong support that they will continue to offer to us, as an extension of their consent, which, through God's will, has brought us to the summit of the Apostolic Office;

—To all the bishops of the church of God, "who represent their own church, whereas all, together with the Pope, represent the entire church in a bond of peace, love and unity" (*Lumen Gentium* 23), and whose collegiality we strongly value. We value their efforts in the guidance of the universal church both through the synodal structure and through the curial structure, in which they share by right according to the norms established;

—To all of our coworkers called to a strict response to our will and thus to an honored activity which brings holiness of life, called to a spirit of obedience, to the works of the apostolate, and to a most exemplary love of the church. We love each of them, and we encourage them to stay close to us as they were to our predecessors in proven faithfulness. We are certain to be able to rely on their highly esteemed labors, which will be for us a great joy.

—We salute the priests and faithful of the diocese of Rome, given to us upon our succession to the chair of Peter and to the unique and singular title of this Roman chair, "which presides over universal love."

We salute in a special way the members of the dioceses of Venice and Belluno, those who are remembered as most beloved sons and daughters, and those of whom we think now with a sincere concern, conscious of their magnificent work for the church and of their common commitment to the cause of the Gospel.

And we embrace all priests—especially parish priests and those dedicated to the direction of souls, often in difficult conditions or genuine poverty, yet radiating the grace of their vocation in their heroic following of Christ, "the pastor of our souls" (1 Pet. 2:25).

We salute religious men and women, those in both contemplative and active life, who continue to make present in the world a hymn of total commitment to the Gospel ideal; and we ask them to continue to "see well to it that the church truly shows forth Christ through them with ever-increasing clarity to believers and unbelievers alike" (*Lumen Gentium,* 46).

We salute the entire missionary church, and we extend to all men and women who in their outposts of evangelization dedicate themselves to the care of their brothers our encouragement and our most loving recognition. They should know that, among all who are dear to us, they are the dearest; they are never forgotten in our prayers and thoughts, because they have a privileged place in our heart.

To the associations of Catholic Action, as to the movements of various denominations which contribute with new energy to the renewal of society and the "consecration of the world" as a leaven in the mass (Mt. 13:33)—to them go all support and encouragement, because we are convinced that their work, carried out in collaboration with the hierarchy, is indispensable for the church today.

We salute young people, the hope of tomorrow—a better, a healthier, a more constructive tomorrow—that they might know how to distinguish good from bad and, with the fresh energy that they possess, bring about the vitality of the church and the development of the world.

We greet the families, who are the "domestic sanctuary of the church" (*Apostolicam actuositatem* 11), and indeed a true, actual "domestic church" (*Lumen Gentium*), in which religious vocations can flourish and holy decisions be made. It is there that one is prepared for the world of tomorrow. It is there that one can raise defenses against those destructive ideologies of hedonism which stamp out life and can instead form a vibrant source of generosity, of balance, of dedication to the common good.

We extend a particular greeting to all who are now suffering—to the sick, to prisoners, to exiles, to the persecuted; to those who are unemployed, or who have bad fortune in life; to all upon whom restraints are placed in their practice of the Catholic faith—which they cannot freely profess except at the cost of the basic human rights of free men and of willing, loyal citizens. In a special way our thoughts turn to the tortured land of Lebanon, to the situation in the homeland of Jesus, to the area of Sahel, to India, a land that is so tried—indeed, to all those sons, daughters, brothers, and sisters who undergo privations in their social and political life or as a result of natural disasters.

My brothers and sisters—all people of the world!

We are all struggling to raise the world to a condition of greater justice, more stable peace, more sincere cooperation. We invite all of you and encourage you, from the humblest, who are the underpinning of nations, to heads of state responsible for each nation—we encourage you to build up an efficacious and responsible structure for a new order, one more just and honest.

A dawn of hope spreads over the earth, although it is sometimes touched by sinister merchants of hatred, bloodshed, and war with a darkness which sometimes threatens to obscure the dawn. This humble Vicar of Christ, who begins in fear, yet trust in his mission, places himself at the disposal of the entire church and all civil society. We make no distinction as to race or ideology but seek to secure for the world the dawn of a more serene and joyful day. Only Christ could cause this dawn of a light which will never set, because he is the "sun of justice" (Mal. 4:2). He will indeed oversee the work of all. He will not fail us.

We ask all our sons and daughters for the help of their prayers, for we are counting on them; and we open ourselves with great trust to the assistance of the Lord, who, having called us to be his representative on earth, will not leave us without his all-powerful grace. Mary Most Holy, Queen of the Apostles, will be the shining star of our pontificate. Saint Peter, the foundation of the church (S. Ambrose Exp. Ev. sec. Lucam, IV, 70: CSEL 32, 4, p. 175), will support us through his intercession and with his example of unconquerable faith and human generosity. Saint Paul will guide us in our apostolic efforts directed to all the people of the earth. Our holy patrons will assist us.

In the name of the Father and of the Son and of the Holy Spirit, we impart to the world our first, most loving Apostolic Benediction.

Acceptance Message of John Paul II

On the morning of Tuesday 17 October, the day after his election as Supreme Pontiff, Pope John Paul II celebrated mass together with the College of Cardinals in the Sistine Chapel. At the end of the mass, His Holiness spoke as follows to the cardinals and to the world.

Our Venerable Brothers, beloved children of Holy Church, and all men of goodwill who listen to us:

One expression only, among so many others, comes immediately to our lips at this moment, as after our election to the See of the Blessed Peter, we present ourself to you. The expression, which, in evident contrast with our obvious limitations as a human person, highlights the immense burden and office committed to us, is this: "O the depth . . . of the wisdom and knowledge of God! How unsearchable are his judgments and how inscrutable his ways!" (Rom. 11:33). In fact, who could have foreseen, after the death of Pope Paul VI whom we always remember, the premature decease of his most amiable successor, John Paul I? How could we have been able to foresee that this formidable heritage would have been placed on our shoulders? For this reason, it is necessary for us to meditate upon the mysterious design of the provident and good God, not indeed in order to understand, but, rather, that we may worship and pray. Truly we feel the need to repeat the words of the Psalmist who, raising his eyes aloft, exclaimed: "From whence does my help come? My help comes from the Lord," (Ps. 120:1–2).

These totally unforeseen events, happening in so brief a time, and the inadequacy with which we can respond to that invitation impel us to turn to the Lord and to trust completely to him. But they also prevent us from outlining a programme for our Pontificate which would be the fruit of long reflection and of precise elaboration. But to make up for this, there is to hand a certain compensation, as it were, which is itself a sign of the strengthening presence of God.

It is less than a month since all of us, both inside and outside these historic walls of the Sistine Chapel, heard Pope John Paul speaking at the very beginning of his ministry, from which one might have hoped much. Both on account of the memory that is yet fresh in the mind of each one of us and on account of the wise reminders and exhortations contained in the allocution, we consider that we cannot overlook it. That same address, as in the circumstances in which it was given, is truly apposite and clearly maintains its validity here and now at the start of this new pontifical ministry to which we are bound and which, before God and the church, we cannot avoid.

We wish, therefore, to clarify some basic points which we consider to be of special importance. Hence—as we propose and as, with the help of God, we confidently trust—we shall continue these not merely with earnestness and attention but we shall also further them with constant pressure, so that ecclesial life, truly lived, may correspond to them. First of all, we wish to point out the unceasing importance of the Second

Vatican Ecumenical Council, and we accept the definite duty of assiduously bringing it into effect. Indeed, is not that universal Council a kind of milestone as it were, an event of the utmost importance in the almost two-thousand-year history of the church, and consequently in the religious and cultural history of the world?

However, as the Council is not limited to the documents alone, neither is it completed by the ways of applying it which were devised in these post-conciliar years. Therefore we rightly consider that we are bound by the primary duty of most diligently furthering the implementation of the decrees and directive norms of that same Universal Synod. This indeed we shall do in a way that is at once prudent and stimulating. We shall strive, in particular, that first of all an appropriate mentality may flourish. Namely, it is necessary that, above all, outlooks must be at one with the Council so that in practice those things may be done that were ordered by it, and that those things which lie hidden in it or—as is usually said—are "implicit" may become explicit in the light of the experiments made since then and the demands of changing circumstances. Briefly, it is necessary that the fertile seeds which the Fathers of the Ecumenical Synod, nourished by the word of God, sowed in good ground (cf. Mt. 13:8, 23)—that is, the important teachings and pastoral deliberations—should be brought to maturity in that way which is characteristic of movement and life.

This general purpose of fidelity to the Second Vatican Council and express will, in so far as we are concerned, of bringing it into effect, can cover various sections: missionary and ecumenical affairs, discipline, and suitable administration. But there is one section to which greater attention will have to be given, and that is the ecclesiological section. Venerable Brethren and beloved sons of the Catholic world, it is necessary for us to take once again into our hands the "Magna Charta" of the Council, that is, the Dogmatic Constitution *Lumen Gentium*, so that with renewed and invigorating zeal we may meditate on the nature and function of the church, its way of being and acting. This should be done not merely in order that the vital communion in Christ of all who believe and hope in him should be accomplished, but also in order to contribute to bringing about a fuller and closer unity of the whole human family. John XXIII was accustomed to repeat the following words: "The Church of Christ is the light of the nations." For the church—his words were repeated by the Council—is the universal sacrament of salvation and unity for the human race (cf. Const. *Lumen Gentium*, n. 1; 48; Decr. *Ad Gentes*, n. 1).

The mystery of salvation which finds its center in the church and is actualized through the church; the dynamism which on account of that same mystery animates the People of God; the special bond, that is, collegiality, which "with Peter and under Peter" binds together the sacred Pastors; all these are major elements on which we have not yet sufficiently reflected. We must do so in order to decide in face of human needs, whether these be permanent or passing, what the church should adopt as its mode of presence and its course of action. Wherefore, the assent to be given to this document of the Council, seen in the light of Tradition and embodying the dogmatic formulae issued over a century ago by the First Vatican Council, will be to us Pastors and to the faithful a decisive indication and a rousing stimulus, so that—we say it again—we may walk in the paths of life and of history.

In order that we may become better informed and more vigilant in undertaking our duty, we particularly urge a deeper reflection on the implications of the collegial bond. By collegiality the Bishops are closely linked with the Successor of the blessed Peter, and all collaborate in order to fulfil the high offices committed to them: offices of enlightening the whole People of God with the light of the Gospel, of sanctifying them with the means of grace, of guiding them with pastoral skill. Undoubtedly, this collegiality extends to the appropriate development of institutes—some new, some updated—by which is procured the greatest unity in outlook, intent, and activity in the work of building up the body of Christ, which is the church (cf. Eph. 4:12; Col. 1:24). In this regard, we make special mention of the Synod of Bishops, set up before the end of the Council by that very talented man, Paul VI (cf. Apostolic Letter, given "motu proprio," *Apostolica Sollicitudo: AAS* LVII, 1965, pp. 775–780).

But besides these things, which remind us of the Council, there is the duty in general of being faithful to the task we have accepted and to which we ourself are bound before all others. We, who are called to hold the supreme office in the church, must manifest this fidelity with all our might and for this reason we must be a shining example both in our thinking and in our actions. This indeed must be done because we preserve intact the deposit of faith, because we make entirely our own the commands of Christ, who, after Peter was made the rock on which the church was built, gave him the keys of the kingdom of heaven (cf. Mt. 16:18–19), who bade him strengthen his brethren (cf. Lk. 22:32), and to feed the sheep and the lambs of his flock as a proof of his love (cf. Jn. 21:15–17). We are entirely convinced that in no inquiry which may take place today into the "ministry of Peter" as it is called—so that what is proper and peculiar to it may be studied in greater depth every day—can these three important passages of the holy gospel be omitted. For it is a question of the various parts of the office, which are bound up with the very nature of the church so that its internal unity may be preserved and its spiritual mission placed in safe hands. These parts were not only committed to Saint Peter but also to his lawful successors. We are also convinced that this high office must always be related to love as the source from which it is nourished and, as it were, the climate in which it can be expanded. This love is as it were a necessary reply to the question of Jesus, "Do you love me?" So we are pleased to repeat these words of Saint Paul, "The love of Christ constraineth us" (2 Cor. 5:14), because we want our ministry to be from the outset a ministry of love, and want to show and declare this in every possible way.

In this matter we will strive to follow the meritorious examples of our immediate predecessors. Who does not remember the words of Paul VI, who preached "the civilization of love" and almost a month before his death declared in a prophetic way: "I have kept the faith" (cf. Homily on Feast of SS. Peter and Paul: *AAS* LXX, 1978, p. 395), not indeed to praise himself but after fifteen years full of apostolic ministry to examine his conscience more strictly?

But what can we say of John Paul I? It seems to us that only yesterday he emerged from this assembly of ours to put on the papal robes—not a light weight. But what warmth of charity, nay, what "an abundant out-pouring of love"—which came forth from him in the few days of his ministry and which in his last Sunday address before the Angelus he desired should come upon the world. This is also confirmed by his wise instructions to the faithful who were present at his public audiences on faith, hope and love.

Beloved brothers in the Episcopate and dear children, fidelity, as is clear, implies not a wavering obedience to the Magisterium of Peter especially in what pertains to doctrine. The "objective" importance of this Magisterium must always be kept in mind and even safeguarded because of the attacks which in our time are being leveled here and there against certain truths of the Catholic faith. Fidelity too implies the observance of the liturgical norms laid down by ecclesiastical Authority and therefore has nothing to do with the practice either of introducing innovations of one's own accord and without approval or of obstinately refusing to carry out what has been lawfully laid down and introduced into the sacred rites. Fidelity also concerns the great discipline of the church of which our immediate predecessor spoke. This discipline is not of such a kind that it depresses or, as they say, degrades. It seeks to safeguard the right ordering of the mystical body of Christ with the result that all the members of which it is composed united together perform their duties in a normal and natural way. Moreover, fidelity signifies the fulfilment of the demands of the priestly and religious vocation in such a way that what has freely been promised to God will always be carried out in so far as the life is understood in a stable supernatural way.

Finally, in so far as the faithful are concerned—as the word itself signifies—fidelity of its very nature must be a duty in keeping with their condition as Christians. They show it with ready and sincere hearts and give proof of it either by obeying the sacred Pastors whom the Holy Spirit has placed to rule the church of God (cf. Acts 20:28), or by collaborating in those plans and works for which they have been called.

Nor at this point must we forget the brethren of other churches and Christian confessions. For the cause of ecumenism is so lofty and such a sensitive issue that we may not keep silent about it. How often do we meditate together on the last wish of Christ, who asked the Father for the gift of unity for the disciples (cf. Jn. 17:21–23)? Who does not remember how much Saint Paul stressed "the unity of the spirit" from which the followers of Christ might have the same love, being of one accord, of one mind (cf. Phil. 2:2, 5–8)? Therefore one can hardly credit that a deplorable division still exists among Christians. This is a cause of embarrassment and perhaps of scandal to others. And so we wish to proceed along the road which has happily been opened and to encourage whatever can serve to remove the obstacles, desirous as we are that through common effort full communion may eventually be achieved.

We turn also to all men who as children of almighty God are our brothers whom we must love and serve, to make known to them without any sense of boasting but with sincere humility our intention to really devote ourself to the continual and special cause of peace, of development and justice among nations. In this matter we have no desire to interfere in politics or to take part in the management of temporal affairs. For just as the church cannot be confined to a certain earthly pattern, so we, in our approach to the urgent questions of men and peoples, are led solely by religious and moral motives. Following him who gave that perfect way to his followers, so that they might be the "salt of the earth" and the "light of the world" (Mt. 5:13–16), we wish to strive to strengthen the spiritual foundations on which human society must be based. We feel that this duty is all the more urgent the longer that discords and dissensions last, which, in not a few parts of the world, provide material for struggles and conflicts and even give rise to the more serious danger of frightful calamities.

Therefore it will be our constant care to direct our attention to questions of this kind and to deal with them by timely action forgetful of our own interests and motivated by the spirit of the Gospel. One may at this point at least share the grave concern which the College of Cardinals during the interregnum expressed concerning the dear land of Lebanon and its people. For it we all greatly desire peace with freedom. At the same time we wish to extend our hand to all peoples and all men at this moment and to open our heart to all who are oppressed, as they say, by any injustice or discrimination with regard to either economic or social affairs, or even to political matters, or even to freedom of conscience and the freedom to practice their religion, which is their due. We must aim at this: that all forms of injustice which exist today should be given consideration by all in common and should be really eradicated from the world, so that all men may be able to live a life worthy of man. This also belongs to the mission of the church which has been explained in the Second Vatican Council, not only in the dogmatic Constitution *Lumen Gentium* but also in the pastoral Constitution *Gaudium et Spes.*

Brothers, dear sons and daughters, the recent happenings of the church and of the world are for us all a healthy warning: how will our pontificate be? What is the destiny the Lord has assigned to his church in the next years? What road will mankind take in this period of time as it approaches the year 2000? To these bold questions the only answer is: "God knows" (cf. 2 Cor. 12:2–3).

The course of our life which has brought us unexpectedly to the supreme responsibility and office of apostolic service is of little interest. Our person—we ought to say—should disappear when confronted with the weighty office we must fill. And so a speech must be changed into an appeal. After praying to the Lord, we feel the need of your prayers to gain that indispensable, heavenly strength that will make it possible for us to take up the work of our predecessors from the point where they left off.

After acknowledging their cherished memory, we offer to each one of you, our Venerable Brothers, who we remember with gratitude, our greeting. We extend a greeting which is both trusting and encouraging to all our brothers in the Episcopate, who in different parts of the world have the care of individual churches, the chosen sections of the People of God (cf. Dec. *Christus Dominus*, n. 11) and who are coworkers with us in the work of universal salvation. Behind them, we behold the order of priesthood, the band of missionaries, the companies of religious men and women.

At the same time we earnestly hope that their numbers will grow, echoing in our mind those words of the Saviour, "The harvest is great, the labourers are few" (Mt. 9:37–38; Lk. 10:2). We behold also the Christian families and communities, the many associations dedicated to the apostolate, the faithful who even if they are not known to us individually, are not anonymous, not strangers, nor even in a lower place, for they are included in the glorious company of the church of Christ. Among them we look with particular affection on the weak, the poor, the sick, and those afflicted with sorrow.

Now, at the beginning of our universal pastoral ministry, we wish to open to them our heart. Do not you, brothers and sisters, share by your sufferings in the passion of our Redeemer, and in a certain way complete it? (cf. Col. 1:24). The unworthy successor of Saint Peter, who proposes to explore "the unsearchable riches of Christ" (Ephes. 3:8), has the greatest need of your help, your prayers, your devotedness or "sacrifice," and this he most humbly asks of you.

We also wish, most beloved brothers and sons who hear us, because of our undying love for the land of our birth, to greet in a very special way all the citizens of Poland, "ever faithful," and the bishops, priests, and people of the church of Cracow. United in this greeting by an indissoluble bond are memories, affections, the sweet love of the fatherland, and hope.

In this grave hour which gives rise to trepidation, we cannot do other than turn our mind with filial devotion to the Virgin Mary, who always lives and acts as a Mother in the mystery of Christ, and repeat the words "Totus tuus" (all thine), which we inscribed in our heart and on our coat of arms twenty years ago on the day of our episcopal ordination. We cannot but invoke Saints Peter and Paul and all the Saints and Blesseds of the universal church.

In this same hour we greet everyone, the old, those in the prime of life, adolescents, children, babes newly born, with that ardent sentiment of fatherhood which is already welling up from our hearts. We express the sincere wish that all "may grow in the grace and knowledge of our Lord and Saviour Jesus Christ," as the Prince of the Apostles desired (2 Pet. 3:18). And to all we impart our first Apostolic Blessing that it may procure not only for them but for the whole human family an abundance of the gifts of the Father who is in heaven. Amen.

Index

Index

Index

Index

O'Donnell, Cletus, 204
Oggi, 102
O'Grady, Desmond, 62, 85
On Being a Christian, 138, 163. *See also* Küng, Hans
"On Electing a Supreme Pontiff," 17
Opus Dei, 3, 19–20, 26
Oriental Congregation, 252 n. 5
Orwell, George, 7
Osservatore della Domenica, 207
Osservatori, 69
Ostpolitik, 1–2, 60, 251 n. 1
Ottaviani, Alfredo, 260, 262; and birth control, 45–46; as August papabile, 42
Otunga, Maurice, 189
Our Sunday Visitor, 248

P

Pacelli, Eugenio. *See* Pius XII
Palazzini, Pietro, 50, 252 n. 2(d); biographical information on, 3; in National Opinion Research Center poll, 189
Panciroli, Romeo, 69, 216, 218
Panorama, 83, 102
papacy, 34–36, 39, 128–31; job description for, 87–89, 277–80; mystique of, 43
Pappalardo, Salvatore, 252 n. 2(d); biographical information on, 4; and John Paul II, 224; supporting Albino Luciani, 139; in National Opinion Research Center poll, 188; as August papabile, 38, 58, 71, 127, 148; as October papabile, 192, 205
Parecattil, Joseph, 135
Paris-Match, 83
Pasqualina, Madre, 69, 84, 86
Paul VI, 1–5 passim, 7, 38, 58, 81, 86, 123, 129; view of American church, 3; assessment of, 15–16, 22, 24–25, 33–34, 35–36, 51–52, 98–101, 130; and birth control encyclical, 27, 45–47; and appointment of cardinals, 19, 49, 50, 190, 257; and Christian traditionalists, 50–51; and clerical education, 56–57; and John Cody, 91, 92; Curia of, 251 n. 2(b), 251 n. 2(d); death of, 95–96, 264 n. 2; deterioration of, 74, 83–84; election of, 260–62; funeral of, 113–15; and John XXIII,

257; and John Paul I, 162; and papal election rules, 17–18, 64–66, 141, 150–51, 153; wake for, 105–07
Pellegrino, Michele, 252 n. 2(d); biographical information on, 4; and John Paul II, 225; in National Opinion Research Center poll, 189; as August papabile, 36, 148
Petrarch, 157
Pignedoli, Sergio, 49, 192, 252 n. 2(d); biographical information on, 4; at October conclave, 213; in National Opinion Research Center poll, 187, 188; as August papabile, 21, 27, 39, 40, 55, 60, 62, 71, 75, 101, 104, 105, 106, 110, 112, 113, 122, 127, 128, 137, 148, 151–53
Pinocchio, 164, 165
Pironio, Eduardo, 124, 238; biographical information on, 4; appointed cardinal, 49; at October conclave, 217; in National Opinion Research Center poll, 189; as August papabile, 21, 53, 55, 58, 59, 71, 75, 101, 109, 113, 127, 137, 148, 151; as October papabile, 196
Pius VII, 255, 257
Pius IX, 57, 257
Pius X, 58, 111, 165, 255, 256, 257, 260; election of, 258 n. 3, 262
Pius XI, 9, 58, 111, 256, 258, 260, 262
Pius XII, 22, 28, 39, 68, 69, 84, 86, 99, 111, 123, 125, 138–39, 256, 260, 265, 279
Poletti, Ugo: biographical information on, 4; and Communism, 19; in National Opinion Research Center poll, 189; as August papabile, 21, 113, 127; as October papabile, 195, 205, 212
Poma, Antonio, 187, 224, 252 n. 2(d)
Pompili, Cardinal, 258 n. 3
Pontifical Ecclesiastical Assembly, 4
Potter, Philip, 125
Prefecture of Economic Affairs, 5, 266
Primeau, Ernie, 23, 137, 167, 175, 214, 252 n. 3

Q

Quinn, John, 81
Quintero, José, 263 n. 3

300

Index